Negating Negation

Negating Negation

*Against the Apophatic Abandonment
of the Dionysian Corpus*

Timothy D. Knepper

CASCADE *Books* · Eugene, Oregon

NEGATING NEGATION
Against the Apophatic Abandonment of the Dionysian Corpus

Copyright © 2014 Timothy D. Knepper. All rights reserved. Except for brief quotations in critical publications or reviews, no part of this book may be reproduced in any manner without prior written permission from the publisher. Write: Permissions, Wipf and Stock Publishers, 199 W. 8th Ave., Suite 3, Eugene, OR 97401.

Cascade Books
An Imprint of Wipf and Stock Publishers
199 W. 8th Ave., Suite 3
Eugene, OR 97401

www.wipfandstock.com

ISBN 13: 978-1-62564-250-9

Cataloguing-in-Publication data:

Knepper, Timothy D.

    Negating negation : against the apophatic abandonment of the Dionysian corpus / Timothy D. Knepper.

    xviii + 152 pp. ; 23 cm. Includes bibliographical references and index.

    ISBN 13: 978-1-62564-250-9

    1. Pseudo-Dionysius, the Areopagite. 2. Negative theology. 3. Neoplatonism. 4. Mysticism. I. Title.

BR65.D66 K526 2014

Manufactured in the U.S.A.

For John

Contents

List of Tables viii
Preface ix
Introduction xi

1 The Divine Names Are Not Names 1
2 Negation Does Not Negate 35
3 Ranks Are Not Bypassed; Rites Are Not Negated 69
4 The Ineffable God Is Not Ineffable 103
   Conclusion 132

Bibliography 137
Subject Index 141

Tables

1 The Divine Names of *Divine Names* 5–13   16
2 The Logic of Apophasis   64
3 Terms of Affirmation and Negation in the Dionysian Corpus   66
4 Hierarchical Sciences, Orders, and Activities   73

Preface

I DID NOT BEGIN READING the Dionysian corpus until the second semester of my doctoral program. Having just completed courses in early Jewish mysticism (with Steven Katz) and Wittgenstein's *Philosophical Investigations* (with Juliet Floyd), I had already determined to write my dissertation on the grammatical techniques and rules of mystical discourse. But I had not yet decided where to look for such techniques and rules. I had wanted to work with Nāgārjuna's *Mūlamadhyamakakārikā*. But my advisor (Wesley Wildman) convinced me that unless I wanted to add years to my degree, I was better off working in a language I already knew. As with so many other matters, his advice was sage.

Although I read and reread the Paulist Press translation of the Dionysian corpus during the remaining years of my doctoral program, the interdisciplinary nature of my dissertation prevented me from working all that closely with the critical edition of the corpus. Thus it was not until after the defense of my dissertation that I began chasing down all the occurrences of certain technical terms in the Dionysian corpus, translating the sentences in which they appeared. Part of what I discovered in the process was what so many other Dionysian scholars already knew: the Paulist Press edition is more paraphrase than translation. But my other discovery seemed relatively unique: the Dionysian corpus does not negate all things of an absolutely ineffable God; rather, it negates very few things of a God that is only qualifiedly ineffable.

This book is the culmination of that process. In it I will try to show you that the "popular" interpretation and appropriation of the Dionysius corpus is mistaken: Pseudo-Dionysius the Areopagite does *not* abandon all things to apophasis, and therefore cannot serve as a poster boy for our (post)modern projects in religious pluralism or anti-onto-theology. Quite

Preface

the contrary, the Dionysian corpus gives reason for suspicion of such projects, especially when they relativize or metaphorize religious belief and practice in the name of absolute ineffability.

This process of discovery did not of course occur in a vacuum. Among the many thanks that are in order, the first and foremost goes out to my former editor, John N. Jones, whose life of kindness and insight was tragically cut short a year ago. It was John who first sought out my dissertation, who eventually encouraged me to write a book on just the Dionysian corpus, and who shepherded me through this process. Not only is this book unimaginable without him, so also is my maturity as a Dionysian scholar.

After John, I thank my former students Blake Brown and Michael Scully for their research assistance with various aspects of this project; Drake University for making possible this research assistance with a Provost Research Grant and an Arts and Sciences Research Assistantship; Eric Perl, Brad Herling, and Thomas Carroll for their critical feedback of various aspects of this project; John Finamore for directing my entrée into Proclus during a research semester; Drake University's Center for the Humanities not only for granting me this research semester along with access to Thesaurus Linguae Graecae but also for a research scholar award to support the writing of this book and for a services support grant to support the indexing of this book; Wesley Wildman for his guidance of a much earlier version of this project; Robin Parry for his masterful editing of the manuscript; and my family for showing me why this book does and does not matter.

Some of the material from some of these chapters appeared elsewhere first (although most of it has been thoroughly reworked, and some of it has been substantively reconceived): *American Catholic Philosophical Quarterly* ("Not Not: The Method and Logic of Dionysian Negation," 82.4 [2008] 619–37), *Religious Studies* ("Three Misuses of Dionysius for Comparative Theology," 45.2 [2009] 205–21), *Quaestiones Disputatae* ("Ineffability Now and Then: The Legacy of Neoplatonic Ineffability in Twentieth-Century Philosophy of Religion," 2.1–2 [2011] 263–76), and in *Logic in Orthodox Christian Thinking* ("Techniques and Rules of Ineffability in the Dionysian Corpus," edited by Andrew Schumann, 122–173, Berlin: De Gruyter, 2012). But in the case of chapter 3, almost all of this material appeared elsewhere first: *Modern Theology* ("Ranks Are Not Bypassed; Rituals Are Not Negated: The Dionysian Corpus on Return," forthcoming). I thank all these publishers for allowing me to draw on this material here.

Introduction

How can that which is absolutely ineffable be or do something in particular? How, for that matter, can it be anything at all? For if it is or does anything at all, then something can be said of it. And if nothing can be said of it, then it cannot be or do anything at all.

This is the predicament in which recent interpreters of the Dionysian corpus have found themselves, having to explain the many positive details of the corpus on the one hand, but wanting to proclaim the absolute and unqualified ineffability of the Dionysian God on the other. Their solution, although varying in grounds and ends, is more or less the same—*apophatic abandonment*, the ultimate and complete negation of all things of an absolutely and unqualifiedly ineffable God.

Among these grounds, two general strategies stand out; both, however, fall short. The first consigns the many positive details of the Dionysian corpus to the linguistic realm of the non-literal.[1] Here, for example, the divine names of God or ecclesiastical rituals of the church are said to be metaphors that are not literally true of God or means that are merely useful at attaining some salvific goal. Here it is said that God is metaphorically predicable as the divine names or soteriologically accessible through the ecclesiastical rituals, while remaining literally absolutely ineffable. The second strategy instead relegates the positive details of the Dionysian corpus to the ontological realm of the non-ultimate.[2] Here the divine names and ecclesiastical rituals are said to pertain only to the

---

1. Examples of this strategy that I will consider below include John Hick, Denys Turner, and Paul Rorem. See my introductions to all four chapters, but particularly those of the first three chapters.

2. Examples of this strategy that I will consider below include John D. Jones, Eric Perl, and Andrew Louth. See my introductions to chapters 2 and 4.

Introduction

realm of "being" or only to the God of causation. Here it is said that God is predicable with respect to the things of being that God causes, while remaining ultimately absolutely ineffable.

Both strategies come up short. In the case of the first, such metaphorical-pragmatic predications rest on literal understanding. We can only know that God is metaphorically the divine name *life* or that the liturgical rite of baptism is soteriologically efficacious given some sort of appropriate literal understanding of what God actually is and does—e.g., that God actually causes life in things that live, or that baptism symbolizes the actual death and resurrection of Jesus. And in the case of the second strategy, such ontological segregations also presuppose some sort of understanding of what God ultimately is and does. We can only know that the divine names and ecclesiastical rituals pertain only to the realm of being or the God of causation if we understand God to be the cause of being.

There is a simpler solution: the Dionysian God is *not* absolutely and unqualifiedly ineffable; rather, the Dionysian God is ineffable only *in certain respects* and *for certain reasons* and *to certain ends*. This solution is not only simpler; it is also sounder, better fitting of the Dionysian corpus itself. Or so this book will argue.

Our pervasive (post)modern misunderstanding of the Dionysian corpus begins with the divine names. So will this book, showing in chapter 1 how the divine names are not mere names, let alone metaphors, but the divine causes of the intelligible properties in which beings participate. Dionysian divine names are therefore something like Platonic forms (especially in their late Neoplatonic instantiation): the divine name *life-itself* is the cause of the property of life in things that live. This means that since the divine names themselves are responsible for the basic parameters of reality, they must be precise in order and number (or at least not culturally or personally arbitrary). This also means that every divine name has (at least) two senses: a primary sense that pertains to the divine name itself *qua* cause of its property (e.g., life-itself), and a secondary sense that pertains to the property caused by its divine name itself (e.g., life). Thus, when a divine name is removed (*aphairesis*) from God, it is logically possible for it to be removed only as effect or also as cause.

Chapter 2 argues at length for the former: when divine names are *aphairetically* removed from God, they are removed only as effects and not also as causes. This must be so for (at least) four reasons. First, Dionysius tells the reader that removals from God must be interpreted preeminently

Introduction

(*hyperochē*) rather than privatively, where *hyperochic* preeminence reveals the priority of causes over their effects. Second, when Dionysius removes divine names from God, he never *auto*-prefixes them, as he often does to the divine names themselves when distinguishing them as causes rather than effects. Third, Dionysius calls those things that are removed from God "beings"; but the divine names themselves *qua* causes are "divine unities" that transcend the realm of being. Fourth, since the divine names themselves are God's means of causation, and since Dionysius never denies causation of God, Dionysius logically cannot deny the divine names themselves of God.

Chapter 3 then places these findings within the context of the hierarchical structure and ritual practice (*hierurgy*) of the ecclesiastical hierarchy, demonstrating how the Dionysian corpus gives no indication that such hierarchical order or hierurgical ritual should be subjected to negation but instead suggests that the *aphairetic* removal of divine names functions as both theological preparation for and theurgical component of the liturgical rites. Negative theology is not the means by which hierarchical order and hierurgical ritual are negated and overcome; rather it is *a* means by which hierarchical uplifting and hierurgical union are affirmed and accomplished.

Finally, chapter 4 maintains that given all this, given everything the Dionysian corpus tells us about supposedly "ineffable" and "unknowable" things, Dionysian ineffability and unknowability not only are not, but also *cannot* be, absolute and unqualified in nature. Although completely ineffable and unknowable by "ordinary" cognitive means, ineffable divine things are partially effable and knowable as divinely revealed, hierarchically disseminated, and hyper-intellectually (*hyper-noētically*) understood.

We need not, therefore, resort to theo-logical contortions in order to explain how Dionysius says all this (and more) about an unsayable God. Nor need we admit that Dionysius just did not appreciate the logic of ineffability. Instead, we can read the Dionysian corpus for what it is: the explication of a highly detailed and culturally specific metaphysics and ecclesiology, some aspects of which are said to be unspeakable in certain ways and for certain reasons, no aspect of which is absolutely and unqualifiedly ineffable.

But more is at stake here than just getting the Dionysian corpus right. Also at stake is letting the Dionysian corpus be, and listening to what the Dionysian corpus can teach.

Introduction

Chief among the variety of contemporary ends or uses of the Dionysian corpus alluded to above rank religious pluralism and anti-onto-theology.[3] But if the Dionysian corpus offers a highly detailed and culturally specific metaphysics and ecclesiology, as I have claimed above and will demonstrate below, then it stands witness for neither. Since the Dionysian corpus does not metaphorize or relativize all religious doctrine and ritual of an absolutely ineffable God, it does not evince any program of religious pluralism that claims that the religious traditions hold such a "God" in common. And since the Dionysian corpus does not criticize, but rather proffers, a metaphysics of divine things, it also does not support any anti-onto-theology that turns away all attempts to reason about the nature of the divine.

In light of these misinterpretations and misappropriations of the Dionysian corpus, it is tempting simply to say that we should just let the Dionysian corpus be, that we should respect its alterity, refraining from compelling it to testify on behalf of our (post)modern agendas. But I believe that to hear it in its otherness, rather than collapsing it into our sameness, is to allow it not only to speak but also to teach. And I believe that what it has to teach us most concerns those very ways in which we have misinterpreted and misappropriated it worst—religious pluralism, anti-onto-theology, and the notion that often stands behind them: *absolute ineffability*.

Simply put, the notion of absolute ineffability is not only incoherent but also useless. Incoherent, because nothing that is in some way something for us—even something that is beyond things—can be absolutely and unqualifiedly ineffable. Absolutely ineffable gods cannot be gods, not even ones beyond divinity or causality or being; absolutely ineffable experiences cannot be experiences, not even ones beyond experience or event or mediation. The notion of absolute ineffability is therefore absolutely useless, because that which isn't anything can't do anything. Insofar, then, as the (post)modern programs of religious pluralism or anti-onto-theology require the notion of an absolutely ineffable God either as a common religious core or a rationally inscrutable other, these programs will fail.

Ineffability, rather, is always relative—some particular "thing" that cannot be spoken in some particular respect for some particular reason toward some particular end. Philosophy of religion is well advised to pay attention to these details. They matter. Without them we cannot hope to know the precise ways in which ultimate realities and experiences are and are not putatively ineffable and therefore the precise ways in which ultimate

3. See the following note.

Introduction

realities and experiences are similar and different. Without them we cannot hope to know anything about the ultimacies that are ultimized or the ultimizers that ultimate them.

Let me finally clarify a few points about the book you are about to read. Regarding its organization: each of its four chapters will begin with an explication of the strongest *types* of arguments for the apophatic abandonment of the Dionysian ideas and practices in question, then go on to offer textual evidence against these arguments. This means, on the one hand, that I will be arguing more against arguments than against arguers. The aim of this book is to offer a textually compelling critique of and counter to a general picture of the Dionysian corpus, not to defeat any one Dionysian scholar's claim about any one Dionysian issue.[4] And on the other hand, it means that my focus will be squarely on the text itself, not its supposed historical-cultural context or its author's conjectured motives and agendas. I would like to allow the Dionysian corpus to "speak for itself" as much as possible, insofar as possible, in

---

4. When such a picture is drawn, it is usually drawn by generalist philosophers of religion, one leading example of which is John Hick. About *Mystical Theology* 5 in particular, Hick asserts: "Here and elsewhere Denys says in as emphatic and unqualified a way as he can that the Godhead, the ultimate One, is absolutely ineffable, eluding all our human categories of thought" ("Ineffability," 38). See my "Three Misuses of Pseudo-Dionysius for Comparative Theology" and "Ineffability Now and Then" for a critique of Hick's appropriation of Dionysius. Note that Hick has, in private correspondence, identified Denys Turner as the source of his interpretation of Dionysius. Interestingly, though, whereas Hick marshals this interpretation for the ends of combating religious pluralism, Turner's ends are more "anti-onto-theological" in nature. See Turner's *The Darkness of God* and "The Art of Unknowing"; but see also Turner's more recent "How to Read the Pseudo-Denys Today?" in which he says he "will no longer misrepresent the pseudo-Denys as a derridean deconstructionist *avant la lettre*" (438). The list of anti-onto-theological appropriations of Dionysius is considerable—Christos Yannaras, Jean-Luc Marion, John Caputo, Kevin Hart, Thomas Carlson, Mary-Jane Rubenstein, and even, depending on whose opinion it is, Jacques Derrida himself. But for a clear example of an (Heideggerian) anti-onto-theological appropriation of the Dionysian corpus by a Dionysius scholar, see John D. Jones's introduction to his translation of the *Divine Names, Mystical Theology*, and *Epistles 1–5*. In brief, Jones maintains that the mystical negative theology espoused by Dionysius constitutes a "radical denial" of both affirmative theology in particular and metaphysics in general insofar as it denies of God all reference to being, not in order to affirm God's preeminence over beings, but rather to deny of God all eminence and causality/support in general ("Introduction," 25, 20 n. 20, 97). (Note that I use "onto-theology" in this wider, more distinctly postmodern sense, *not* as "a theology that subordinates God to a more fundamental category of being." Pseudo-Dionysius would certainly oppose *that* kind of onto-theology. My thanks to Professor John Milbank for suggesting that I clarify this distinction.) I will have much more to say about both Hick's and Jones's appropriations of the Dionysian corpus below, particularly in my introductions to chapters 1 and 2.

Introduction

all of its possibility; for all too often is it overwhelmed by strong interpretive rubrics, be they historical or personal in nature.[5]

Regarding Pseudo-Dionysius the Areopagite: I am not going to spend much time here or elsewhere puzzling over possible identities.[6] Suffice it to say that although the author of the Dionysian corpus claimed to be the first-century Dionysius, whom the book of Acts reports converting to Christianity after hearing the apostle Paul's sermon about the unknown God at the Areopagus in Athens (Acts 17:34), contemporary scholarship has definitively dated this unknown author's work to the late-fifth or early-sixth century and conclusively established its dependence on both late Neoplatonic and patristic texts and motifs. (I see no merit in agendas that champion one such dependence to the neglect or dismissal of the other.)

Regarding the Dionysian corpus: a little more needs to be said up front, and much more as I go along. The extant works include four treatises—*Celestial Hierarchy* (*CH*), *Ecclesiastical Hierarchy* (*EH*), *Divine Names* (*DN*), and *Mystical Theology* (*MT*)—and ten epistles (*EP*).[7] Of these four treatises, the former two are usually underappreciated, if not outright ignored, resulting in an apophatic-centric understanding of the corpus. It will be the burden of chapter 3 to argue that it is in fact these hierarchical treatises that address the matter of how humans make their "return" to God. Without the ranks and orders of angelic beings and ecclesiastical offices as well as the

---

5. Due to the literal inaccuracy of Colm Luibheid's Paulist Press translation of the Dionysian corpus, I have translated all quoted passages from the Dionysian corpus directly from the critical edition of the Dionysian corpus. (See Eric Perl's *Theophany* [ix] for the charge that the Paulist Press translation is more paraphrase than translation.) In doing so, I have worked closely with the 1897–99 translation of John Parker, which, despite using outdated language, usually preserves the grammatical structure of the Greek. I have also consulted the translations Thomas Campbell, John D. Jones, Ronald Hathaway, and Colm Luibheid.

6. For book-length, English-language treatments of Dionysius or the Dionysian corpus, see especially the following: Arthur, *Pseudo-Dionysius as Polemicist* (2008); Perl, *Theophany* (2007); Wear and Dillon, *Dionysius the Areopagite and the Neoplatonic Tradition* (2007); Golitizin, *Et Introibo Ad Altare Dei* (1994); Rorem, *Pseudo-Dionysius* (1993); Louth, *Denys the Areopagite* (1989); and Hathaway, *Hierarchy and the Definition of Order in the Letters of Pseudo-Dionysius* (1969). For an interesting, recent conjecture about the identity of the author, see Arthur's *Pseudo-Dionysius as Polemicist*.

7. Note, though, that these works mention an additional seven works, all of which are likely fictitious though possibly lost: *Symbolic Theology, Theological Representations, Conceptual and Perceptible, Divine Hymns, Concerning Justice and the Judgment of God, Properties and Ranks of the Angels, Concerning the Soul*. Many scholars assume these works fictitious since their omission does not significantly hinder comprehension of the overall corpus.

sacramental rites and symbols there is no such return—union is accomplished by hierarchical mediation and liturgical ritual, not by apophatic abstraction and solitary meditation. But chapter 3 will also hypothesize that the theological positioning and removing of divine names that occurs in the latter two treatises (*Divine Names* and *Mystical Theology*, respectively) in fact function as both theological preparation for and ritual component of the sacramental rites. To repeat: negative theology is a means by which one prepares for and performs the sacraments, not the means by which one negates and overcomes them.

Finally, regarding my intended audience: that I have been so brief with my introduction to the author and contents of the Dionysian corpus indicates that my model reader comes to this work with a basic familiarity of Pseudo-Dionysius the Areopagite. Still, I write this book more for generalist philosophers of religion than Dionysian scholars. More particularly, this book is for those philosophers of religion who have read some of the English-language scholarship on the Dionysian corpus or have read the Dionysian corpus itself in English-language translation, but who have not had the opportunity to spend time with the Greek critical edition of the corpus. And this is because my primary concern is with the appropriation of the Dionysian corpus in contemporary philosophy of religion. In short and in closing, I would like to see such scholars think twice before reading Dionysius with apophatic abandon.

Chapter 1

The Divine Names
Are Not Names

THIS CHAPTER IS ABOUT names that are not names—divine names, which, despite appearances, are not merely or primarily names for God. Dionysian divine names are much more than this. They are divine processions that source and sustain the basic properties of the cosmos. The divine name *being* is the cause of being in all that exists; the divine name *power*, of all capacities to act in existing beings; the divine name *unity*, of all activities by which existing beings enjoy degrees of internal and external unification. Thus it is only because divine names are firstly and primarily *causes of properties* that those properties can be attributed to or denied of those beings that do or do not participate in them.

Not unsurprisingly, this is one of the more common misunderstandings of the Dionysian corpus. The casual reader fails to notice that Dionysius restricts the application of the technical term *divine name* (*theōnumia*) to intelligible names (e.g., being, power, unity) and does not use it of perceptible symbols (e.g., a fire, a rock, a worm). Such a reader therefore overlooks the fact that whereas perceptible symbols are metaphors drawn from the realm of sensation, intelligible divine names are divine causes of intelligible properties. Worse, this reader assumes that by *names* Dionysius means something similar to what we (post)moderns do—arbitrary signifiers that arbitrarily denote some arbitrary signified. Thus this reader takes the divine names to be in the eye of the beholder—a means of naming God among other means of naming God, a means of naming God that serves

1

Negating Negation

some particular time and place but not other times and places, a means of naming God that is soteriologically useful but not metaphysically true, a means of naming God that says more about the humans who use those names than it does about the God that is so named.

Some of these claims are in fact quite prevalent in the writings of those who deploy one of the arguments for the apophatic abandonment of the divine names.[1] This argument begins with a textual conundrum—how can the Dionysian God be all the things that Dionysius says it is and still be absolutely and unqualifiedly ineffable? To this conundrum, it offers a stark solution: all of Dionysius' affirmations about God fall into the realm of the non-literal—that which is literally false though metaphorically apt or soteriologically useful. Here, this argument partially blurs, if not entirely expunges, the distinction between perceptible symbols and divine names, drawing on passages that address the "metaphorical" nature of the former to generalize over *all* "names" of God (including not only intelligible divine names but also individual Trinitarian persons and general thearchic functions).[2] Then, it goes on to suggest that since Dionysius states that anything caused by God can be taken to name God, Dionysius' "names" for God enjoy no special privilege; they are but one of many ways

---

1. See, for example, John Hick, who has maintained such an interpretation of the divine names in a series of writings since 1999 (*The Fifth Dimension*, "Ineffability," *The New Frontier*, and *Who or What is God?*). (Note that Dionysius appears only once—and there in a note—in Hick's 1986-87 Gifford Lectures, *An Interpretation of Religion* [250 n. 5.].) Hick's "Ineffability" in particular maintains that it is only by calling the language of Scripture metaphorical—and *language of Scripture* is here inclusive of both perceptible symbols and intelligible names—that Dionysius avoids the "direct contradiction" of asserting both God's absolute and unqualified ineffability and God's positive revelation in Scripture ("Ineffability," 38, 39). Dionysian divine names are not therefore "eternal truths" but rather "useful means" of uplifting humans to God (ibid., 39). Of course, Hick is not a Dionysian scholar *per se*. He has, though, in private correspondence, defended his interpretation of Dionysius as inspired by Denys Turner, whose *Darkness of God* (1995) predictably commits a similar apophatic abandonment of the divine names. Unlike Hick, Turner does, at times, draw a distinction between divine names and perceptible symbols. This distinction, though, is chalked up to degree of similarity to God: divine names are more similar to God ("similar similarities"), whereas perceptible symbols are less similar to God ("dissimilar similarities") (*Darkness of God*, 26–27). Nowhere is there a whiff of the causal function of the divine names. Moreover, Turner maintains that since all things preexist in God, any name at all can possibly serve as a divine name: "to name God adequately, we not only may, but must, name God by all the names of creatures" (ibid., 23–24, 24). *Every* name is here equally true *and* equally false of the Dionysian God.

2. Among such passages are *CH* 1.2, *CH* 2.1–3, and *EP* 9.1.

of inadequately naming an unnamable God.³ In sum, the divine names are but human attempts at naming an unnamable God—literally false and infinitely inadequate, historically accidental, and culturally relative. In the words of one proponent of this argument, kataphatic theology is here but a "verbal riot, an anarchy of discourse in which anything goes."⁴

At first glance, the second argument for the apophatic abandonment of the divine names appears not to fit the mold, maintaining, on the contrary, that the divine names in fact are real divine attributes.⁵ Now what is meant here by *attribute* is not entirely clear. But what is clear is the repeated refrain that *qua* attributes, the divine names are qualitatively different from the henads of pagan Neoplatonism.⁶ And this, according to at least one proponent of the argument, is but one flank of Dionysius' two-pronged assault on the Neoplatonic doctrine of emanation. Thus we find such a Dionysius "insisting" not only that divine names are merely divine attributes but also that God creates out of nothing and without intermediaries.⁷ As I will explain later, I do not find either of these claims convincing—like divine names, henads are attributes of the first principle; like henads, divine names play a role in the procession of being and its most basic properties. But my concern here is with how this argument sometimes ends up resembling

---

3. Among such passages are *DN* 1.6, *DN* 1.7, and *EP* 9.1.

4. Turner, *The Darkness of God*, 20.

5. See especially Andrew Louth's *Denys the Areopagite*, about which more will be said below. But see also Paul Rorem's *Pseudo-Dionysius* and Christian Schäfer's *The Philosophy of Dionysius Areopagite*.

6. The henads of late or "pagan" Neoplatonism are pluralizations of the One (that were often identified with the Greek gods). See section IV for more on Neoplatonic henads and Dionysian divine names.

7. Louth, *Denys*, 85, 86. In the former case (viz., divine names are just divine attributes) Louth quotes *DN* 11.6, 953C–956A in text (ibid., 86) and also cites *DN* 2.1, 636C–637C and *DN* 5.2, 816C–817A (ibid., 97 n. 15); I'll spend time with all of these passages below. In the latter case (viz., God creates out of nothing and without intermediaries) Louth admits that Dionysius does not speak much of creation in general and never speaks of creation *ex nihilo* in particular. (Louth instead argues for the doctrine of creation on theological grounds, asserting that it is necessary to Dionysius' understanding of the world as theophany since if the cosmos emanated from God [via "lesser beings"], then the cosmos could not serve to display God's glory and draw everything into contemplation of God's beauty but rather would serve as an "obstacle" to such ends [ibid., 85–86].) Still, Louth provides two pieces of textual evidence for the claim that the Dionysian God creates all being immediately: *DN* 2.11, 649BC and *DN* 5.4, 817C. I'll spend some time with the first of these passages below; the second—a discussion of the divine name *being-itself*—doesn't seem to support Louth's position.

the previous argument for the nominal nature of the divine names. Such resemblance is born in two stages: first, *qua* attributes the divine names are removed from God's nature to God's activity in the world (and, at that, to activity that is illuminative, not causal); second, *qua* illuminative activities the divine names are relegated to the domain of human meaning rather than divine truth. Granted, unlike the argument of the last paragraph, this argument does not go so far as to say that the divine names are, for Dionysius, one among many ways in which humans name God, each of which is literally false though metaphorically apt or pragmatically useful. Such a conclusion might, however, be a short step from the position that divine names are merely means by which meaning is conveyed. For in both cases divine names are no longer sown into the fabric of reality; they are, rather, in the eyes of their beholders. And even if not so subjective, divine names are in the very least not part of the nature of God; they are, rather, merely a way in which God chooses to relate to creation.

This chapter argues instead for a "positively different" understanding of the Dionysian God, one that does not sacrifice God's divine names at the altar of apophatic abandon as inadequate metaphors or impotent attributes, one that instead locates the divine names in God as the pluralized divine unities and transcendent divine causes that they are. To do so, it develops the following four points, each in one of the following four sections of this chapter. First, divine names are not perceptible symbols; rather they are divine causes of intelligible properties and therefore are neither primarily linguistic nor thoroughly metaphorical in nature. Second, the organization of the divine names in the *Divine Names* is not arbitrary and vague but rather purposeful and exact; indeed divine names must be of a precise number and order if they are to account for the most basic properties of participating beings. Third, both the divine names and the properties they source are pre-contained in God in a *hyper*-unified and *hyper*-existent manner; thus there are important respects in which the divine names are true even of the transcendent God. Finally, although Dionysian divine names are not pagan deities, they are in many other ways remarkably similar to the henads of pagan Neoplatonism; notably, as processive causes and divine unities, divine names are much more than mere "attributes" of God.

I. Divine Names Are Not Perceptible Symbols, Not Metaphors, Not Even (Primarily) Names

Although the Dionysian corpus often employs the general term *name* (*onoma*) inclusively of both the divine names and the perceptible symbols, it always restricts the application of the technical term *divine name* (*theōnumia*) or *intelligible divine name* (*noētē theōnumia*) to the divine names and does not use it of the perceptible symbols (*aisthētai symbola*). Occasionally, such exclusion is explicit. *Divine Names* 9.5, after lapsing into a brief discussion of some of "the manifold shapes of God in the many formed visions," reminds the reader that such perceptible symbols both are not the concern of the *Divine Names* and should not be confused with the incorporeal divine names.

> But so that we do not lose ourselves in the explanation of the diverse shapes and forms by bringing together in thought the incorporeal divine names (ἀσωμάτους θεωνυμίας) with those given through the perceptible symbols (ταῖς διὰ συμβόλων αἰσθητῶν), we have discussed these things in the *Symbolic Theology*.[8]

Mystical Theology 3, in delineating the respective content of the three "kataphatic" treatises,[9] specifies that whereas the *Theological Outlines* hymns the Trinitarian nature of God and the *Divine Names* explicates the intelligible divine names, the *Symbolic Theology* discusses "changes of name" (*metonymies*) from the sensible to the divine.

> And so in the *Theological Outlines* we hymned the most principal things of kataphatic theology—how the divine and good nature is called one; how it threefold, saying what fatherhood and sonhood are in it; what the theology of the spirit is meant to show; how the core lights of goodness generated from the immaterial and indivisible good and in this upshooting remained most unalienated from their coeternal abiding in it, in themselves, and in each other; how the *hyper*-being of Jesus became a being of true human nature, and whatever other revelations of Scripture are hymned in the *Theological Outlines*. And in the *Divine Names* we hymned how it is named good, being, life, wisdom, power; and whatever

---

8. *DN* 9.5, 913B.

9. Two of these treatises are, of course, either lost or fictional. The content of the *Theological Outlines* is summarized in *MT* 3 and *DN* 1.4; the content of the *Symbolic Theology*, in *MT* 3, *DN* 1.6, *CH* 15, and *EP* 9. For a little bit more about the lost/fictitious treatises of Dionysius the Areopagite, see note 7 of the Introduction.

else is of the intelligible divine names (τῆς νοητῆς θεωνυμίας). And in the *Symbolic Theology* we hymned what are the changes of name (μετωνυμίαι) from the sensible to the divine, what are the divine forms, what are the divine figures and parts and organs, what are the divine places and worlds, what are the angers, what are the griefs and rages, what are the drunkennesses and hangovers, what are the oaths and what are the curses, what are the sleeps and what are the wakefulnesses, and whatever other sacredly-imaged forms are of the symbolic divine-impression.[10]

And the bookend chapters of the *Divine Names* first iterate that its treatise explicates only the intelligible divine names (and not also the perceptible symbols) and then reiterate that the divine names are explicated only in the *Divine Names* (and not also in the *Symbolic Theology*).

Indeed, not only do the theologians rank first those divine names (θεωνυμίας) that are given either from universal or particular providences or from that which is providenced, but they also name the *hyper*-brilliant and *hyper*-named goodness from certain occasional divine visions that have illuminated the initiated or the prophets in the sacred temples or elsewhere for all sorts of reasons and means. They bestow upon it human or fiery or amber forms and shapes, and they hymn its eyes, ears, hair, face, hands, wings, feathers, arms, backparts, and feet. They form around it crowns, thrones, cups, mixing bowls, and other mystical things, about which we will speak as best as able in the *Symbolic Theology*. But now, collecting from the writings whatever is important for the present inquiry, and employing what has been said as a canon, and examining about them, let us proceed to the unfolding of the intelligible divine names (νοητῶν θεωνυμιῶν).[11]

Having collected these intelligible divine names (νοητὰς θεωνυμίας), we have unfolded them to the best of our ability, falling short not only of their precision (for even the angels might truly say this), nor only of their angelic hymning (for even the greatest of our theologians fall short of the lowest angels), nor, indeed, of the theologians themselves or their disciples and companions, but

---

10. MT 3, 1032D–1033B. I leave the Greek preposition/prefix *hyper* untranslated here (and most elsewhere) since I believe it conveys two different spatial and logical relations: a sense of being *beyond* or *across* something (horizontal distance) and therefore of exceeding beyond the having of that thing, and a sense of being *over* or *above* something (vertical height) and therefore of having that thing in excessive measure. For more on this semantic bivocity, see chapter 2.

11. DN 1.8, 597AB.

> also exceedingly and inferiorly of those who are of the same rank as us. So that if what was spoken may be right, and if we have really reached the divine-name (θεωνυμικῆς) unfolding in our thinking, we must attribute this to the cause of all goods which first gives the power to speak, then, to speak well. [. . .] Let these things be held and spoken in a way that is pleasing to God, and let this be our end to the intelligible divine names (νοητὰς θεωνυμίας). Being led by God, we will now proceed to the *Symbolic Theology*.[12]

At least this much seems clear: perceptible symbols are not divine names.

But this is to put matters modestly. There is not merely *a* difference between the divine names and the perceptible symbols; there is a *qualitative* difference between the divine names and the perceptible symbols. In fact, as the above passages attest, there are *two* qualitative differences between the divine names and the perceptible symbols: whereas perceptible symbols are drawn from occasional visions, divine names are general providences; and whereas perceptible symbols are "changes of name" from the sensible to the divine, divine names just are divine. Ontologically, this means that divine names are divine causes whereas perceptible symbols are not. Semantically, it means that perceptible symbols need to be interpreted metaphorically whereas divine names do not.

I will have a good deal more to say about the causal nature of the divine names throughout this chapter; here, I limit my comments to the semantics of both the perceptible symbols and the divine names. What does it mean to say that perceptible symbols are "changes of name" (*metonymies*) from the sensible to the divine? Just this: when said of God, perceptible symbols predicate the non-sensible with the sensible (e.g., God is a rock) and therefore must have their sense changed from the literal to the figurative (e.g., God is steadfast).[13] By contrast, divine names, when predicated of God, do not need to "change name" from the sensible to the non-sensible since they are not drawn from the sensible realm and therefore already are "divine."[14] (More on the divine nature of the divine names in sections III

---

12. *DN* 13.4, 981C–984A.

13. If Dionysius is using *metonymy* in deliberate distinction from *metaphor*, then perceptible symbols are changes of name based on contiguity rather than similarity. Perhaps, though *metonymy* refers simply to all "transfers of name" (i.e., all non-literal predication).

14. Of course, if everything unfolds from the Dionysian God, then perceptible symbols are also divine. But, unlike intelligible divine names, perceptible symbols are not divine causes; rather they are divinely-caused effects that must be symbolically interpreted for the purpose of uplifting.

and IV.) This is not to say that the divine names are in all respects literally true of God. Still, even when the divine names are not in some respect God, this respect is not one of sensibility. (More on the respects in which the divine names are and are not God in section III and chapter 2.) This is also not to say that the perceptible symbols are useless or inferior or arbitrary. On the contrary, Dionysius repeatedly extols the perceptible symbols for their necessary efficacy and secrecy, occasionally exclaims that they have greater soteriological utility than divine names, and even refers to the perceptible symbols as "descendants and impressions of the divine stamps."[15] Still, perceptible symbols are "changes of name" from the sensible to the divine, whereas intelligible divine names just are divine.

Just as there is a crucial distinction between the divine names and the perceptible symbols so there is a crucial distinction between the divine names *qua* causes and the divine names *qua* properties. Unlike the previous distinction, however, this one is not always well-marked. Its root—as anyone familiar with Platonic philosophy will know—lies in the fact that since any given divine name is the cause of an intelligible property that bears that divine names' name (i.e., is homonymous), the predication of that divine name can be taken as referring either to a causal source or to a caused property. The divine name *life*, for example, can refer either to the divine cause *life-itself* or to the predicated property of life. Of course, divine names *qua* causes are never predicated of participating beings (e.g., angels, humans, animals, plants) since such beings are not themselves divine causes. But in the case of God things are a bit trickier: when the Dionysian corpus states, e.g., that God is life, it can be interpreted as saying that God is the divine cause *life-itself* or that God possesses the property of life. Of course, the former is more likely since—as anyone familiar with Platonic philosophy will also know—causes do not participate in their effects. Still, since properties are pre-contained in causes and causes are pre-contained in God, there is a sense in which God does possess the

---

15. *EP* 9.2, 1108C. The striking unsuitability ("dissimilarity") of perceptible symbols causes the interpreter to look beneath their perceptible shell to their suitable ("similar") conceptual meaning, thereby serving as an important and necessary means of uplifting perceptible beings from the perceptible to the conceptual. The striking unsuitability of perceptible symbols also serves to protect the mysteries from the "hoi polloi," preventing the uninitiated from learning esoteric knowledge. Thus, Dionysius says that like negations, perceptible symbols honor divine things better than the intelligible divine names (*CH* 2.5, 145A). For more on Dionysius' perceptible symbols, see *CH* 2.2–3 and *EP* 9.1–2 as well as Rorem's *Biblical and Liturgical Symbols*.

properties that the divine names source. (More on self-predication and pre-containment in section III.)

Now when Dionysius is precise, he marks this distinction the way any good Platonist would—viz., prefixes the divine names *qua* causes with the Greek intensive *auto* (which is translated as the English suffix *itself*). Thus, as the following passage from *Divine Names* 5.5 states, the divine name *life-itself* is the source of the property of life in living beings.

> And if you wish to say that life-itself (αὐτοζωὴν) is source of what lives as living, and similarity-itself (αὐτοομοιότητα) is source of what is similar as similar, and unity-itself (αὐτοένωσιν) is source of what is unified as unified, and order-itself (αὐτοτάξιν) is source of what is ordered as ordered, and whatever participates in this or that or both or many is this or that or both or many, you will find the participations-themselves (αὐτομετοχὰς) first themselves participating of being and existing with respect to being, then existing as sources of this or that, and both existing and being participated by participating in being. And if these are by participating of being, this is much more so of that which participates of them.[16]

But as mentioned above, Dionysius doesn't always mark this distinction.[17] And more significantly, Dionysius never *auto*-prefixes divine names when he removes them from God, thereby leaving it up to the reader to decide whether he is removing these divine names only *qua* properties or also *qua* causes.[18] As I will argue a little in section III of this chapter and a lot in section III of the next chapter, it makes a good deal more sense to read these removals as applying only to the properties that the divine names source and not also to divine names as sources. For now, though, I would like simply to draw some conclusions from and respond to an objection about the above distinctions.

One important—and hopefully obvious—consequence of the distinction between divine names *qua* causes and divine names *qua* properties is that the latter is dependent upon and derivative from the former. This means that it is only because divine names themselves source properties to

---

16. *DN* 5.5, 820BC. For more passages that *auto* prefix divine names, see note 51.

17. He does, however, mark it whenever he differentiates between causes and effects. See, for example, *DN* 2.8, 645CD; *DN* 5.5, 820BC; *DN* 11.6, 953C–956B.

18. Although Dionysius never removes auto-prefixed divine names, he does sometimes *auto* prefix the *hyper*-prefixed divine names (*DN* 5.2, 816C; *DN* 5.6, 820C). But as I'll explain later (section III), this is just to speak about a respect in which God pre-contains the divine names themselves prior to them being substanced from out of God.

Negating Negation

participating beings that divine names can be taken as properties to be predicated. Without divine names themselves such as *being-itself* and *power-itself* and *peace-itself*, there would be no properties of *being* and *power* and *peace*, and therefore no possibility of predicating anything as *being* and *power* and *peace*. And this means that divine names are not (primarily) names—they are first and foremost the causes of "names" (i.e., properties).[19] But it also means that when some instance of a divine name is taken as a property to be predicated, its meaning is determined by its corresponding divine name. To say that something exists or possesses power or peace is to say that it is a participating instance of the divine name *being-itself* or *power-itself* or *peace-itself*. Of course, this does not mean that the participant is an exact replication of the participated. Nevertheless, as *Divine Names* 2.6 observes, divine names themselves give themselves whole and the same to that which participates in them.

> And yet someone might say that the seal is not whole and the same in all its impressions. But the seal is not the cause of this, for it gives itself whole and the same to each, but the difference of the participants makes the impressions unlike the one and whole and same archetype. For instance, if it is soft and impressionable and smooth and unstamped, and neither resistant and hard nor easily dissolved and incohesive, that which is to be impressed receives a clear and distinct impression. But if it lacks any of the fitness mentioned above, this will be the cause of the imparticipatable and indistinct and whatever else arises from its inaptitude for participating.[20]

Thus we see once again why divine names *qua* predicable properties are not "changes of name from the sensible to the divine." They are non-sensible

---

19. Although the Dionysian corpus employs a considerable number of synonyms for the term *divine name*, all of them reveal the causal nature of divine names. A divine name is a procession (*proodos: DN* 1.4, 589D; *DN* 2.4, 640D; *DN* 2.5, 641D–644A; *DN* 2.11, 649B; *DN* 2.11, 652A; *DN* 3.1, 690B; *DN* 5.1, 816B; *DN* 5.2, 816D; *DN* 5.2, 817A; *DN* 11.6, 956B), power (*dynamis: DN* 2.7, 645A; *DN* 11.6, 956A), radiation (*phaos: DN* 1.4, 592BC; *CH* 1.1, 120B), flowing (*chusis: DN* 9.2, 909C; *DN* 11.6, 956AB), and manifestation (*ekphansis: DN* 2.4, 641A) from God. It is a providence (*pronoia: DN* 1.8, 597A; *DN* 5.2, 817A), giving (*-dotis, -ōsis: DN* 2.5, 644A; *DN* 5.2, 816C; *DN* 11.6, 956A), gift (*dōrea: DN* 2.3, 640C; *DN* 2.5, 644A; *DN* 3.1, 680B; *DN* 5.5, 820B; *DN* 5.6, 820C; *DN* 11.6, 956B), production (*-poios: DN* 2.5, 644A; *DN* 5.2, 816C; *DN* 11.6, 956B), and imparting (*metadosis: DN* 2.5, 644A; *DN* 2.11, 649C) of God. It is a source (*archē: DN* 5.5, 820BC; *DN* 5.6, 820D; *DN* 11.6, 956A) and cause (*aitia: DN* 2.3, 640B; *DN* 5.2, 816C; *DN* 11.6, 956A) of properties.

20. *DN* 2.6, 644BC.

The Divine Names Are Not Names

imprints of or participations in divine names themselves. Thus even when considered as properties or names, divine names are not metaphors.

As mentioned in the introduction to this chapter, one of the arguments *for* the arbitrary-metaphorical nature of the divine names is Dionysius' assertion that since God is the cause of all things, any thing can be used to name God—not only all the names of the Dionysian corpus but also all the names that never make their way into the Dionysian corpus, all the "divine names" of the other. A passage that frequently gets cited in support of this position is *Divine Names* 1.6.

> Knowing this, the theologians hymn it as nameless (ἀνώνυμον) and out of all names. On the one hand, [they hymn it as] nameless (ἀνώνυμον), when they say the thearchy itself, in one of the mystical sights of the symbolic theophany, rebuked him who asked, "What is your name?" and, leading him away from all divine name knowledge (θεονυμικῆς γνώσεως), said, "Why do you ask my name?" and "It is wondrous." Is not this really the wonderful name, "the name *hyper* all," the nameless (ἀνώνυμον), that which is established above "every name that is named," whether "in this age" or "in that which is to come"? On the other hand, [they hymn it as] many-named, when they again introduce it as saying "I am the being," "the life," "the light," "the God," "the truth," and the theosophists themselves many-namely hymn the cause of all out of all that is caused as good, as beautiful, as wise, as beloved, as god of gods, as lord of lords, as "holy of holies," as eternity, as being and cause of eternity, as provider of life, as wisdom, as mind, as logos, as knower, as before having all treasures of every knowledge, as "power," as powerful, as king of kings, as ancient of days, as unaging and un-changing, as "salvation," as "justice," as sanctification, as redemption, as preeminent of all in greatness, and as in the gentle breeze. Moreover, they say that it is in minds and in souls and in bodies and in heaven and in earth, and at the same time as this it is in itself, in the cosmos, around the cosmos, *hyper*-cosmos, *hyper*-heaven, *hyper*-being, sun, air, "fire," "water," "spirit," dew, cloud, stone-itself, and "rock," all beings and nothing of beings.[21]

But a careful reading of this passage—informed by an awareness of the rigid distinction that Dionysius draws elsewhere between divine names and perceptible symbols—militates against such an interpretation. For nowhere in this passage does Dionysius explicitly include perceptible symbols in the category *divine name*, be they actual Dionysian perceptible symbols

---

21. *DN* 1.6, 596ABC.

or other logically possible perceptible symbols.[22] Of course it is true for Dionysius that since God is the cause of all things and God can be named by anything that God has caused, God can be named by all things. But this does not mean that these names should be included in the category *divine name*. There is, as I have shown above, an inviolable distinction between those names that are divine names and those names that are not. Moreover, as I will now go on to show, those names that are divine names are of a precise number and order. This is to say that there can be no other (types of) divine names than those listed and ordered in the *Divine Names*. The category *divine name* is a closed set (at least with respect to its basic types).

II. Divine Names Are Not Arbitrary in Number and Order

As indicated above, the argument that the divine names are merely nominal often serves under the flag of a certain religious pluralism, one that holds not only that there are many different ways of "naming" ultimacy but also that since these many ways are all literally false of an ineffable and unknowable God, they are functionally equivalent. Regardless of the independent merit of this hypothesis, it is an egregiously mistaken interpretation of the Dionysian corpus. For not only are divine names not primarily names, they are also of a precise number and order. Indeed, they must be, since the divine names bear the sole responsibility for causing all the intelligible properties in which beings participate so as to be what they are and do what they do. Put differently, the number and order of the divine names is constrained by the basic parameters of reality.

At first glance this position seems at odds with the text. For there are moments in the Dionysian corpus, moments such as the passage from *Divine Names* 1.6 quoted above, when Dionysius appears to offer up a veritable smorgasbord of divine names.[23] Moreover, the divine names that are actually identified and explicated as such in the *Divine Names* appear to be of a nearly dizzying number and somewhat random order. But it is

---

22. Although the adjective *divine name* (*theonumikēs*) is used to modify the noun *knowledge* (*gnōseōs*) in the second paragraph, there is no indication that the perceptible symbols listed in the last sentence of the third paragraph qualify as such divine-name knowledge, let alone divine names.

23. The other "smorgasbord" of names in the *Divine Names* is at *DN* 1.8. But as Dionysius indicates, the names listed here are perceptible symbols, not intelligible divine names.

The Divine Names Are Not Names

also the case that the *Divine Names* informs the reader that the theologians always order the divine names with respect to the procession of the thearchy.

> You will find, so to say, that every sacred hymning of the theologians manifestingly and hymningly sets in order the divine names (θεωνυμίας) with respect to the good-working procession (πρoόδους) of the thearchy.[24]

And as I will now show, the divine names of the *Divine Names* are of a certain specific number and order. So what appears to be smorgasbord-like is in fact a carefully planned nine-course meal!

It is not the divine names of *Divine Names* 4–7 that are the problem. These are easily recognized as a variant of the first and second hypostases of Athenian Neoplatonism—*good* (ch. 4), *being* (ch. 5), *life* (ch. 6), and *wisdom* (ch. 7). Rather, it is the divine names of the remainder of the treatise (chs. 8–13) that seem to be of random number and order—*power, justice, salvation,* and *redemption* (ch. 8); *great, small, same, other, like, dislike, rest, motion,* and *equality* (ch. 9); *almighty* and *ancient of days* (ch. 10); *peace* (ch. 11); *holy of holies, king of kings, lord of lords,* and *god of gods* (ch. 12); *perfect* and *one* (ch. 13).[25] I believe, though, that two keys unlock the organization of these divine names. The first is the basic principle that since divine names are the sources of the intelligible properties of the cosmos, they must be ordered with respect to the types of properties that they source: properties that carve out basic ontological types fall into one category; those that empower proper hierarchical ordering and functioning, into another category; those that enable the achievement of proper unificatory ends, into yet another. The second is Dionysius' well-established affinity for triads of triads: if Dionysius elsewhere goes to great length to massage "recalcitrant data" into a triadic structure,[26]

---

24. *DN* 1.4, 589D.

25. See Schäfer's *The Philosophy of Dionysius Areopagite* for a helpful explication and representation of the ordering schemes of Thomas Aquinas, Hans Urs von Balthasaar, and Endre von Ivánka, as well as a compelling presentation and defense of his own organization of the divine names (which arranges the divine names into three groups: those that concern procession [chs. 4–7], those that concern remaining [chs. 8–11], and those that concern reversion [chs. 12–13]). Although my organization of the divine names shares some obvious points of similarity with Schäfer's (though predates awareness of it), it differs in its interpretation of the divine name *peace* as well as its analysis of the divine names contained in *DN* 4. See note 27 for more.

26. I'm thinking especially of the ways in which Dionysius contorts the hierarchies to fit them into triads of triads—e.g., by positing a "legal" hierarchy to accompany the ecclesiastical and celestial hierarchies, by combining the heterogeneous theurgical rituals and ecclesiastical roles into the ecclesiastical hierarchy, and by forcing the angelic hierarchy

and if the divine names of chapters 5–7 clearly cohere as the divine names responsible for the procession of basic types of beings, then it bears searching for similar cohesion among the divine names of chapters 8–10 and 11–13.

This is most evident in chapters 11–13, each of which contains divine names that enable the unification of beings. Chapter 11 unfolds the divine name *peace* as the power of unification—that which returns all things by uniting them not only within and between themselves but also with divine knowledge and the divine being.[27] Chapter 12 explicates the reduplicated divine names *holy of holies, king of kings, lord of lords*, and *god of gods* as various ways of denoting not only the goal or end of unification *qua* deification but also the divine names themselves *qua* the sources or means of unification and deification.[28] And chapter 13 presents the divine names *perfect* and *one* as the actual perfection and unification of all things. Together these names make it possible for beings to achieve their proper end—unificatory return.

Although not as initially evident, such cohesion is also present among the divine names of chapters 8–10, together which source the properties that empower beings to function as the particular kinds of hierarchically ordered beings that they are. The divine names of chapter 8 (*power, justice, salvation, redemption*) do this by distributing and preserving functional order in general. More particularly, the divine name *power* accompanies the procession of being, life, and wisdom into all things, thereby enabling all things to

---

into the triadic mold of the ecclesiastical hierarchy (three sacraments, three initiators, three initiateds). For more about this, see chapter 3.

27. *DN* 11.1, 948B, 949A, 949B; *DN* 11.2, 949C–952A; *DN* 11.3, 952B. Contra Schäfer's *The Philosophy of Dionysius Areopagite* (100–112)—which asserts that *peace* is "a synonym of the *monē*," emphasizing its ordering or abiding or steadying aspects, and therefore grouping it with the divine names of *DN* 8–10—I find the unifying aspects of *peace* not only first but also foremost in *DN* 11.

28. For the former, see *DN* 12.3, 972A and *DN* 12.4, 972B. For the latter, note that *DN* 12 states its intention up front as that of declaring what the divine names *themselves* are and what is meant by their *reduplication* (*DN* 12.1, 969AB). In fact, Dionysius discusses the divine names themselves not only in *DN* 12 but also at the very end of *DN* 11. The latter denotes the divine names themselves with *auto*-prefixes; the former, with reduplication as well as the term *autometochai* (participations-themselves). These three techniques are just different ways of referring to the same "thing"—divine names in themselves, which exist absolutely and primarily (*DN* 11.6, 953C), which are the sources of beings and properties (*DN* 11.6, 953D–956B; *DN* 12.4, 972AB), and which are unities according to divine difference (*DN* 2.11, 649AB, 652A; *DN* 5.2, 816C; *DN* 2.5, 641D–644A). As will be argued in section IV, these Dionysian divine names are almost metaphysically indistinguishable from Neoplatonic henads. Thus, one could also read *DN* 11–13 thusly: before discussing the One itself in *DN* 13, Dionysius explicates the divine names *qua* henadic-like unities-in-difference both in *DN* 12 and at the end of *DN* 11.

function properly and consequently achieve proper order;[29] the divine name *justice* distributes proportion, beauty, rank, arrangement, and order, and preserves the nature of everything in its proper place and order;[30] and the divine names *salvation* and *redemption* ensure that beings are preserved and maintained in proper being and order.[31] The divine names of chapters 9 and 10 then source those properties that pattern basic similarities and differences in hierarchically ordered beings. The divine names of chapter 10 (*almighty, ancient of days*) order the cosmos into a temporal perceptible realm and an eternal intelligible realm. More particularly, God possesses the divine name *ancient of days* as both the eternity and the time of all things, the former of which applies to the intelligible realm, the latter of which, to the perceptible realm.[32] And the divine names of chapter 9 (*great, small, same, other, like, dislike, rest, motion, equality*) rank beings within these realms by sourcing what Neoplatonists considered to be the most general Forms.[33] These divine names serve to explain the basic similarities and differences between beings by virtue of properties such as *same* and *other, great,* and *small* (e.g., *x* is other than *y* by virtue of some greatness).

Finally, although obviously cohesive as the sources of the basic ontological categories of being, life, and wisdom, the divine names of chapters 5–7 here require a triad of clarifications (since some of these clarifications will figure prominently in this and later chapters). First, as Dionysian scholars have long observed,[34] whereas the divine names of chapters 5–7 are the names of the second hypostasis in traditional Neoplatonism (with the sole exception that Dionysius substitutes *wisdom* for *mind*), there is no such hypostasis in Dionysian metaphysics (unless that hypostasis is the intellectual-intelligible realm of the celestial minds). Thus all Dionysian divine names are of the first hypostasis—i.e., are God or the Good or the One in pluralized form. (More

---

29. *DN* 8.3, 892B; *DN* 8.5, 892C. See also *CH* 13.4, 321A, which says that *power* holds all things together.

30. *DN* 8.7, 893D–896A; *DN* 8.7, 896B.

31. *DN* 8.9, 896D, 897B.

32. *DN* 10.2, 937B; *DN* 10.3, 940A. Note, however, that *DN* 10 leads with the name *almighty* (*pantokratora*), which is said to preserve and embrace the world (*DN* 10.1, 936D), to generate and return all (*DN* 10.1, 936D–937A), and to hold all things together in total control (*DN* 10.1, 937A). In doing so, Dionysius seems to be reiterating the content of *DN* 8 (power) within the context of a discussion of eternity and time.

33. These names were central to Plato's *Parmenides*, and therefore were considered by Neoplatonists to be among the most general or highest of the Forms.

34. See for example Gersh's *From Iamblichus to Eriugena*.

Negating Negation

on this in section IV.) Still, and second, Dionysius' exposition of the divine name *being* makes it clear that there is a hierarchy of sorts among the divine names. Not only do individual beings participate in being-itself (in order to exist at all), but other divine names also participate in being-itself (in order to exist at all).[35] And third, although being-itself is the cause of both the property of being in general and the being of the other divine names, it is the *paradeigmata* or *logoi* of being-itself that are the causes of individual beings.[36] Of course, in both cases this causation need not be "horizontal" or intentional; nevertheless, some sort of causation is required in order to explain not only why there is anything at all but also why there are the individual things that there are. (More on this in chapter 2.)

What we have then is a triad of triads of divine names, the first of which sources those properties that define basic types of beings (chs. 5–7), the second of which sources those properties that empower the proper hierarchical ordering and functioning of those beings (chs. 8–10), the third of which sources those properties that enable the enactment of unificatory ends by those beings (chs. 11–13).

Table 1: The Divine Names of *Divine Names 5–13*

Divine Names of Ontological Procession	Being (ch. 5)
	Life (ch. 6)
	Wisdom (ch. 7)
Divine Names of Functional Ordering	Power, Justice, Salvation, Redemption (ch. 8)
	Great, Small, Same, Other, Like, Dislike, Rest, Motion, Equality (ch. 9)
	Almighty, Ancient of days (ch. 10)
Divine Names of Unificatory Return	Peace (ch. 11)
	Holy of holies, King of kings, Lord of lords, God of gods (ch. 12)
	Perfect, One (ch. 13)

35. See especially *DN* 5.5; see also *DN* 5.4 and 11.6. Of course, it is also the case that there is a hierarchy of sorts between the divine names *being*, *life*, and *wisdom* due to the fact that only a subset of existing things live and only a subset of living things possess reason and intellect.

36. *DN* 4.7, 701C–704C; *DN* 5.7, 821AB; *DN* 5.8, 821C, 824C; *DN* 5.9, 824D; *DN* 7.3, 869D; *DN* 7.4, 872C. For more on *paradeigmata*, see Perl, "Dionysius," 546.

The Divine Names Are Not Names

Of course, one obvious question here is, what about the divine names of *Divine Names* 4 (*good, light, beautiful,* and *love*)? At least two interpretations of these names are possible. On the one hand, since each of these names is responsible for all three of the basic processional functions above,[37] and since these names are sometimes equated with one another,[38] these names might be different names for God *qua* divine subsistence itself, the source of every source, the cause of all being and non-being.[39] On the other hand, since each of these names is associated primarily with only one these three processional functions—*good* sources beings and non-beings,[40] *beauty* orders beings,[41] *love* returns beings[42]—and since *light* is just an image of *good*,[43] and *love* seems to be a synonym for *one*,[44] these names might effectively constitute the triad *good-beauty-one*,[45] each name of which is identified with one of the three types of processional functions and correlative triads of chapters.[46]

For the sake of my central argument, it hardly matters which of these interpretations is correct, nor even, really, that either is correct. In fact, I do not even need to be right about my proposed organization of the divine names in chapters 5–13 (although I do think there is something to it). It suffices simply to show that as divine causes of intelligible properties, divine names must be of a certain number and order. Without divine names such as *being, life,* and *wisdom,* there would be no beings, living beings, and intelligent beings, respectively; without divine names such as *power, great/*

---

37. *DN* 4.4, 700AB; *DN* 4.7, 704ABC; *DN* 4.10, 705D; *DN* 4.10, 708AB; *DN* 4.14, 712C–713A.

38. The Good and the Beautiful are identified in *DN* 4.7, and eros is assimilated with both in *DN* 4.12.

39. *DN* 2.1, 636C; *DN* 4.1, 693B; *DN* 4.3, 697A; *DN* 4.7, 704BC; *DN* 4.10, 708A; *DN* 5.2, 817A.

40. *DN* 4.1–3, 693B–697A.

41. *DN* 4.7, 701C; see also *CH* 2.4, 144B; *CH* 3.1, 164D; *CH* 3.2, 165B.

42. *DN* 4.10, 708A; *DN* 4.12, 709CD.

43. *DN* 4.4, 697C.

44. *DN* 4.12, 709CD.

45. *DN* 4.7, 704B; *DN* 4.14, 712C.

46. Thus as the procession of beings, God is named *good/light* as well as the related names *being, life,* and *wisdom* (*DN* 5–7); as the order of beings, God is named *beautiful* as well as the related names *power, justice, salvation, redemption, great, small, same, other, like, dislike, rest, motion, equality, almighty,* and *ancient of days* (*DN* 8–10); and as the return of beings, God is named *one/love* as well as the related names *peace, holy of holies, king of kings, lord of lords, god of gods,* and *perfect* (*DN* 11–13).

Negating Negation

small, and *almighty*, there would be no hierarchical order among beings; and without divine names such as *peace, god of gods*, and *one*, there would be no divine unification among beings. Divine names must be able to account for the basic contours of reality and therefore cannot be arbitrary or relative in nature.

The primary objection here is not unlike that of the previous section.[47] If divine names are of a precise number and order, why does Dionysius sometimes offer up what appears to be a random sampling of divine names, and why do these samplings sometimes include names that are not among those explicated in chapters 4–13 of the *Divine Names*?[48] I think, though, that if one works through these passages, one will find not only that the divine names included in them are not so random after all but also that the divine names included in them either are among or reduce to those explicated in chapters 4–13 of the *Divine Names*. I do not have the space here to demonstrate this in all relevant passages. I will though register the fact that it is true of the smorgasbord-like passage quoted above, *Divine Names* 1.6. And I will show in the next chapter that it is true of the passage in which Dionysius removes intelligible divine names from God, *Mystical Theology* 5. Moreover, even if it were the case that Dionysius' "divine names" sometimes either exceed the formal list of divine names explicated

---

47. Another possible objection might be the concern that Dionysius shows at the end of the *Divine Names* regarding a possible imprecise explication of some of the divine names and outright omission of other divine names. This, though, is just characteristic Dionysian humility. (And it might also reflect the fact that investigation of the most basic principles of reality was, for Platonists, an on-going dialectical enterprise.)

48. For some indication of the diversity of divine names consider that such names include traditional Neoplatonic concepts such as cause (*DN* 1.4, 592A; *DN* 1.6, 596B), source (*DN* 1.6, 596B), power (*DN* 1.6, 596B; *DN* 8.1, 889C), truth (*DN* 1.6, 596A), logos (*DN* 1.6, 596B), knowledge (*DN* 1.6, 596B), light (*DN* 1.6, 596A), eternity (*DN* 1.6, 596B), and time (*DN* 1.6, 596B); Neoplatonic hypostases such as god (*DN* 1.6, 596A), one (*DN* 13.4, 977C), good (*DN* 1.6, 596B; *DN* 5.1, 816B), henad (*DN* 1.4, 589D), monad (*DN* 1.4, 589D), being (*DN* 1.6, 594A; *DN* 5.1, 816B), life (*DN* 1.6, 596A; *DN* 5.1, 816B), and mind (*DN* 1.6, 596B); Platonic forms such as beauty (*DN* 1.4, 592A; *DN* 1.6, 596B; *DN* 4.7, 701C), justice (*DN* 1.6, 596B; *DN* 8.1, 889C; *DN* 9.10, 917A), eros (*DN* 4.12, 709B), great (*DN* 1.6, 896B; *DN* 9.1, 909B), small (*DN* 9.1, 909B), same (*DN* 9.1, 909B; *DN* 9.6, 913C; *DN* 9.10, 917A), other (*DN* 9.1, 909B), like (*DN* 9.1, 909B), unlike (*DN* 9.1, 909B), rest (*DN* 9.1, 909B), motion (*DN* 9.1, 909B), and equality (*DN* 9.10, 917A); and terms especially germane to Christianity such as Trinity (*DN* 1.4, 592A), human-loving (*DN* 1.4, 592A), agape (*DN* 1.6, 596B; *DN* 4.7, 701C), wisdom (*DN* 1.4, 592A; *DN* 1.6, 596B; *DN* 5.1, 816B), god of gods (*DN* 1.6, 596B), lord of lords (*DN* 1.6, 596B), holy of holies (*DN* 1.6, 596B), king of kings (*DN* 1.6, 596B), salvation (*DN* 1.6, 596B; *DN* 8.1, 889C), sanctification (*DN* 1.6, 596B), and redemption (*DN* 1.6, 596B; *DN* 8.1, 889C).

in chapters 4–13 of the *Divine Names* or fall outside the categories of divine names proposed above, it would still be the case that since every divine name must source some intelligible property in which beings participate, no divine name can be socially-historically accidental. Dionysian divine names are neither primarily linguistic or metaphorical nor culturally arbitrary or relative.

III. Divine Names Are Not Inessential, Impotent Divine Attributes

The preceding two sections offered evidence against the claim that the divine names are merely names and therefore metaphorical, accidental, or arbitrary. This section and the next turn to the charge that the divine names are merely attributes and therefore not essential, processional, or divine. Against it, I will again be providing evidence for the fact that the divine names source intelligible properties—including existence—to participating beings. But I will also be drawing in evidence both that the divine names are, in some respect, the transcendent triune thearchy in the highest respect and that the divine names, as divine unities, bear a number of striking similarities to Neoplatonic henads. Overall my argument is simply this: to call the divine names *attributes* is misleading if this term functions in such a way as to demote the divine names to a non-essential, non-processional, non-transcendent status.

Just as there is a complexity and coherence to the divine names as a whole, so there is a complexity and coherence to each individual divine name—a complexity and coherence that is, of course, threefold. In this latter case Dionysius employs three different grammatical devices to designate three different respects in which each divine name serves as a divine source of intelligible properties: divine names are prefixed with *hyper* (beyond) to refer to them as they are precontained in and substanced out of God prior to or independent of their causal roles; they are prefixed with *auto* (itself) to refer to them as causes apart from the participation of beings in them; and they are suffixed with *ōsis* (making)—or, less frequently, *poiēsis* (producing), *gonos* (begetting), or *dōros* (giving)—to refer to them as they actually flow forth to participating beings. (Note that these three ways of referring to divine names themselves do not constitute three different types or levels of divine names; rather they denote three different respects in which any given divine name is and is said of God—as substanced out of God, as existent "in itself," and as flowing forth to beings.[49]) Although this terminology shows up repeatedly throughout the Dionysian corpus, it receives its most systematic exposition in *Divine Names* 11.6, the longest treatment of the divine names as such in the Dionysian corpus. Here, in response to two *aporiai* concerning divine names, Dionysius details these three different respects in which the divine names "exist" with respect to God and function with respect to that which they cause.

In response to the first *aporia*—How is God both the divine names and the substance of the divine names?—Dionysius says that God is, on the one hand, the divine names as cause of all beings and, on the other hand, that which gives substance to the divine names as *hyper* all beings.

> But since you once asked me by letter what I mean by being-itself (αὐτοεῖναι), life-itself (αὐτοζωήν), and wisdom-itself (αὐτοσοφίαν), and since you also said that you were at a loss about how I say sometimes that God is life-itself (αὐτοζωήν) and other times that God gives substance to life-itself (τῆς αὐτοζωῆς ὑποστάτην), I thought it necessary, sacred man of God, to release you from this difficulty. First, in order that we may now repeat what I have said a thousand times before, there is no contradiction in saying that God is power-itself (αὐτοδύναμιν) or life-itself (αὐτοζωήν) and that which gives substance (ὑποστάτην) to life-itself (αὐτοζωῆς) or peace or power. For the former is said with respect to beings and especially with respect to the first beings as cause of all beings, while the latter is said *hyper*-beingly *hyper*-be-ing *hyper* all and the first beings.[50]

This much seems easy enough: As the cause of all beings, God is named by the *auto*-prefixed divine names themselves;[51] as that which gives substance

---

49. Thus, the final sentence of *DN* 11.6 (the preceding sentences of which will be exposited below) collapses these distinctions: "Here some of our divine instructors say that the *hyper*-good and *hyper*-divine is the substance (ὑποστάτην) of goodness-itself and divinity[-itself], saying goodness-itself and divinity[-itself] are good-producing and divinity-producing gifts that have proceeded from God, and beauty-itself [is] the beauty-itself-producing flow and the whole beauty and the partial beauty and the things wholly beautiful and the things partially beautiful and whatever other things are said or will be said in the same way, showing that the providences and goodnesses proceeding out of the unparticipated God and flowing over in an ungrudging stream are participated in by beings, precisely so the cause of all may be beyond all, and the *hyper*-being and *hyper*-nature may be altogether preeminent of all things of any kind of being and nature whatever" (*DN* 11.6, 956AB).

50. *DN* 11.6, 953BC.

51. For passages that auto-prefix divine names, see the following: *DN* 2.1, 636C;

The Divine Names Are Not Names

to the divine names themselves, God is named by the *hyper*-prefixed divine names.[52] With respect to the latter (I'll return to the former below), I begin by recognizing that although the connection between the *hyper*-prefixed divine names and God as the substance of divine names does not come out so clearly in the passage above, it does elsewhere, most notably in the last paragraph of *Divine Names* 11.6.

> Here some of our divine instructors say that the *hyper*-good and *hyper*-divine is the substance (ὑποστάτην) of goodness-itself and divinity[-itself].[53]

Beyond this, I emphasize two things. First, as a number of passages indicate, these *hyper*-names are applicable of God even in the "highest" respect.

> As we showed in the *Theological Outlines* with many examples from the Scriptures, the things unified (ἡνωμένα) of the whole divinity are the *hyper*-good, the *hyper*-divine, the *hyper*-being, the *hyper*-life, and the *hyper*-wise, and whatever else is of the preeminent removal [...].[54]
>
> For example, this is unified and common to the henarchic (ἐναρχικῇ) trinity with respect to the divine unity (ἡνωμένον)

DN 2.8, 645D; *DN* 4.16, 713C; *DN* 4.21, 724C; *DN* 5.5, 820ABC; *DN* 6.1, 825C; *DN* 6.1, 856B; *DN* 6.2, 856C; *DN* 6.3, 857C; *DN* 7.1, 865B, 868A; *DN* 8.2, 889D; *DN* 9.6, 916A; *DN* 9.10, 917A; *DN* 11.2, 949C; *DN* 11.6, 953B–956B. (On the peculiarity of some of these terms, see Wear and Dillon, *Dionysius the Areopagite*, 11.) For passages that refer to particular divine names as the sources or causes of particular properties, also see the following: *DN* 4.1, 693B; *DN* 4.4, 697CD; *DN* 4.7, 701C; *DN* 4.12, 709CD; *DN* 5.1, 816B; *DN* 5.2, 816C; *DN* 6.3, 857B; *DN* 7.1, 868A; *DN* 8.7, 893D–896A; *DN* 8.9, 896D; *DN* 9.6, 913D; *DN* 9.8, 916B; *DN* 10.3, 940A; *DN* 11.1, 948D–949A; *DN* 12.4, 972AB; *DN* 13.2, 977C–980A. For passages that refer to divine names as the sources or causes of properties in general, note 19 above.

52. For passages that call God the substance of the divine names, see *DN* 2.1, 636C; *DN* 2.8, 645D; *DN* 4.16, 713C; *DN* 4.21, 724C; *DN* 5.5, 820ABC; *DN* 6.1, 825C; *DN* 6.1, 856B; *DN* 6.2, 856C; *DN* 6.3, 857C; *DN* 7.1, 865B, 868A; *DN* 7.2, 868C; *DN* 8.2, 889D; *DN* 9.6, 913D; *DN* 9.6, 916A; *DN* 9.10, 917A; *DN* 11.2, 949C; *DN* 11.6, 953B–956B; *EP* 2, 1068A–1069A. For passages that associate God *qua* substance of divine names with *hyper*-prefixed divine names, see the following: *DN* 11.6, 956A; *EP* 2, 1068A–1069A. For passages that associate *hyper*-prefixed divine names with divine unity, see the following: *DN* 2.3, 640B; *DN* 2.4, 640D, 641A. For passages that rank God's causality of the divine names prior to the subsistence of the divine names, see the following: *EP* 9.2, 1108D; *DN* 6.3, 857B.

53. *DN* 11.6, 956A. See also the relevant references in the preceding note.

54. *DN* 2.3, 640B. For more applications of *hyper*-names to God, see the following: *DN* 1.1, 588B; *DN* 2.3, 640B; *DN* 2.4, 640D–641B; *DN* 5.2, 816C; *DN* 11.6, 953C–956B; *MT* 1.1, 997B.

Negating Negation

> *hyper*-beingness: the *hyper*-being subsistence, the *hyper*-divine divinity, the *hyper*-good goodness, the identity beyond all of the whole identity beyond all, the *hyper* henarchic unity (ἡ ὑπὲρ ἐναρχίαν ἑνότης), the unspeakable, the much-speaking, the unknowable, the all-intelligible, the positing of all, the removal of all, the *hyper* all positing and removal, the remaining and foundation of the henarchic substances (ἐναρχικῶν ὑποστάσεων) in one another (if I may so speak), wholly *hyper*-unified (ὑπερηνωμένη) and in no part comingled [...].[55]

Second, as some other passages suggest, these *hyper*-names designate the manner in which the divine names themselves are pre-contained (*prolambanō*) or pre-held (*proechō*) or pre-existent (*proeimi, proneimi*) or pre-subsistent (*prohyphistmi, prouparxō*) in God in a unified, unlimited, transcendent, and superabundant manner.[56]

> For it is not only the cause of cohesion or life or perfection such that the *hyper*-name goodness should be named from one or another of its providences. But it also has pre-contained (προείληφε) all beings absolutely and limitlessly in itself in the all-perfect goodness of its one and all-causing providence, and it is fittingly hymned and named out of all beings.[57]

> Suitably, then, more principally than all the others, God is hymned as being from the elder of his other gifts. For pre-having (προέχων) even pre-being (προεῖναι) and *hyper*-being (ὑπερεῖναι) and *hyper*-having (ὑπερέχων) being, God pre-hypostatized (προϋπεστήσατο) all being, I say being itself of itself (αὐτὸ καθ αὐτό), and hypostatized (ὑπεστήσατο) everything whatsoever that exists in being

---

55. *DN* 2.4, 641A.

56. The register of the critical edition of the Dionysian corpus lists one occurrence of *pro-hyparxis* (*DN* 4.10, 708B) and nine occurrences of *pro-hypostasis* (*DN* 1.4, 592D; *DN* 4.7, 704A; *DN* 4.12, 709D; *DN* 5.5, 820B; *DN* 5.6, 820D; *DN* 5.8, 824C [two appearances]; *DN* 6.3, 857B; *DN* 7.2, 869B). Thesaurus Linguae Graecae lists nine occurrences of *pro-(en)eimi* (*DN* 2.8, 645D; *DN* 4.14, 712C; *DN* 5.5, 820A [three appearances]; *DN* 5.5, 820B; *DN* 5.8, 821D; *DN* 5.8, 824A; *EP* 9.5, 1112C), thirteen occurrences of *pro-echō* (*DN* 1.6, 596B; *DN* 2.10, 648C; *DN* 4.6, 701B; *DN* 4.7, 704A; *DN* 5.5, 820B; *DN* 5.8, 824B; *DN* 5.9, 825A; *DN* 5.10, 825B; *DN* 7.2, 869B; *DN* 8.2, 889D; *DN* 8.6, 893C; *DN* 9.4, 912C; *DN* 13.1, 977B), and twelve occurrences of *prolambanō* (*DN* 1.4, 593A; *DN* 1.5, 593A; *DN* 1.7, 597A; *DN* 4.12, 709B; *DN* 5.4, 817D; *DN* 5.8, 824B; *DN* 5.8, 824C; *DN* 7.2, 869A; *DN* 7.2, 869B; *DN* 7.4, 872C; *DN* 9.10, 917A; *DN* 13.3, 980B).

57. *DN* 1.7, 596D–597A.

itself. And so, all the sources of beings, by participating in being, both are and are sources, and first are and then are sources.⁵⁸

To say that God is the *hyper*-names is therefore to say more than that God is beyond the divine names themselves; it is also to say that God pre-contains or pre-holds the divine names themselves in a *hyper*-unified and *hyper*-existent manner. And this is to say that there are important senses in which God, even in the most transcendent respect, *is* the divine names.

This takes us into Dionysius' response to the second *aporia*: What is a divine name in general and which divine name is the first to be given substance from God? Here, in spite of Dionysius' claim that his explanation is "simple and direct," the solution is not as clear.

> But you ask, what really do we say is being-itself (αὐτοεῖναι) or life-itself (αὐτοζωήν) or whatever exists simply and primarily, and what do we posit as first to subsist (ὑφεστηκέναι) from out of God? But we say this is not oblique but rather has a simple and direct explanation. For we say that being-itself (αὐτοεῖναι), cause of the being of all beings, is not some divine or angelic being (for only that which is *hyper*-being is source, being, and cause of all beings and being itself), nor do we say that another divinity besides the *hyper*-divinity is both life-production for all that lives and life-cause of life-itself, nor, to speak summarily, do we say that the sources and demiurges of beings are beings and substances (ὑποστάσεις), which some superficial people describe as gods and demiurges of beings, whom, to speak truly and properly, neither they nor "their fathers" "knew" since they do not exist. But rather we say that, with respect to source and divinity and cause, being-itself (αὐτοεῖναι) and life-itself (αὐτοζωήν) and divinity-itself (αὐτοθεότητά) are the one *hyper*-source and *hyper*-being source and cause of all, but we say that, with respect to participation, the providential powers given forth out of the unparticipated god are being-itself-giving (αὐτοουσίωσιν), life-itself-giving (αὐτοζώωσιν), and divinity-itself-giving (αὐτοθέωσιν), in which beings, participating in a manner appropriate to themselves, both are and are said to be existing and living and deified and the rest in the same way. Thus, the Good is said to be the substance (ὑποστάτης) first of them, then of the whole of them, then of the parts of them, then of those that participate wholly in them, then of those that participate partially in them.⁵⁹

58. *DN* 5.5, 820B.
59. *DN* 11.6, 953C–956A.

Negating Negation

This passage seems to make two overall points. The first half of the paragraph argues simply that the divine names themselves are not gods or angels: being-itself—which is the source, being, and cause of the being of all beings, and therefore is the first divine name to receive substance from God—just is the *hyper*-being God. (About this claim in particular and the similarities and differences between Dionysian divine names and Neoplatonic henads in general, see the following section.) With this in mind, the second half of the paragraph makes quite a bit more sense. With respect to causation, the divine names themselves just are God (not gods or angels); whereas with respect to participation, the divine names themselves are powers that flow forth from God and are participated in by beings. The divine names in this latter respect are suffixed with *ōsis* (giving), thereby grammatically illustrating their ontological procession out to participating beings.[60] Of course, this is one variation of the general Neoplatonic solution to how a cause can be both unpartipcated and participated.[61] What interests me more here, though, is a bit more superficial. It is the simple fact that it is due to participation in the divine names that beings, first exist at all; second, exist as the types of beings that they are; and third, can be said to be the types of beings that they are. This fact should again make it clear that divine names are not primarily names and, even when they are considered as properties or names, are not metaphors. It should also show that the divine names are not mere attributes—if, that is, *attributes* is meant to imply that the divine names are not processional causes. Finally, given that just as divine names themselves preexist in God so also the properties that divine names themselves source preexist "exceedingly and essentially" in the divine names themselves, it should continue to demonstrate that there are important respects in which the transcendent thearchy *is* the divine names. This is true, *Divine Names* 2.8 declares, even if the divine names

---

60. Although *ōsis*-suffixed divine names are most common, *poiēsis* (producing), *gonos* (begetting), and *dōros* (giving) suffixed divine names are also present in the Dionysian corpus. For other occurrences of such divine names, see the following: *DN* 2.4, 640D; *DN* 2.5, 641D–644B; *DN* 2.7, 645A; *DN* 2.11, 649AB, 652A; *DN* 4.7, 701C; *DN* 11.6, 956AB. For passages that refer to the transcendent God as unparticipated, see the following: *DN* 2.5, 641D–644B; *DN* 12.4, 972AB. Note that although divine names *qua* causes are (usually) *auto*-prefixed, they are nevertheless participated (*DN* 2.5, 644A). Thus, Dionysius uses the interesting term *autometochai* (participateds-themselves) to refer to divine names in themselves (*DN* 12.4, 972AB; *DN* 5.5, 820BC). (Thesaurus Linguae Graecae reveals no prior usage of this term.)

61. Note that Dionysius' variation, like that of other Neoplatonists, is quite complex, including ranks of whole and partial participateds and participations (*DN* 11.6, 956AB).

The Divine Names Are Not Names

themselves do not actually possess the properties that they source (i.e., cannot be self-predicated).

> If someone should say that life-itself (αὐτοζωὴν) lives or that light-itself (αὐτοφῶς) is lit, he does not speak rightly in my view, unless he should say this in another manner, [namely] that those things that are produced by causes pre-exist (προένεστι) abundantly and essentially in their causes.[62]

As *hyper*-named, the transcendent God precontains not only the pre-subsistent divine names themselves but also the properties that those divine names source.

Here the objection to my position points to the rigorous removal of divine names in the *Mystical Theology*: if it is the case that all these divine names are removed from the transcendent God, then how can the transcendent God *be* these divine names in some respect? Let me begin my response by noting that a proper consideration of what it means to say that God is *not* the divine names is the concern of the next chapter, my chapter on negation. Still, I can at least point out here that when Dionysius removes some divine name from God, it is logically possible for Dionysius to be removing (a) only the divine-name-itself, (b) only the property sourced by the divine-name-itself, or (c) both the divine-name-itself and the property sourced by the divine-name-itself. So (b) is logically possible. Moreover, as I'll argue in the next chapter, (b) is evidentially stronger. But here I want to observe that even if (c) is evidentially stronger, it is still the case that the transcendent God must pre-contain both the divine-names-themselves and the properties they source and therefore must *be* the divine names in precisely this manner. There are respects in which divine names just cannot be removed from God—not if God is, as Dionysius repeatedly declares, the cause of all.

---

62. *DN* 2.8, 645D. See also *DN* 2.7, 645A for the assertion that in applying the divine names to God "we intellect (νοοῦμεν) nothing other than the divinizing powers (δυνάμεις) that are brought forward out of it into us, the being-producings or life-begettings or wisdom-givings," even though what these divine names are in "their proper source and foundation" exceeds being and intellect. Note also that the passage above (*DN* 2.8, 645D) seems to be Dionysius' position on the classic Platonic problem of self-predication (see also *DN* 4.7, 701C–704A; *DN* 9.6, 913CD).

IV. Divine Names Are Not Qualitatively Different From Neoplatonic Henads

Although the argument that Dionysian divine names are "merely" attributes is sometimes used to drive a wedge between the nameless essence of God and the inessential-impotent attributes of God, it is more frequently enlisted to distinguish Dionysian divine names from Neoplatonic henads. A Christian such as Dionysius, it assumes, could not possibly have given credence to the notion that anything other than God is responsible for causation (which is often assumed to be a creation out of nothing), let alone the notion that such things are divine. Thus, it exclaims, Dionysius transformed the Neoplatonic doctrine of divine names into a doctrine of divine attributes.[63] Consequently, it proclaims, Dionysian divine names are essentially impotent—functionless manifestations of the glory of God that serve no necessary causal role (since everything is created immediately by God).[64]

I hope to have shown above that at least some of these claims are evidentially weak. There is no evidence in the Dionysian corpus of *creatio ex nihilo*; rather, the divine names, the properties they source, and the beings that participate in them, all preexist in and process from God.[65] Moreover, there is an abundance of evidence that the divine names are responsible for the causation of all intelligible properties, *being* included (whereas the *paradeigmata* or *logoi* of the divine name *being-itself* are responsible for the causation of individual beings). Given that I have already provided this evidence, I turn my efforts here to the claim that Dionysian divine names and Neoplatonic henads are qualitatively different, arguing instead that although Dionysian divine names are not independently existing "gods," they are practically equivalent to Neoplatonic henads in every other important way. Indeed, it is more accurate to say that the divine names are processive divine unities than that they are impotent divine attributes.

---

63. Louth, *Denys*, 86. See also Rorem, *Pseudo-Dionysius*, 140, 154, 161, 163–64; and Golitzin, *Et Introibo Ad Altare Dei*, 55–59.

64. Louth, *Denys*, 86.

65. Moreover, this procession seems to be necessary or "automatic" (*DN* 4.1, 693B). Note that in speaking about God's causal relationship with the cosmos, Dionysius almost always prefers the impersonal vocabulary of Neoplatonism—*cause, source, flow-over, bubble-over*—to the personal language of the Bible (*ktizō*).

My first argument is simply that Dionysian divine names do almost everything that Neoplatonic henads do.[66] Henads—literally, *ones* or *units*—pluralize the One (just as minds pluralize Mind and souls pluralize Soul); so too do divine names, which are processions from God that not only are unified and divine but also precede the further procession of God into the realm of mind (angels) and soul (humans). As pluralized unities, henads are attempts to bridge the gulf between the first principle and everything else; so too are divine names, which, locate multiplicity within God, making it possible both for everything to be pre-contained in God (in a *hyper*-unified, *hyper*-existent manner) and for everything to participate in God (by participating in the divine names rather than God *per se*). Henads are not only pluralized unities but also transcendent Forms;[67] so too are divine names, which, although preexistent in God, source intelligible properties to participating beings.[68] Finally, henads provide an object of worship for pagan Neoplatonists; so too do divine names, which, although not pagan deities, nevertheless serve as objects of contemplative praise and union.[69]

---

66. This brief explication of henads is heavily dependent on Dodds' commentary on Proclus' *Elements of Theology* (257–84) as well as Siorvanes' introduction to the person and thought of Proclus (*Proclus*).

67. According to Dodds, Proclus held that whereas Forms proper (with respect to causation) inhabit the second hypostasis, Forms with respect to transcendent unity are henads ("Commentary," 258). Sheldon-Williams ("Henads and Angels") saw things differently, arguing that although Proclus' predecessor and teacher, Syrianus, held that henads are both pluralized unities/divinities and transcendent forms/causes, Proclus believed that henads were only pluralized unities/divinities and not also transcendent forms/causes. (For this reason, Sheldon-Williams found Dionysius' doctrine of divine names closer to Syrianus' doctrine of henads than to Proclus'.) According to Sheldon-Williams, this earlier, dual understanding of henads has its ultimate roots in Plato, who used the term twice, once to refer to gods (*Timaeus* 41ABC), and once to refer to Forms (*Philebus* 15A).

68. Here lies one important difference between divine names and henads—divine names do all the sourcing of intelligible properties, needing no "help" from beings below the henadic level (e.g., the angels), whereas henads are just the initial point in a long chain of processional activity. Indeed, the only "Form-like" entity in Dionysian metaphysics is the divine names (which "inhabit" the henadic level), whereas in Procline metaphysics the "Forms proper" reside in the first tripartization of the second hypostasis.

69. Praise, in that the entire *Divine Names* is a hymn to the divine names; union, in that the *aphairetic* union with the divine rays is effectively a union with the divine names. For the latter, see section IV of chapter 3. Compare Eric Perl's claim that the most significant difference between Dionysian divine names and Procline henads is not metaphysical but soteriological: although Proclus hymns the many modes of unity as a multiplicity of gods, Dionysius hymns God as the many modes of unity (*Theophany*, 68).

Negating Negation

My second argument is that divine names are structured similarly to henads, both individually and collectively. As causes, Procline henads exist in three different respects: according to causation (*kat aitian*), subsistence (*kath hyparxin*), and participation (*kata methexin*);[70] so too do Dionysian divine names, which, as *hyper*-prefixed, are precontained in and caused from out of God; as *auto*-prefixed, subsist from out of God; and as *ōsis*-suffixed, make themselves available to participating beings. Procline henads are also ordered into three series, the first of which presides over the existence of beings; the second, over the power of beings; the third, over the activity of beings;[71] so too are Dionysian divine names, the first set of which sources properties that process being in its most basic gradations; the second set of which sources properties that empower beings to be the particular kind of hierarchically-ordered beings that they are; and the third set of which sources properties that enable beings to achieve appropriate degrees of internal and external unification.

My final argument is just the language that Dionysius uses in speaking about the divine names. Since Dionysian divine names not only process directly from the unparticipated first principle but also just are the first principle in a pluralized and participated form, they are spoken of as divine unities. This language comes out strongest in *Divine Names* 2, an extended treatment of unity and difference in God. Here, after *Divine Names* 2.1 establishes that every divine name applies equally to the entire triune thearchy, *Divine Names* 2.2 and 2.3 begin using the language of unity to refer to the divine names (in both their transcendent and causal senses) as that which is common to the entire triune thearchy, reserving the language of difference for the particular members of the Trinity.

> As we showed in the *Theological Outlines* with many examples from the writings, the things unified (ἡνωμένα) of the whole divinity are the *hyper*-good, the *hyper*-divine, the *hyper*-being, the *hyper*-life, and the *hyper*-wise and whatever else is of the preeminent removal, with which also [are included] all those that have a

---

70. See proposition 65 of Proclus' *Elements of Theology* for the assertion that everything that subsists in some fashion does so as cause (*kat aitian*) or as substance (*kath hyparxin*) or as participant (*kata methexin*). For similar language in the Dionysian corpus, see *EP* 9.2, 1108D and *DN* 6.3, 857B.

71. Proclus, *Elements of Theology*, secs. 151–53. See also, Rosán, *The Philosophy of Proclus*, 136–37; and Siorvanes, *Proclus*, 100–110. Compare the Dionysian claims both that the rays of the Good are responsible for all beings, powers, and activities (*DN* 4.1, 693B) and that the triad *being-power-activity* exists in all divine minds (*CH* 11.2, 284D).

The Divine Names Are Not Names

causal sense—the good, the beautiful, the being, the life-genesis, the wise, and whatever else the cause of all goods is named from its good-fitting gifts. But the things differentiated (διακεκριμένα) are the *hyper*-being name and property of Father and Son and Spirit, in which no interchange or community is in any way introduced. But in addition to this, the all-complete and unaltered subsistence of Jesus amongst us and the essential mystery of his love for humans through it are differentiated.[72]

This is all good and well until *Divine Names* 2.4 calls for new beginning to the inquiry, one that systematically takes up what is proper in the matter of divine unity (*henōseōs*) and difference (*diakriseōs*), rejecting "the various unwise things that are said." Now we are told that the divine unions are "the hidden and non-proceeding *hyper*-establishments of a *hyper*-ineffable and *hyper*-unknowable constancy," whereas the divine differences are "the good-formed processions and manifestations of the thearchy." Moreover, we are told that there are "certain specific unions and differentiations" with respect to this union and differentiation.

> For as I said elsewhere, the sacred initiators of our theological tradition call the divine unions the hidden and un-proceeding *hyper*-establishments (ὑπεριδρύσεις) of a *hyper*-ineffable (ὑπεραρρήτου) and *hyper*-unknowable (ὑπεραγνώστου) constancy, but they call the [divine] differences the good-formed processions and manifestations of the thearchy. And, following the sacred Scriptures, they say there are certain specific unions and differentiations that are proper to the union and differentiation spoken about in turn.[73]

This gives us, then, four logically distinct categories:

1a divine unions with respect to the divine union (i.e., with respect to the hidden and permanent *hyper*-establishments);

1b divine differences with respect to the divine union;

2a divine unions with respect to the divine difference (i.e., with respect to the good-formed processions and manifestations);

---

72. *DN* 2.3, 640BC.

73. *DN* 2.4, 640D–641A. The remainder of *DN* 2.4 and 2.5 make a good deal more sense if the phrase "spoken about earlier" is taken as referring to the understanding of union and difference mentioned immediately above (as *hyper*-establishments and processions) rather than the earlier understanding of union and difference (as divine names and persons of the Trinity). Paul Rorem prefers the latter interpretation (*Pseudo-Dionysius*, 138–41).

Negating Negation

  2b divine differences with respect to the divine difference.

Dionysius begins his explication of these categories with the divine unities of the divine unity (1a). These are what I identified earlier as the *hyper-*prefixed divine names—the divine names as they preexist in God in a *hyper-unified* and *hyper-existent* manner. They are common to the members of the Trinity in general, constituting a set of pluralized unities within the triune thearchy.

> For example, this is unified and common to the henarchic (ἐναρχικῇ) Trinity with respect to the divine unity (ἡνωμένον) *hyper*-beingness: the *hyper*-being subsistence, the *hyper*-divine divinity, the *hyper*-good goodness, the identity beyond all of the whole identity beyond all, the *hyper* henarchic unity, the unspeakable, the much-speaking, the unknowable, the all-intelligible, the positing of all, the removal of all, the *hyper* all positing and removal, the remaining and foundation of the henarchic substances (ἐναρχικῶν ὑποστάσεων) in one another (if I may so speak), wholly *hyper*-unified (ὑπερηνωμένη) and in no part comingled [. . .].[74]

Next come the divine differences of the divine unity (1b). These are the persons of the Trinity in their distinctness, each of which is, nevertheless, "purely and unconfusedly founded in the unity itself." (Note that this means that the members of the Trinity are not just another part of the procession of God—they are God *per se*.[75])

> The distinction in the *hyper*-being theologies is not only what I have said, namely that each of the henarchic substances (ἐναρχικῶν ὑποστάσεων) is purely and unconfusedly founded in the unity (ἕνωσιν) itself, but also that that which pertains to the *hyper*-being theogonies are not convertible with respect to one another. The Father is the only source of the *hyper*-being divinity, since the Father is not the Son and the Son is not the Father. Thus the hymns reverently guard that which is proper to each of the thearchic substances (θεαρχικῶν ὑποστάσεων).[76]

After a brief recapitulation of these first two categories, Dionysius then continues on to the third and fourth categories—the divine unions and differences of the divine difference (2a, 2b). Here, the "unifieds according to

 74. *DN* 2.4, 641A.

 75. This is in contrast to Rorem's interpretation (*Pseudo-Dionysius*, 139–40). See note 5 in the next chapter for more on the status of the Trinity in the Dionysian corpus.

 76. *DN* 2.5, 641D.

The Divine Names Are Not Names

the divine difference" are identified as processive divine names (e.g., being-makings, life-makings, and wisdom-producings) that are participated in but do not themselves participate in God, whereas the differences according to the divine difference are, by default, the participants that participate in these divine names.

> These then are the unions (ἑνώσεις) and differences according to the unspeakable unity and subsistence. But if divine difference is the good-showing procession of the divine union (ἑνώσεως), which *hyper*-unitarily makes itself many and multiplies itself by goodness, then unifieds (ἡνωμέναι) according to the divine difference are the irrepressible impartings, the being-makings, the life-makings, the wisdom-producings, the other gifts of the cause of the goodness of all, according to which the unparticipatedly participateds (τὰ ἀμεθέκτως μετεχόμενα) are hymned out of the participants (μετοχῶν) and the participatings (μετεχοντων).[77]

The divine names therefore are divine unities in not one but two respects—they are divine unities according to divine unity with respect to their hidden and permanent *hyper*-establishment in God, and they are divine unities according to divine difference with respect to their good-formed procession from God. And as divine unities, the divine names are henad-like.

Here, the objection produces the two passages from the Dionysian corpus that appear to openly rebuke the Neoplatonic doctrine of henads. The first, the second paragraph from *Divine Names* 11.6, has already been observed above (in the context of my argument that God is the divine names "through and through"). But here it is again in full.

> But you ask, what really do we say is being-itself (αὐτοεῖναι) or life-itself (αὐτοζωήν) or whatever exists simply and primarily, and what do we posit as first to subsist (ὑφεστηκέναι) from out of God? But we say this is not oblique but rather has a simple and direct explanation. For we say that being-itself (αὐτοεῖναι), cause of the being of all beings, is not some divine or angelic being (for only that which is *hyper*-being is source, being, and cause of all beings and being itself), nor do we say that another divinity besides the *hyper*-divinity is life-production for all that lives and life-cause of life-itself (τῆς αὐτοζωῆς αἰτίαν ζωὴν), nor, to speak summarily, do we say that the sources and demiurges

---

77. *DN* 2.5, 641D–644A. John D. Jones is correct in saying that this fourth category is not identified as such ("Introduction," 34–35); nevertheless, it seems implicit in the brief mention of participants and their participatings.

of beings are beings and substances (ὑποστάσεις), which some superficial people describe as gods and demiurges of beings, whom, to speak truly and properly, neither they nor "their fathers" "knew" since they do not exist. But rather we say that, with respect to source and divinity and cause, being-itself (αὐτοεῖναι) and life-itself (αὐτοζωήν) and divinity-itself (αὐτοθεότητά) are the one *hyper*-source and *hyper*-being source and cause of all, but we say that, with respect to participation, the providential powers given forth out of the unparticipated god are being-itself-giving (αὐτοουσίωσιν), life-itself-giving (αὐτοζώωσιν), and divinity-itself-giving (αὐτοθέωσιν), in which beings, participating in a manner appropriate to themselves, both are and are said to be existing and living and deified and the rest in the same way. Thus, the Good is said to be the substance (ὑποστάτης) first of them, then of the whole of them, then of the parts of them, then of those that participate wholly in them, then of those that participate partially in them.[78]

This passage is often interpreted as averring that divine names are not divine or angelic beings and therefore not henads. But it might in fact be saying something different. (It's not exactly Dionysius at his clearest![79]) If the operative word here is *being*—being-itself is not a being (whether divine or angelic) since being-itself is *hyper* being—then there is nothing here that is necessarily critical of henads, since henads also are not beings (whether divine or angelic) but rather "exist" at the henadic level and are therefore *hyper* being. In short, neither divine names nor henads are "beings" (whether divine or angelic). So saying that being-itself is not some divine or angelic being is hardly a manifest critique of the henads. That said, the overall point of this paragraph seems to be that the ultimate cause of the properties that the divine names source is God. Being-itself and life-itself and divinity-itself just are the one *hyper*-source and *hyper*-being source of all. Again, though, I fail to see how this constitutes a direct or overt critique of the henads, since it is also the case in late Neoplatonism that the ultimate cause of all is the first principle.

---

78. DN 11.6, 953C–956A.

79. What I find baffling here, given Dionysius' claim elsewhere that God is the substance of or gives substance to the divine names (see note 52 above), is the declaration that the divine names are not "substances" (ὑποστάσεις). Perhaps, though, this is just to say that the divine names and God are of the same hypostasis—i.e., that the divine names are not located at the "hypostasis" of mind or soul.

The Divine Names Are Not Names

Much of this also applies to the second passage that appears to object to henads, *Divine Names* 5.2 (which I again provide in full).

> And so, the discourse seeks to hymn these manifested divine names (θεωνυμίας) of providence. It does not profess to describe the goodness, being, life, and wisdom, which is *hyper*-being-itself (αὐτοῦπερούσιον), of the divinity, which is *hyper*-being-itself (αὐτοῦπερούσιου), and which is established above in hiddenness, as the Scriptures say, *hyper* all goodness, divinity, being, life, and wisdom. Rather, it hymns the manifested good-producing providence, preeminent goodness and the cause of all goods and being and life and wisdom; the being-producing and life-producing and wisdom-giving cause of that which participates in being and life and mind and reason and sensation. It does not say that goodness is one, being another, and life or wisdom yet another, nor that there are many causes and other productive divinities that are superior and inferior of another, but rather that the entire good processions and the divine names (θεωνυμίας) celebrated by us are of one God, the first of which is descriptive of the entire providence of the one God, the others of which are descriptive of its more general and specific providences.[80]

Again, it seems that no late pagan Neoplatonist would challenge Dionysius' claim that "the entire good processions and the divine names celebrated by us are of one God."[81] Again, though, Dionysius' overall point seems clear: divine names should not be identified with pagan deities.

This is of course one very important difference between Dionysian divine names and Neoplatonic henads. And it is most likely the reason why Dionysius seems generally allergic to the Greek term *henad*, preferring instead to refer to the divine names as *unities* (*henōseis*) or *things unified* (*henōmenai*).[82] Still, my point remains: beyond this fact—as well as

80. *DN* 5.2, 816C–817A.

81. For Proclus, the One is the first source and cause of all things (*Elements of Theology* 11, 12, 56) as well as the substance of other monads (*Platonic Theology* II.6, II.10; *Elements of Theology* 99–100).

82. The term *henad* is used just seven times in the Dionysian corpus—six times in the singular (*DN* 1.1, 588B [which contains two occurrences]; *DN* 1.4, 589D; *DN* 1.5, 593B; *DN* 2.1, 637A; *CH* 7.4, 212C), and just one time in the plural (*DN* 8.5, 892D). Additionally, the term *henarchia* appears just one time (*DN* 2.4, 641A), and the term *henarchikos* appears four times (*DN* 2.4, 641A [which contains two occurrences]; *DN* 2.5, 641D; *DN* 4.4, 700A). In general these uses don't seem to convey anything more than a sense of unity (or super-unity). Sometimes they are applied of God in general (*DN* 1.1, 588B; *DN* 1.4, 589A; *DN* 2.1, 637A; *DN* 4.4, 700A), other times of God as triune unity

Negating Negation

the fact that for Dionysius, nothing below the henadic level plays a role in the procession of properties and beings[83]—there are not any significant differences between Dionysian divine names and late Neoplatonic henads, surely not any that would support the broadside on henads by Dionysian scholars. What's at stake here? First, obviously, the orthodoxy of Dionysius: if Dionysius is a Christian and henads are pagan deities, then Dionysian divine names cannot be henads. I suspect, though, that an issue of "apophatic abandon" may also be at stake: if the divine names are attributive or linguistic in nature, then they cannot be part of the architecture of both the cosmos and the divine and therefore cannot be henadic-like in both their unitive-divine and causal-formal aspects. But with respect to the matter of orthodoxy, it is a theistic error of overcorrection to have Dionysius "insisting" that God creates all things out of nothing and without intermediary and that the divine names therefore play no role whatsoever in the procession of beings and their powers and activities. And with respect to the issue of abandon, it is a (post)modern error of interpretation to have Dionysius completely sweeping away the divine names in the removal of all things from God.

(*DN* 1.5, 593B; *DN* 2.4, 641A; *DN* 2.5, 641D; *CH* 7.4, 212C), and even once of the angels (*DN* 8.5, 892D).

83. See *DN* 5.8 for a possible exception to this.

Chapter 2

Negation
Does Not Negate

If Dionysian divine names are mere names and the Dionysian God is nameless, then Dionysius' negation of divine names is just what it seems to be. But as the last chapter argued, Dionysian divine names are much more than names. And as this chapter will argue, Dionysian negation is not what is commonly thought of as negation. Dionysius' negation of divine names is not what it seems to be.

But this chapter is about more than just the negation of divine names. It begins with an explication of Dionysian negation in general, arguing that a proper understanding of it requires an informed appreciation of the principal terms that constitute it—*aphairesis* (removal), the method by which Dionysius removes predicate-terms from God; and *apophasis* (negation), the logic by which these negated predicate-terms are interpreted.[1] (Note that among these terms are not only divine names and perceptible symbols but also Trinitarian properties and properties pertaining to knowing and speaking in general.) Since the logic of *apophasis* interprets these negated terms "*hyperochically*" (preeminently) rather than "*steretically*"

---

1. When translating from the Dionysian corpus, I have translated *aphairesis* as *removal* and *apophasis* as *negation* as seems to be common translational practice. (The Paulist Press translation translates *aphairesis* as *denial*; this, however, does not properly preserve the semantic distinction between *aphairesis* and *apophasis*.) I have always left the Greek term *apophasis* un-translated in the main body of the chapter so that the English term *negation* can function inclusively of both *apophasis* and *aphairesis*. For stylistic ease, however, I have sometimes translated *aphairesis* as *removal* in the main body of the chapter.

(privatively), the chapter next takes up an exposition not only of *hyperochē* but also of some of the other *hyper*-prefixed terms in the Dionysian corpus, showing how such terms register two different spatial and logical meanings—that of being beyond or separated from (logical inapplicability), and that of being above or more than (metaphysical preeminence). The chapter then argues that this ambiguity should not be resolved by relegating the latter meaning to the "lower" causal God of the divine names; rather the *hyper*-being God is the cause of all by means of the divine names and, as such, it both utterly transcends the properties that the divine names source with respect to being and preeminently pre-contains these properties in a *hyper*-unified, *hyper*-existent manner. Finally, the chapter translates all this back into the language of Dionysian negation: *aphairesis* removes the properties that the divine names source from God with respect to being, thereby revealing, through the logic of *apophasis*, their *hyper*-beingly preeminent pre-containment in God.

I will position these four claims in opposition to two general arguments for apophatic abandonment, the first of which involves the form and logic of Dionysian negation, the second of which concerns the content and reach of Dionysian negation. With regard to the former, it is necessary first to observe that the distinction between *aphairesis* (removal) and *apophasis* (negation) is rarely detected, and even when detected, usually downplayed.[2] More significant, though, is the general assumption that Dionysian negation is roughly equivalent to our ordinary language concept of negation.[3] By "ordinary language concept of negation," I have in mind what logicians call wide-scope propositional negation, where Rush

---

2. The majority of Dionysian scholars do the former, failing to recognize the distinction between *aphairesis* and *apophasis*, and thereby tacitly assuming that both terms roughly equate to the English word *negation*. This is true not only of both older scholarship (e.g., Andrew Louth, Denys Turner) and more recent scholarship (e.g., Eric Perl, Sarah Wear) but also of the Paulist Press translation of the Dionysian corpus. A smaller second category of scholars recognizes the distinction but denies its significance. Paul Rorem, for example, has quipped that *aphairesis* and *apophasis* are surely "the same" (*Pseudo-Dionysius*, 193), whereas H. A. Wolfson has argued that *aphairesis* and *apophasis* function "indiscriminately" ("Negative Attributes," 137). This leaves only a handful of recent scholars who have suggested that there is a meaningful difference between *aphairesis* and *apophasis*. John N. Jones, for example, has maintained that *apophasis* is synonymous with *aphairesis of all beings* ("Sculpting God"), whereas Janet Williams has proposed that *apophasis* culminates and negates the dialectic of *thesis* and *aphairesis* ("The Apophatic Theology"). See note 67 for a brief discussion of Jones' and Williams' positions.

3. For a recent interesting exception to this assumption, see Rojek's "Toward a Logic of Negative Theology."

is not wise is, under normal circumstances, taken to mean *It is not the case that Rush is wise*. (Of course, our ordinary language forms of negation do not all reduce to wide-scope propositional negation; nevertheless I think that this is what most people have in mind when they think of the concept of negation.) So when Dionysius writes that God is not wise, Dionysius is read as saying that it is not the case that God is wise, that wisdom is literally false of God. Granted, careful readers of the Dionysian corpus do not make the mistake of thinking that this negation implies its corresponding contrariety (e.g., God is stupid). Still, such readers often assume that when Dionysius removes wisdom of God, Dionysius means simply and only that it is not the case that the transcendent God is wise. And, even though the careful reader also recognizes that Dionysius removes positing (*thesis*) and removal themselves, this reader usually assumes that such removal indicates simply and only that the transcendent God ultimately cannot be posited of or removed from at all.

Although this first argument for apophatic abandonment usually comes off less as argument than as assumption, the second argument is full-blooded. In fact, it contains two different arguments, each of which attempts to show how Dionysian negation is all-encompassing. The first and more general points to passages in the Dionysian corpus where Dionysius removes from God either a panoply of divine names and perceptible symbols or the methods of positing and removal themselves, inferring from these passages that *nothing whatsoever* is literally true of the Dionysian God, that everything whatsoever that can be thought or said about the Dionysian God is ultimately false of a God that transcends all human categories and activities.[4] The second and more specific draws a similar conclusion, though

---

4. Here I'm thinking again of the work of John Hick and Denys Turner. Hick believes that since all "names" of God are only metaphorically true of God, Dionysian negation states their literal falsity of God. Thus Dionysius' negation of perceptible symbols and divine names in *MT* 4–5 is effectively a declaration that God is absolutely ineffable or transcategorial. No category or name is literally true of God: "Here and elsewhere Denys says in as emphatic and unqualified a way as he can that the Godhead, the ultimate One, is absolutely ineffable, eluding all our human categories of thought" ("Ineffability," 38). Unlike Hick, Turner doesn't find all of the symbols and names of *MT* 4–5 to be metaphorical in nature: although all the symbols of *MT* 4 and half the names of *MT* 5 are metaphorical, the other half of the names in *MT* 5 are not. These names—which Turner believes consist of two different sub-types: predicates that Platonists took to be true of everything (e.g., *being, good, true, one*), and predicates that Platonists took to be absolute rather than relational (e.g., *equality, inequality, similarity, dissimilarity*)—are, for Turner, secondhand descriptions of the logic of negation itself. As such, they state God's infinite transcendence and incommensurateness; they say what God is not. But since

Negating Negation

does so by arguing against those aspects of the Dionysian God that are least obviously denied—divine causation, in particular.[5] Here it is claimed both that if Dionysius denies of God all reference to beings, then Dionysius must deny of God the causation (*aitia*) or support (*hyparxis*) of beings,[6] and that

---

those symbols and names that are essentially metaphorical also exhibit the total failure of language, Turner, much like Hick, ends up averring the literal falsity of all "names" of God (*The Darkness of God*, 39). (See note 18 below, for more on Turner's classification of the "names" of *MT* 5.)

5. Here I'm thinking especially of John D. Jones' arguments against causality in his introduction to his translation of the *Divine Names*, *Mystical Theology*, and *Epistles* 1–5. (Eric Perl also offers some interesting arguments against divine causality—see note 55 below as well as both the introductory and fourth sections of chapter 4.) Note that Jones also argues that Dionysius also denies of God the persons of the Trinity. (See his older "Introduction" [ibid., 91–92] as well as his more recent "An Absolutely Simple God.") Although I find Jones mistaken about this, I will not be arguing so in the main body of my text (due to this book's focus on more traditionally philosophical issues). But I will here observe that whereas Dionysius may deny of God the properties of threeness, oneness, fatherhood, sonship, and spirit, Dionysius never denies of God the persons of the Trinity. And here I will also provide the following in the way of textual evidence: passages that identify Trinity with the *hyper*-being God (*DN* 1.5, 593B; *DN* 2.4, 641A; *DN* 2.5, 644A; *DN* 3.1, 680B; *DN* 13.3, 980B; *MT* 1.1, 997A; *EH* 1.3, 373CD); passages that adamantly declare that all the divine names, even in their transcendent respects, apply to each of the members of the Trinity (*DN* 2.1; *DN* 2.6); and passages that qualify the denial of Trinitarian properties as pertaining only to human conceptions of Trinity (*DN* 13.3, 980D–981A; *MT* 5, 1048A). For the claim that the Dionysian God is Trinitarian through and through, see the more sustained arguments of John N. Jones ("The Status of the Trinity") and Alexander Golitzin (*Et Introibo*, 51–54).

6. Jones, "Introduction," 89–95. Textually, Jones leans on four passages in particular (*DN* 1.5, 593CD; *DN* 5.8, 824A; *DN* 13.3, 980C–981A; *MT* 5, 1048B), though also draws in three additional passages (*DN* 5.1, 816BC; *DN* 11.1, 949BC; *DN* 1.4, 589B). All of these passages have or will be examined at some point in this book. But here let me point out that none of these passages explicitly asserts that God is not the cause or support of all. Indeed, Jones himself admits as much, devoting his efforts instead to developing a couple of interpretive rubrics that he uses to try to show that these passages implicitly deny causality/support of God. The first such rubric argues that since Dionysius equates both the divine name *goodness* and the persons of the Trinity with the functions of causation (*aitia*) and subsistence/support (*hyparxis*), Dionysius effectively denies causation and subsistence of God when he denies of God the divine names *goodness* and the persons of the Trinity. The second rubric instead argues that since Dionysius opposes God *qua* beyond (*hyper*) all to God *qua* cause of all, Dionysius effectively denies causation of God in affirming the beyond-all transcendence of God. Crucial here is Jones' claim that the Greek preposition *hyper* and many of the words that it prefixes—most importantly *hyperochē* (literally "beyond-having," commonly "preeminence")—function as negations in the Dionysian corpus (ibid., 31). So when Dionysius says that God is *hyper* wise, Dionysius means that it is not the case that God is wise. And when Dionysius says that negations should be interpreted in a *hyperochic* manner, Dionysius means that God is

Negation Does Not Negate

if Dionysius denies of God "all logos," then Dionysius must "radically deny" all affirmative and metaphysical theology in general (especially insofar as it is concerned with divine causation).⁷

Although I will position my four claims against these two arguments, these claims and arguments will not line up as evenly as the claims and arguments of chapter 1. Rather, I will be mounting a cumulative-case

---

beyond the having of anything. In this latter case Jones recognizes that *hyperochē* is usually used in Greek philosophy to express the preeminence of a cause over what it causes; still he maintains that *hyperochē* is, for Dionysius, "fundamentally ambiguous," serving to express the preeminence of divine causes with respect to metaphysical negative theology, while denying causality altogether with respect to mystical negative theology (ibid., 94–95). Here, we circle back to Jones' logical argument: since Dionysius supposedly denies of God all reference to beings, Dionysius must deny preeminence of God. Mystical negative theology therefore "must" translate *hyperochē* as "beyond-having" or "beyond-preeminence" (ibid., 95). My arguments otherwise appear throughout this chapter, but see section III in particular.

7. Jones, "Introduction," 95–103. Jones maintains that the mystical negative theology supposedly espoused by Dionysius constitutes a "radical denial" of both affirmative theology in particular and metaphysics in general (ibid., 25, 20 n. 20). Here Jones distinguishes mystical negative theology from metaphysical negative theology, the latter of which functions strictly within affirmative theology as a means of expressing the preeminence of the divine causality celebrated by affirmative theology (ibid., 20 n. 20). Mystical negative theology by contrast denies of God all reference to being, not in order to affirm God's preeminence over beings, but rather to deny of God all eminence and causality/support (ibid., 97). Jones qualifies these claims by noting that mystical negative theology is not a declaration that affirmative theology is false or an illusion; rather, it is simply a "going away from" or "indifference to" all beings and all logos (ibid., 101; see also 21, 23, 25, 26). Put differently, negative mystical theology is not one logos among many; it is the denial of every logos or standpoint (ibid., 102). And again, negative mystical theology neither denies of God all knowledge whatsoever nor holds that God is not be-ing in any way whatsoever; instead, it recognizes that there is *hyper*-being knowledge of an overfull God that "exists" in a manner beyond every way of being, simply and unlimitedly (ibid., 25, 32, 54). But it is not clear how exactly to interpret such claims alongside the simultaneous proclamation that mystical negative theology constitutes the radical denial not only of affirmative theology and metaphysics in particular but of all attempts to make God intelligible or to speak of God in general (ibid., 100, 5, 19, 22). On the one hand, the radical denial not only of every attempt to render God intelligible in general but also of particular divine names *qua* causal powers sure looks like a declaration that affirmation theology both in general and in this particular case are false. (It is, for Jones' Dionysius, the case that the transcendent God is *hyperochē* wise *qua* not wise; *hyperochē* cause/support *qua* not cause support.) On the other hand, the discourse of God *qua* overfull, beyond-being, simple, and unlimited sure sounds like a discourse that renders God intelligible. (Indeed, to certain [(post)modern] audiences it renders God even more intelligible than the discourse of God *qua* cause of all.) But of course what matters here is not the coherence of Jones' mystical negative theology but Dionysius' alleged adherence to it.

argument throughout the entirety of this chapter. And so, only toward the end of this chapter should it become clear both why it is not the case that Dionysius denies all things of God and how Dionysian negation differs from our ordinary concept of negation. Only then, therefore, should it also become clear why and how the Dionysian God is not the God of apophatic abandonment—not a God that is utterly removed from all things and utterly devoid of all things, but a God that preeminently pre-contains all things and providentially processes all things.

I. Negation: *Aphairesis* and *Apophasis*

One of the more surprising aspects of the Dionysian corpus is its infrequent use of the term *apophasis*. Whereas *aphairesis* shows up a total of twenty-six times in the corpus, *apophasis* makes just nine appearances, only two of which can be found in the so-called "apophatic" treatise *Mystical Theology*, neither of which falls after the introductory first chapter.[8] The term *apophasis* is therefore entirely absent from the central methodological and performative chapters of the *Mystical Theology* (whereas *aphairesis* is used twelve times in these chapters and fourteen times in the entire treatise). Instead, the chapters on method (chs. 2–3) present *aphairesis* as the privileged means of hymning the *hyper*-being God. And the subsequent performative chapters (chs. 4–5) implement this method, hymning the *hyper*-being God through the removal of perceptible and intelligible properties from God.

Drawing upon the well-known Plotinian metaphor, chapter 2 of the *Mystical Theology* compares the method of *aphairesis* to the *technē* of sculpting.[9] Just as the sculptor chisels away stone to create a statue, the *aphairetic* method removes "beings" to reveal the *hyper*-being darkness of God.

> We pray to come to this *hyper*-light darkness, and through not-seeing and not-knowing to see and to know not to see and to know that which is *hyper* sight and knowledge itself—for this is truly seeing and knowing—and [we pray] to hymn *hyper*-beingly the *hyper*-being through the removal of all beings (τῆς πάντων τῶν ὄντων ἀφαιρέσεως), just as those making a life-like statue lift-out (ἐξαιροῦντες) every obstacle to the pure view of the

---

8. The register of Greek terms in the critical edition of the Dionysian corpus lists twenty-six occurrences of *aphairesis/aphaireō* and eight occurrences of *apophasis/apophaskō*. Thesaurus Linguae Graecae reveals an additional adjectival appearance of *apophasis* (*apophatikais*) at *CH* 2.3, 140D.

9. Plotinus, *Enneads* I.6.9.

> hidden and reveal the hidden beauty in it by the removal alone (τῇ ἀφαιρέσει μόνῃ). It is necessary, I think, to hymn the removals (τὰς ἀφαιρέσεις) oppositely from the positings; for we posit these beginning from the first things and descending through the middle things to the last things; but then we remove everything (τὰ πάντα ἀφαιροῦμεν) making the search for the highest principles from the last things, so that we may unhiddenly know this unknowing that is covered by all the knowledge among all beings, and we may see this *hyper*-being darkness that is hidden by all the light among beings.[10]

Turning next to the traditional Neoplatonic interpretation of negation in Plato's *Parmenides*, *Mystical Theology* 3 specifies the sequence in which "beings" are to be removed from God.[11] Whereas the method of *thesis* posits beings of God in order of closeness, *aphairesis* removes beings from God in reverse order of accuracy.

> But why in short, you say, having posited the divine positings from the first thing, do we begin the divine removal (τῆς θείας ἀφαιρέσεως) from the last things? Because when positing that which is *hyper* all positing it is necessary to posit the attributive affirmation from the more akin to it; but when removing that which is *hyper* all removal (τὸ ὑπὲρ πᾶσαν ἀφαίρεσιν ἀφαιροῦντας) it is necessary to remove (ἀφαιρεῖν) from the farthest away from it. Is it not life and goodness more than air and stone? And not drunkenness and not anger more than not speaking and not intellecting?[12]

Together these chapters present a fairly uncomplicated picture of *aphairesis*. *Aphairesis* is a hymning of the *hyper*-being God. *Aphairesis* removes or abstracts "beings" from God (whereas *thesis* posits them of God). *Aphairesis* removes such beings sequentially, from last or furthest to first or closest (whereas *thesis* posits them of God in order of accuracy). And *aphairesis* removes *all* such beings. (This is the meaning of the phrase *aphairesis of all [beings]*, one of a few special usages of *aphairesis*.[13]) Paradoxically, however,

10. *MT* 2, 1025AB.

11. See especially Proclus' *Commentary on Plato's* Parmenides, 1088–89.

12. *MT* 3, 1033CD.

13. The phrase *aphairesis of all (beings)* occurs a total of seven times in the Dionysian corpus—twice in the above excerpt from *MT* 2, and five times in the *Divine Names* (*DN* 1.5, 593BC; *DN* 2.4, 641A; *DN* 4.3, 697A; *DN* 4.7, 704B; *DN* 7.3, 872A). (Note that the phrase *apophasis of all [being]* is never used in the Dionysian corpus.) Although I am indebted to John N. Jones' explication of this phrase ("Sculpting God," 360–63), I prefer to think of the *removal of all (beings)* as a methodological goal rather than a methodological

Negating Negation

this removal of all does not sculpt away everything whatsoever; rather, it reveals an underlying statue of sorts, yielding true "knowing" and "seeing" of the unknowable divine darkness. (More on this later.)

Mystical Theology 4 and 5 then put this *aphairetic* method into practice, hymning "the cause of all and being *hyper* all" by removing predicate-terms from it. Chapter 4 begins with four alpha-privative divine names.

> And so we say that the cause of all and being *hyper* all is not being-less (ἀνούσιός), not life-less (ἄζωος), not logos-less (ἄλογος), and not mind-less (ἄνους).[14]

After this, chapter 4 turns to the perceptible symbols (i.e., properties that pertain to corporeal objects only).

> It is not body or figure, it has not form or quality or quantity or mass. It is not in a place, is not visible, and does not have sensible contact. It does not perceive nor is perceived. It has not disorder or confusion, overwhelmed by material passion. It is not powerless, subjected by disturbances to perception. It is not lacking light. It is not and has not alteration or destruction or division or privation or diminution or anything else of the senses.[15]

Next, chapter 5 "rises higher," removing from "the cause of all and being *hyper* all" both the intelligible divine names and the Trinitarian properties. (*Apropos* of last chapter, note that all these intelligible divine names are either actual divine names or analogues of actual divine names.)

> Again, rising higher we say that it is neither soul nor mind. It does not have imagination or opinion or reason or intellection. It is not speech or intellect, nor is it spoken or intellected. It is neither number nor order, neither greatness nor smallness, neither equality nor inequality, neither similarity nor dissimilarity. It has neither standing nor motion nor rest. It does not have power nor is it power or light. It does not live nor is it life. It is neither being nor eternity nor time. There is neither intellectual nor scientific

---

shortcut. Other special usages of *aphairesis* include the phrases *aphairesis alone*, *hyper-having aphairesis*, and *hyper aphairesis*. *Aphairesis alone* occurs just once (see above, *MT* 2, 1025B) and seems merely to mean that only removal is necessary to reveal the hidden beauty itself-by-itself. *Hyper-having aphairesis*, which occurs two times (*DN* 1.5, 593C; *DN* 2.3, 640B), will be discussed in section IV of this chapter. *Hyper aphairesis*, which occurs four times (*DN* 2.4, 641A; *MT* 1.2, 1000B; *MT* 3, 1033C; *MT* 5, 1040B), will be discussed in chapter 4.

14. *MT* 4, 1040D. For more on these terms, see note 69 below.
15. *MT* 4, 1040D.

Negation Does Not Negate

> touching of it. It is neither truth nor kingship nor wisdom. It is neither one nor oneness, neither divinity nor goodness. It is not spirit as understood by us, nor is it sonship or fatherhood or something else known to us or some other beings. It is not something of non-being, nor is it something of being. Beings do not know it as it is, nor does it know beings as they are.[16]

Finally, chapter 5 concludes both the treatise and its aphairetic ascent by removing that which pertains to thinking and speaking, including, notably, the methods of *thesis* and *aphairesis* themselves.

> There is neither speech nor name nor knowledge of it. It is neither darkness nor light, neither error nor truth. There is neither positing nor removal (ἀφαίρεσις) of it at all. Making positings and removals (ἀφαιρέσεις) of what comes after it, we neither posit nor remove (ἀφαιροῦμεν) of it, since the perfect and singular cause of all is *hyper* all positing, and the preeminent (ὑπεροχὴ) absolutely free of all and beyond the whole is *hyper* all removal (ὑπὲρ πᾶσαν ἀφαίρεσιν).[17]

In these chapters the picture of *aphairesis* sketched above gets filled in a bit more. The "beings" that are removed from God are, for the most part, sensible and intelligible properties. (Note that if they are "beings," then they cannot be divine names themselves, which are *hyper* being—more on this in sections III and IV.) Such properties are removed from God in sequential order: first alpha-privative prefixed intelligible properties (e.g., being-less, life-less), then sensible properties, then intelligible and Trinitarian properties, and finally properties pertaining to thinking and speaking about God.[18] And the grammatical means by which such properties are removed is that of negative particles, each of which precedes and therefore applies to one of the predicate terms above (rather than preceding the verbs and therefore applying to the entire predicate). According

---

16. *MT* 5, 1045D–1048A.

17. *MT* 5, 1048AB.

18. See Turner's *The Darkness of God* for a different attempt at organizing the properties of *MT* 5 (albeit one that fails to take account of their Neoplatonic context). Turner classifies these names into four categories: (1) names of perceptual attributes (*kingship, sonship, fatherhood, greatness, smallness, darkness, light*); (2) names of intrinsically created things (*speech, imagination, number, order*); (3) names that Platonists took to be true of everything (*being, good, true, one*); (4) names that Platonists took to be absolute rather than relational (*equality, inequality, similarity, dissimilarity*). Turner believes that those of the first two categories are metaphorical in nature, whereas those of the second two categories are secondhand descriptions of the logic of negation itself.

to Laurence Horn's encyclopedic *Natural History of Negation*, such syntax is indicative of the marked word order of narrow-scope predicate-term negation (rather than the normal word order of wide-scope predicate denial). And predicate-term negation, according to Aristotle, yields contrary opposition (rather than contradictory opposition) in which the law of the excluded middle does not obtain in the cases of vacuous reference and category mistakes.[19] If, for example, the property of life is a category mistake of God, then it is both false that God is life and false that God is not-life. Thus, there need not be any contradiction when Dionysius asserts at the beginning of *Mystical Theology* 4 that *God is not lifeless* and then later asserts in *Mystical Theology* 5 that *God is not life*. I will return to this crucial analysis of Dionysian negation later (section IV), after an analysis of *apophasis* and *hyperochē* is in place. For now, before moving on to an analysis of *apophasis*, I simply underscore that *apophasis* is nowhere present in these chapters of the *Mystical Theology—apophasis* is not proffered as a method of hymning the *hyper*-being God, *apophasis* is not implemented as a method of hymning the *hyper*-being God, and *apophasis* is not itself negated or removed of God.[20]

When *apophasis* does make its appearances in the Dionysian corpus, it does so not as a method of negating predicate-terms but as a logic of interpreting negative predicate-terms "*hyperochically*" (preeminently) rather than "*steretically*" (privatively). This understanding of *apophasis* comes out particularly well when several of the passages in which it appears are read together. According to *Celestial Hierarchy* 2.3, *apophatic* predicate-terms such as *invisible*, *infinite*, and *inseparable* signify not what God *is* but what God is *not*. In hymning God as invisible, the theologians deny that God possesses the attribute of visibility (with respect to being) rather than affirming that God possesses the attribute of invisibility.

> [God] is *hyper*-cosmically hymned in negative (ἀποφατικαῖς) revelations by the Scriptures themselves, named invisible (ἀόρατον), infinite (ἄπειρον), ungraspable (ἀχώρητον), and that which

---

19. According to Aristotle, both infinite/indefinite names (e.g., not-wise) and alpha privatives (e.g., wise-less or un-wise) yield contrary opposition. See Aristotle's *Categories* 11b17ff, 11b38ff, 13b12ff; *On Interpretation* 19b20ff, 20a31ff; and *Prior Analytics* 51b5ff. See also Horn, *A Natural History of Negation*, 6–21, 102–3, 110.

20. In fact, nowhere in the entire Dionysian corpus is *apophasis* itself either removed or negated. (Moreover, *CH* 2.3, 140D–141A and *CH* 2.5, 145A call it "true.") But this is hardly surprising if *apophasis* is a logic for interpreting negative predicate-terms rather than a method of negating predicate terms.

signifies not what it is but what it is not. For this, I think, is more appropriate to it, since, as the secret and sacred tradition has instructed, we speak truly of it as not being according to things of being, but we do not know of its incomprehensible and ineffable (ἄρρητον) *hyper*-being and indeterminacy. Therefore, since the negations (ἀποφάσεις) are true of the divine while the affirmations (καταφάσεις) are unfitting to the hiddenness of the inexpressible things, the manifestation through dissimilar shapings is more fitting to the invisible.[21]

Divine Names 7.1 then develops this, asserting that *apophatic* predicate-terms such as *invisible, ineffable, unnamable, incomprehensible,* and *inscrutable* indicate not God's lack but God's excess. In calling God invisible, the theologians attest to God's abounding luminosity (i.e., all-shining light) rather than God's deprivation of (ordinary) visibility: God is invisible in the sense that God is other than (ordinary) visibility *qua* excessive or exceeding visibility.

> [. . .] it is customary for theologians to negate (ἀποφάσκειν) the things of privation (τὰ τῆς στερήσεως) with respect to God in an opposite sense. Thus Scripture calls the all-shining light invisible (ἀόρατόν), and the many-hymned and many-named ineffable (ἄρρητον) and unnamable (ἀνώνυμον), and that which is present in all things and discoverable from all things incomprehensible (ἀκατάληπτον) and inscrutable (ἀνεξιχνίαστον). In this way, even now, the divine apostle is said to have hymned as foolishness of God that which appears unreasonable and paradoxical in itself, but which uplifts us to the ineffable truth before all reason.[22]

And *Epistle* 4 maintains that affirmations about Jesus' love for humanity have the power of preeminent negation (*hyperochikēs apophaseōs*). In saying that Jesus was non-human, we maintain that Jesus is *hyperochē* or *hyper* human: Jesus is not-human in the sense that Jesus is other than (ordinary) humanity *qua* excessive or exceeding humanity.

> Why should one go through the remaining things, which are numerous? Through them the one who sees divinely will know *hyper* mind that the affirmations (καταφασκόμενα) about Jesus' love for humanity have the power of preeminent negation (ὑπεροχικῆς ἀποφάσεως). So we may say briefly, he was not human (οὐδὲ ἄνθρωπος), not as non human (μὴ ἄνθρωπος), but as from humans

21. *CH* 2.3, 140D–141A.
22. *DN* 7.1, 865BC.

Negating Negation

> being beyond humans and as *hyper* human having truly become human, and, as for the rest, not having done the things of God as God, nor the things of humans as human, but administering for us a new theandric activity as God having become human.[23]

In sum: negative predicate-terms signify not privative lack but preeminent excess—an excess that must be understood not ordinarily but extraordinarily.[24]

Two phrases are here of crucial significance. The first, *to negate the things of privation*, states that *apophatic* negation must be sharply differentiated from privative negation (*sterēsis*, or less commonly *elleipsis*). The second, *preeminent negation*, shows that this difference must be understood semantically—*apophatic* negation states preeminence (*hyperochē*), not privation (*steresis*). Thus "negating the things of privation" does not change the syntactic form of a predicate-term negation (which can be of either the alpha-privative [*unwise*] or indefinite [*not-wise*] variety[25]). Rather, it indicates that the predicate-term negation in question should be interpreted preeminently rather than privatively. And as the passages below suggest, when negative predicate-terms are applied to God, we should always interpret them preeminently rather than privatively.

> But as I have often said, one must intellect the divine divinely. For one must arrange in order non-intellection (ἄνουν) and non-sensibility (ἀναίσθητον) of God according to preeminence (ὑπεροχήν) and not defect (ἔλλειψιν), just as we attribute non-reason (ἄλογον)

---

23. *EP* 4, 1072BC. Note that it is the individual who sees divinely *hyper*-mind who knows this. I'll have more to say about such *hyper-nous* knowing in chapter 4.

24. Below (section IV), I'll provide a reading of another passage in which *apophasis* appears (twice)—*MT* 1.2. This leaves three remaining uses, none of which will be examined in the main body of this chapter, but all of which will be mentioned here: (1) *CH* 2.5, 145A maintains that both "true" negations and comparisons with "last things" honor the divine (more than affirmations or similarities); it therefore resembles the excerpt above from *CH* 2.3; (2) *DN* 13.3, 981B speaks of an "ascent through *apophaseōn*" (that stands the soul outside itself and joins it to God); it therefore constitutes a possible exception to the otherwise non-methodological nature of *apophasis* in the Dionysian corpus (perhaps, however, this ascent is not the systematic removal of predicate-terms of *MT* 4–5 but rather an "ascending" interpretation of negative predicate-terms that "rises" from a *steretic* interpretation to a *hyperochic* interpretation); and (3) *DN* 3.3, 684C uses *apophasis* to mean "prohibit."

25. It stands to reason that Dionysius could signify a semantic relationship of privation or lack by means other than predicate-term negation (e.g., by using terms like *weak* and *blind*). Indeed evil is referred to as a privation and lack of the Good throughout *DN* 4.20–35.

> to that which is *hyper* reason, non-perfection (ἀτέλειαν) to that which is *hyper*-perfection and *pro*-perfection, and non-manifest (ἀναφῆ) and non-visible (ἀόρατον) darkness to the inaccessible light according to a preeminence (ὑπεροχὴν) of visible light.[26]
>
> Darkness disappears in the light, the more so, the more light; unknowing is removed by knowledge, the more so, the more knowledge. Having understood this preeminently (ὑπεροχικῶς) rather than by privation (στέρησιν), you will declare *hyper*-truthfully that the unknowing of God escapes those having existing light and knowledge of beings, and that God's transcendent (ὑπερκείμενον) darkness is hidden from all light and concealed from all knowledge.[27]

Of course, it remains to be seen what exactly is meant by the preeminent interpretation of negative predicate-terms. Nevertheless, it should by now be clear that Dionysian negation, which is composed of an *aphairetic* method of removal and an *apophatic* logic of interpretation, does not resemble our "ordinary" understanding of negation. Dionysian negation is not widescope propositional negation: *God is not-wise* (or *un-wise*) is not equivalent to *It is not the case that God is wise*. Dionysian negation does not entail an opposite affirmation: *God is not-wise* does not entail *God is foolish*. Dionysian negation does not exclude a middle: *God is not-wise* does not exclude *God is neither wise nor not wise*. And Dionysian negation may even reveal a non-middle: *God is not-wise* reveals *God is preeminently wise*.

II. Interpretation: *Hyper* and *Hyperochē*

What does it mean to say that negative predicate-terms, interpreted *apophatically*, signify *hyperochic* preeminence rather than *steretic* lack? If Dionysius is using *hyperochē* at all like other Neoplatonists did, then it signifies the preeminence of causes over their effects.[28] Of course, we know (per last chapter) that causes do not possess the properties that they source. (Life-itself is not living.) So a cause is not preeminent in the sense of possessing more of the property that it sources. Rather, a cause is preeminent in the sense of being metaphysically prior to, and therefore pre-containing, its effects. This, in short, is what I will be arguing over the next two sections: to

---

26. *DN* 7.2, 869A.
27. *EP* 1, 1065A.
28. Liddell and Scott, *A Greek-English Lexicon*, 1867; Jones, "Introduction," 94–95.

interpret negative predicate-terms *apophatically* is to see the *hyper*-being God as pre-containing the divine names, which themselves pre-contain their effects, all in a manner that is *hyper*-unified and *hyper*-existent. And this is to say that Dionysian negation does much more than remove; it also *reveals*. It removes the things of being to reveal that which is *hyper* being.

But the next two sections will take the long road, if only to consider the claim not only that *hyperochē* is "fundamentally ambiguous" between inapplicability and preeminence but also that this ambiguity should be resolved by relegating preeminence to the "lower" causal God of the divine names. (To relegate preeminence in such a way would be to say, e.g., that although God is preeminently life with respect to God's causal procession or divine name life-itself, God is utterly and completely beyond life with respect to God's *hyper*-being transcendence.) In fact, I agree with the former of these claims; thus I will work to demonstrate the ambiguity of *hyperochē* in the remainder of this section. But in the next section, I will provide evidence contrary to the latter claim, arguing that the *hyper*-being God is the cause of all and, as such, pre-contains not only the divine names but also that which they source. (To elevate preeminence in such a way is to say, e.g., that the *hyper*-being God is preeminently life as pre-containing both the divine name life-itself and the property of life that it sources.)

One argument for the ambiguity of *hyperochē* is just the morphology of *hyperochē*. Although commonly translated as *preeminence*, *hyperochē* is composed of the preposition *hyper* and the verb *to have* (*echō*) and therefore literally means *hyper-have*. As is the case with most prepositions, however, *hyper* is difficult to translate precisely, possessing a number of different meanings that convey a number of different spatial relations. The ninth edition of Liddell and Scott lists the following meanings for *hyper* (when used with an accusative prepositional object):

1. with respect to place in reference to motion: *over, beyond*;
2. with respect to measure: *above, exceeding, beyond*;
3. with respect to number: *above, upwards*;
4. with respect to time: *beyond* (i.e., *before, earlier than*);
5. in some dialects: *on behalf of, concerning*.[29]

As is also the case with most prepositions, these different meanings reflect different spatial relations, two of which are principal here: a sense of being

29. Liddell and Scott, *A Greek-English Lexicon*, 1858.

beyond or across something (horizontal distance), and a sense of being over or above something (vertical height). And these two different spatial relations convey two different logical meanings: in the first case, the complete inapplicability or falsity of that which one is beyond or across; in the second case, an excessive measure or manner of that which one is over or above. Moreover, these two different logical meanings suggest two different senses of transcendence: removal beyond and superiority above.[30]

As with *hyper*, so with many *hyper*-prefixed terms. The following three in particular—among which stands *hyper-ochē*—typically concern the manner in which a property is predicated, and so register a sense of both lack of possession and preeminent possession, a sense of *both* the logical falsity or inapplicability of the predicate in question *and* the superabundant or excessive measure of that predicate:

- *hyperochē*: literally *hyper-having*, but more commonly *preeminence*—the above-having (excess) or beyond-having (inapplicability) of some property;
- *hyperbolē*: literally *hyper-thrown*, but more commonly *excess*—the throwing-above (excess) or throwing-beyond (inapplicability) of some property;
- *hyperplērēs*: literally *hyper-full*, but more commonly *overfull*—the overfullness (excess) or beyond-fullness (inapplicability) of some property.[31]

---

30. Very similarly, the spatial direction of *up* has two different metaphorical applications in everyday discourse, as it is used to convey both a sense of *more* and a sense of *unknown*. According to Lakoff and Johnson, these two metaphors—*more is up* and *unknown is up*—have very different experiential bases: the former, that of observing rising and falling levels of piles and fluids; the latter, that of finding it easier to grasp something and look at it if it is on the ground (*Metaphors We Live By*, 21; *Philosophy in the Flesh*, 51, 54). For Dionysius' use of height as a metaphor for divine transcendence, see chapter 4.

31. Here are a couple more *hyper*-prefixed terms (that convey more of a sense of placement than possession):
   - *hyperidrusis*: literally *hyper-established*, but more commonly *superior*—the establishing of superior things above inferior things (excess) or the establishing of something beyond all things (inapplicability);
   - *hyperkeimai*, literally *hyper-lie*, but more commonly *lie above*—the positioning of superior things above inferior things (excess) or the positioning of something beyond all things (inapplicability).

The first of these, *hyper-established* may convey utter removal more than any other hyper-prefixed term. Thus it is sometimes used to speak of God as unparticiapted.

> For there is no exact likeness between the causeds and the causes, but rather the causeds have the allowed likenesses of the causes, while the causes themselves are apart from and *hyper*-established (ὑπερίδρυται) the causeds according to the

Negating Negation

Such is the grammatical ambiguity (bivocity) of *hyper* and *hyperochē*.

But it is not merely the case that *hyper, hyperochē,* and many of the other *hyper*-prefixed terms are in themselves grammatically ambiguous; it is also the case that Dionysius uses these terms ambiguously, sometimes to stress *preeminence above*; other times, *removal beyond*, and rarely to mean one to the exclusion of the other. (Thus, for the remainder of this chapter, I will not translate the *hyper* prefixes of these terms so as to allow these resonances to sound out.) Some uses favor a sense of superiority

> ratio of their own proper source. (*DN* 2.8, 645C)

And it is also sometimes used to contrast God *qua hyper*-established *hyper*-being with God *qua hyper*-full and *hyper*-having cause of all.

> And so, the discourse seeks to hymn these manifested divine names of providence. It does not profess to describe the goodness, being, life, and wisdom, which is *hyper*-being-itself (αὐτοϋπερούσιον), of the divinity, which is *hyper*-being-itself (αὐτοϋπερούσιου), and which is established above in hiddenness; as the Scriptures say, *hyper* all goodness, divinity, being, life, and wisdom. Rather, it hymns the manifested good-producing providence, *hyper*-having (ὑπεροχικῶς) goodness and the cause of all goods and being and life and wisdom, the being-producing and life-producing and wisdom-giving cause of that which participates in being and life and mind and reason and sensation. (*DN* 5.2, 816C)

But even *hyper-established* is occasionally ambiguous between establishment-beyond and establishment-above. *Epistle* 1 states that God is *hyper*-established *hyper* mind and being and yet "exists" in a *hyper*-being sense and "is known" in a *hyper*-mind sense, thereby suggesting that *hyper*-establish also connotes established-above.

> But God, *hyper*-established (ὑπεριδρυμένος) *hyper* mind and being, not known and not being in general, exists *hyper*-beingly and is known *hyper*-mind. And the surpassingly complete unknowing is a knowledge of that which is *hyper* everything known. (*EP* 1, 1065A)

And *Divine Names* 12.4, a passage that was quoted in part above, not only states that the unparticipated cause *hyper* all beings is *hyper*-established all participatings and participants but also suggests that such *hyper*-establishment might be understood as establishment above (just as participations-themselves are established above, not beyond, participants and participants are established above, not beyond, non-participants).

> Since the cause of all is *hyper*-full (ὑπερπλήρης) of all according to one *hyper*-having (ὑπερέχουσαν) *hyper*-throwing (ὑπερβολήν) of all, it is hymned holy of holies and the rest according to *hyper*-flowing (ὑπερβλύζουσαν) causality and lifted-out *hyper*-having (ἐξηρημένην ὑπεροχήν), as one might say. Thus, just as beings that are holy or divine or lord or king are *hyper*-having (ὑπερέχουσι) to beings that are not, and the participations-themselves (αὐτομετοχαί) are *hyper*-having to their participants, so that which is *hyper* all beings is *hyper*-established (ὑπερίδρυται) all beings and the unparticipated cause is *hyper*-established all participatings (μετεχόντων) and participants (μετοχῶν). (*DN* 12.4, 972B)

And although *hyper-established* usually does convey a sense of being located beyond, this is not the case for the second term above, *hyper-lie*, which almost always conveys a sense of being located above or superior to.

or preeminence, but only marginally so. *Divine Names* 12.4, for example, states that God is named holy of holies since God is "*hyper*-full of all according to one *hyper*-having *hyper*-throwing of all," thereby implying divine preeminence; but it also goes on to say that God is "*hyper*-established all beings," thereby suggesting complete remove.

> Since the cause of all is *hyper*-full (ὑπερπλήρης) of all according to one *hyper*-having (ὑπερέχουσαν) *hyper*-throwing (ὑπερβολήν) of all, it is hymned holy of holies and the rest according to *hyper*-flowing (ὑπερβλύζουσαν) causality and lifted-out *hyper*-having (ἐξῃρημένην ὑπεροχήν), as one might say. Thus, just as beings that are holy or divine or lord or king are *hyper*-having (ὑπερέχουσι) to beings that are not, and the participations-themselves [are *hyper*-having] to their participants, so that which is *hyper* all beings is *hyper*-established (ὑπερίδρυται) all beings and the unparticipated cause [is *hyper*-established] all participatings (μετεχόντων) and participants (μετοχῶν).[32]

And *Divine Names* 11.1 indicates that for the divine peace and rest to be wholly *hyper*-unified is for it to possess a *hyper*-throwing (excess) of unity but only insofar as it is *hyper*-having (removed from) all.

> It is neither lawful nor desirable to speak or conceive something of beings about the divine peace and rest—whatever it is—which the holy Justus calls unspeakable and unmoved in every known procession, how it rests and is tranquil, how it is in itself and within itself and is wholly *hyper*-unified (ὑπερήνωται) with its wholeness, and how it does not abandon its unity (ἕνωσιν) in going into itself and multiplying itself, but proceeds to all, remaining wholly within through a *hyper*-throwing (ὑπερβολὴν) of unity (ἑνώσεως) *hyper*-having (ὑπερεχούσης) all.[33]

And *Epistle* 5 seems to say that the divine darkness is a preeminent *hyper*-having and excessive *hyper*-throwing of light, while at the same time not ruling out the possibility that the divine darkness is simply beyond the having and throwing of light.

> The divine darkness is the "unapproachable light" in which it is said God lives, being invisible through its *hyper*-having (ὑπερέχουσαν) brightness, and being unapproachable through

---

32. *DN* 12.4, 972AB.
33. *DN* 11.1, 949AB.

Negating Negation

> its *hyper*-throwing of *hyper*-being streaming of light (ὑπερβολὴν ὑπερουσίου φωτοχυσίας).[34]

Other uses of these terms instead favor a sense of removal or separation, again, though, not unambiguously so. *Epistle* 9.5 says that God is beyond all having, fullness, and excess, but in a direction that is apparently excessive.

> But rather one must suppose that the standing-outside of one's wits that follows drunkenness is God's *hyper*-having (ὑπεροχὴν) *hyper* intellection, according to which God is lifted-out (ἐξῄρηται) of intellection, being *hyper* intellection and *hyper* being intellected and *hyper* being itself, and quite simply God is drunk with and standing out of all good things whatsoever, as being *hyper*-full (ὑπερπλήρης) of all them, *hyper*-throwing (ὑπερβολή) every excess, and again dwelling outside of and beyond (ἐπέκεινα) the whole.[35]

Celestial Hierarchy 13.4 states that God is incomparably established-beyond every power in a manner that is beyond all having of all being, yet in a manner that could also be positively characterized as one that is *hyper*-beingly preeminent.

> And so the theologian learned in the vision that the divinity is incomparably *hyper*-established (ὑπερίδρυτο) every visible and invisible power according to all *hyper*-being *hyper*-having (κατὰ πᾶσαν ὑπερούσιον ὑπεροχὴν) and verily that it is lifted-out (ἐξῃρημένον) from all in general, not even resembling the first beings of beings [. . .].[36]

And *Divine Names* 7.1 indicates that although God is *hyper*-full of wisdom in the sense of being over-full of wisdom, God is *hyper*-established wisdom in the sense of being established beyond wisdom.

> For God is not only *hyper*-full (ὑπερπλήρης) wisdom such that "of his understanding there is no number" but also *hyper*-established (ὑπερίδρυται) all reason and intellect and wisdom.[37]

Importantly, this ambiguity is also present in the *hyper*-prefixed divine names. *Divine Names* 4.3, for example, is by no means clear about whether

34. *EP* 5, 1073A.
35. *EP* 9.5, 1112C.
36. *CH* 13.4, 304C.
37. *DN* 7.1, 865B.

Negation Does Not Negate

hyper-prefixed and alpha-privative divine names, when said of the *hyper*-being good, denote excess above or exceeding beyond the name in question.

> If the Good is *hyper* all beings, as it is, the formless produces-form. And in it alone non-being (ἀνούσιον) is *hyper*-throwing (ὑπερβολή) being, non-life (ἄζωον) is *hyper*-having (ὑπερέχουσα) life, and non-intellect (ἄνουν) is *hyper*-raising (ὑπεραίρουσα) wisdom, and whatever is in the Good is of the hyper-having (ὑπεροχικῆς) form-production of that which is formless. And, if it is lawful to say, non being (μὴ ὄν) itself desires the Good *hyper* all beings, and strives somehow to be in the Good, and is truly *hyper*-being with respect to the removal of all (τὴν πάντων ἀφαίρεσιν).[38]

And *Mystical Theology* 1.1 uses several different *hyper*-light variations, each of which is ambiguous between a superabundant excess of light and a complete removal beyond light (thereby rendering the first three hyper-prefixed names ambiguous as well).

> Trinity *hyper*-being and *hyper*-divine and *hyper*-good, overseer of Christians in divine wisdom, guide us to the *hyper*-unknown (ὑπεράγνωστον) and *hyper*-brilliant (ὑπερφαῆ) highest summit of mystical Scripture; there the simple, absolute, and unchanged mysteries of theology are veiled by the *hyper*-light (ὑπέρφωτον) darkness of hidden silence, *hyper*-illuminating (ὑπερλάμποντα) the *hyper*-most-appearing (ὑπερφανέστατον) in the darkest and *hyper*-filling (ὑπερπληροῦντα) the sightless minds with *hyper*-beauty beauties in the wholly imperceptible and invisible.[39]

Even Dionysius' use of the term *hyper-name* (*hyperōnomos*) is ambiguous between being beyond all names and possessing all names in superabundant excess. *Divine Names* 1.5, 593B clearly states that the *hyper*-being divinity is *hyper*-name, while at the same time saying that as *hyper* mind and being, this divinity embraces, gathers, and anticipates all, thereby suggesting that this divinity might possess divine names in some sort of excessive or preeminent fashion.

> And clearly, if it is superior to every expression and every knowledge and is altogether established *hyper* mind and being—being an embracing and gathering and anticipating of all—and it is altogether incomprehensible to all, and there is no sensation, imagination, opinion, name, expression, touch, and science of

---

38. *DN* 4.3, 697A.
39. *MT* 1.1, 997B.

> it, how is the treatise *On Divine Names* to be examined by us, having shown the *hyper*-being divinity to be incomprehensible and *hyper*-name (ὑπερωνύμου)?[40]

And *Divine Names* 13.3 indicates that the *hyper*-name divinity is neither monad nor triad *as distinguished by us or another being*, thereby implying that these names may be true of God in some sort of transcendent way—i.e., as *hypernames*.

> Therefore, the divinity *hyper* all things, which is hymned as monad and triad, is neither monad nor triad as distinguished by us or any other kind of being, but rather in order that we may truly hymn its *hyper*-unity and god-generation, we name the *hyper*-name (ὑπερηνωμένον) with the triadic and unitary divine name, the *hyper*-being with the beings.[41]

Admittedly, context allows us to disambiguate some of these terms better than others. But that is not the point. Rather, it is this: (a) if Dionysius tells us that "to negate the things of privation" means to translate such things *hyperochically*, and (b) if *hyperochē* (as well as *hyper* and other *hyper*-prefixed terms) is grammatically ambiguous between lack of having and preeminent having, and (c) if *hyperochē* is also used ambiguously sometimes to mean a beyond-having and other times to mean a preeminent-having, then (d) we do not know what exactly it means to interpret negative predicate-terms *apophatically qua hyperochically*. More precisely and concretely, we do not know in the case of the following previously quoted passages from *Divine Names* 7.2 whether God does not have reason at all or has reason preeminently.

> But as I have often said, one must intellect the divine divinely. For one must arrange in order non-intellection (ἄνουν) and non-sensibility (ἀναίσθητον) of God according to preeminence (ὑπεροχήν) and not defect (ἔλλειψιν), just as we attribute non-reason (ἄλογον) to that which is *hyper* reason, non-perfection (ἀτέλειαν) to that which is *hyper*-perfection and *pro*-perfection, and non-manifest (ἀναφῆ) and non-visible (ἀόρατον) darkness to the inaccessible light according to a preeminence (ὑπεροχὴν) of visible light.[42]

---

40. *DN* 1.5, 593AB.
41. *DN* 13.3, 981A.
42. *DN* 7.2, 869A.

What we *do* know is that if *hyperochē* is typically used to mean *preeminence* in Neoplatonism and also sometimes used to mean *preeminence* in the Dionysian corpus, then we would have to have a pretty good reason not to believe that Dionysian negation reveals divine preeminence. Do we have such a reason?

III. Resolution: Causality and Pre-containment

Where a reason is given for why Dionysian negation does not reveal divine *hyper*-being preeminence, it goes, as mentioned above, something like this: the ambiguity of *hyperochē* can be resolved by relegating all talk of preeminence to the ("lower") causal God, thereby freeing the ("higher") *hyper*-being God of all such positive impurities.[43] But as I will first argue, such a distinction between the *hyper*-being God and the causal God is suspect, more a product of interpretive bias than textual basis. And as I will then go on to show, the fact that the *hyper*-being God *is* the causal God provides the key to resolving the ambiguity of *hyperochē*.

I begin with an uncontroversial point: the Dionysian God is the cause of all. Repeatedly, Dionysius tells us just this. *Celestial Hierarchy* 4.1 declares that the *hyper*-being thearchy hypostatizes the beings of all beings, bringing them into being.

> First of all, let us say this truth—that through goodness the *hyper*-being thearchy, hypostatizing (ὑποστήσασα) the beings of beings, brought (παρήγαγεν) them into being.[44]

---

43. Jones ("Introduction") undertakes just such a move, recognizing that *hyperochē* is usually employed in Greek philosophy to express the preeminence of a cause over what it causes, while asserting that *hyperochē* is, for Dionysius, "fundamentally ambiguous" and resolving this ambiguity by claiming that *hyperochē* serves, on the one hand, to express the preeminence of divine causes with respect to metaphysical negative theology but, on the other hand, to deny causality altogether with respect to mystical negative theology (ibid., 94–95). This move seems more stipulative than evidential, as Jones asserts that mystical negative theology "must" translate *hyperochē* as "beyond-having" or "beyond-preeminence" (ibid., 95). (At one point in his argument Jones says that the fundamental ambiguity of *hyperochē* can be clarified by introducing a term that Dionysius never used—*proochē* [which is apparently only used once (by Polybius) and therefore can be freely interpreted]—inferring that if God is *proochē* in the sense of being before the having of anything, then God must be *hyperochē* in the sense of being beyond the having of anything.)

44. *CH* 4.1, 177C.

Negating Negation

Ecclesiastical Hierarchy 3.III.4 says sacred Scripture teaches, among other things, the generated constitution and order of things from God.

> For every sacred tablet of Holy Scripture—either the generated constitution (γενητὴν ὕπαρξίν) and ordering of beings out of God, or the legal hierarchy and polity, or the distributions and possessions of the inheritances of the people of God, or the prudence of the sacred judges or wise kings or inspirited priests, or the philosophy of men of old who were unshakable in endurance amid numerous and varied things let loose, or the wise treasures for practical conduct, or the songs and inspired images of divine loves, or the prophetic predictions of things to come, or the human theurgies of Jesus, or the divine-transmitted and divine-imitating polities and sacred teachings of his disciples, or the hidden and mystic vision of the beloved and marvelous disciple, or the *hyper*-cosmic theology of Jesus—guided those fit for deification and rooted them in the sacred and godlike upliftings of the sacraments.[45]

Divine Names 1.3, speaking simply, asserts that God is the source and cause of every life and being.

> [. . .] and to speak simply, [it is] the life of that which lives and the being of that which exists, source (ἀρχὴ) and cause (αἰτία) of every life and being, producing (παρακτικὴν) and sustaining (συνοχικὴν) all beings in being through its goodness.[46]

And *Divine Names* 8.2 makes it clear that even though God is in some sense before and beyond power, God is still the cause of every power.

> We say that God is power as pre-having (προέχων) and *hyper*-having (ὑπερέχων) every power in itself, and as cause of every power, producing (παράγων) all in an undeclinable and indefinable power, and as being cause of the being itself of power whether in the universal or the particular, and as unlimited power, not only by the production (παράγειν) of every power, but also by being *hyper* all, even power-itself, and by prevailing over (ὑπερδύνασθαι) and boundlessly producing (παραγαγεῖν) boundless powers other than those that exist, and by the fact that the boundless powers, even when produced (παραγομένας) boundlessly, are not able to blunt the *hyper*-unlimited (ὑπεράπειρον) making of its power-making power.[47]

45. *EH* 3.III.4, 429CD.
46. *DN* 1.3, 589C.
47. *DN* 8.2, 889D–892A.

Negation Does Not Negate

This much, I hope, is not in dispute—the Dionysian God is the cause of all.

What is in dispute, though, is the fact that causal activity is never denied of God. But it is not. Not even in the concluding chapters of the *Mystical Theology* (chs. 4–5), wherein Dionysius removes every ostensibly conceivable property from God, does Dionysius remove from God any variation of *aitia* (cause), *archē* (source/principle), *hypostasis* (substance, give substance to), or *hyparxis* (constitute, make subsist).[48] In fact, all the properties that are removed in these chapters are removed from a God that is said to be at once "cause of all and being *hyper* all."[49] Further, even when *Divine Names* 1.5 predicates thearchy itself as *hyper-hyparxis*, it goes on to say that this *hyper-hyparxis thearchy* is the *hyparxis* of goodness and *hypostasis* of the whole.

> It is permissible for no one who is a lover of the truth *hyper* all truth to hymn the thearchic *hyper*-beingness—whatever is the *hyper*-subsistence (ὑπερύπαρξις) of the *hyper*-goodness—as word, power, mind, life, or being, but as *hyper-havingly* removed (ὑπεροχικῶς

---

48. Although not always clearly differentiated, *hyparxis* usually indicates sheer subsistence or constitution of something (usually of the thearchy or goodness itself: *DN* 1.5, 593D; *DN* 2.1, 636C; *DN* 2.4, 641A; *DN* 2.5, 641D; *DN* 4.1, 693B; *DN* 4.21, 724A; *DN* 5.4, 817C; *CH* 2.3, 140C; *EH* 3.III.4, 429C), whereas *hypostasis* is frequently used to speak about the particular type of existence or nature of something (usually of divine names or members of the Trinity: *DN* 1.4, 592A; *DN* 2.4, 641A; *DN* 2.5, 641D; *DN* 2.11, 652A; *DN* 4.1, 693B; *DN* 4.1, 693B; *DN* 5.5, 820B; *DN* 6.1, 856B; *DN* 7.1, 865B; *DN* 7.1, 868A; *DN* 7.2, 868C; *DN* 9.1, 909B; *DN* 9.6, 916A; *DN* 9.10, 917A; *DN* 11.2, 949C; *DN* 11.6, 953C; *DN* 11.6, 956A; *EH* 2.III.7, 396D; *EH* 5.II.1, 533B). (Although not in complete agreement with them, I am indebted here to Wear and Dillon [*Dionysius the Areopagite*], Jones ["An Absolutely Simple God"], and Pépin ["ΥΠΑΡΞΙΣ et ΥΠΟΣΤΑΣΙΣ en Cappadoce"].)

49. See also *EP* 5, 1076A for Dionysius' claim that the apostle Paul "found that which is *hyper* all and knew *hyper* understanding that it is beyond (ἐπέκεινα) all as the cause of all." Those wanting to hold a distinction between the God *hyper* all and the God that is cause of all often point to passages such as the concluding line of the *Mystical Theology*.

> Making positings and removals of what comes after it, we neither posit nor remove of it, since the perfect and singular cause of all is *hyper* all positing, and the preeminent (ὑπεροχὴ), absolutely free of all and beyond the whole, is *hyper* all removal. (*MT* 5, 1048B)

But it's not clear how this passage warrants a distinction between two levels or respects of God, one of which is a preeminently superabundant cause of all, the other of which is an absolutely ineffable *hyper*-being Godhead. If anything, this passage draws a distinction between, on the one hand, a respect in which God cannot be posited of yet can be removed from and, on the other hand, a respect in which God cannot even be removed from. But the earlier iteration of this passage (at *MT* 3, 1033CD) does not even make this distinction. And as I'll explain in chapter 4, there are better explanations of what it means to say that God is *hyper* positing and removal.

ἀφῃρημένην) from all condition, motion, life, imagination, opinion, name, word, thinking, intellection, being, rest, foundation, unity, limit, non-limit, and whatever else has being. Yet since to it is the cause of all beings and the subsistence (ὕπαρξις) of goodness, one must hymn the good-source providence of the thearchy from all that is caused. And since everything is around it and for the sake of it, "it is before everything, and everything holds together in it." And by its being is the derivation and substance (ὑπόστασις) of the whole, and all desire it—the intellectual and rational knowingly, things inferior to these sensibly, and other things through living movement or real and habitual aptitude.[50]

And further still, although nine passages in the corpus prefix *archē* with *hyper*, none calls into doubt the claim that God is cause and source of all.[51] All but one employ some variation of the phrase *hyper-source source*, thereby suggesting that the *hyper*-being God is a source that is preeminent to ordinary sources, a source transcending being.[52] *Celestial Hierarchy* 7.4, for example, informs us that

> it is monad and tri-hypostatic henad, reaching its most-good providence to all beings, from the first *hyper*-heavenly ranks to the last of the earth, as *hyper*-source source (ὑπεράρχιος ἀρχὴ) and cause of every being, and *hyper*-beingly grasping all in its resistless embrace.[53]

And *Divine Names* 1.3 tells us that

> it is cause and source and being and life of all, a recalling and resurrecting of those who have fallen away from it, a renewal and reformation of those who are slipping away toward the destruction of the divine form, a sacred foundation of those who are tossed about in an unholy perplexity, a steadfastness for those who continue to stand, a guiding hand which is stretched out for those who are being led back to it, an illumination for those who are being illumined, a source of perfection for those who being perfected, a

---

50. *DN* 1.5, 593CD. According to John D. Jones, this may be the only appearance of *hyperhyparxis* in all of ancient Greek literature ("Introduction," 90). See also Wear and Dillon, *Dionysius the Areopagite*, 11.

51. *DN* 1.3, 589D; *DN* 4.10, 708A; *DN* 11.6, 953D–956A; *CH* 1.2, 121B; *CH* 7.4, 212C; *CH* 9.1, 257B; *CH* 10.1, 273A; *CH* 13.4, 304C; *EP* 2, 1069A.

52. The one occurrence of *hyperarchios* that does not use it in the phrase *hyper-source source*—*Celestial Hierarchy* 13.4, 304C—uses this term within the context of a description of Isaiah's vision of the throne room to denote God's transcendence above the angels *qua ruler* (not *source*).

53. *CH* 7.4, 212CD.

Negation Does Not Negate

source of divinity for those who are being divinized, a simplicity for those who are being simplified, an unity for those who being unified, the *hyper*-beingly *hyper*-source source of every source (ἀρχῆς ἁπάσης ὑπερουσίως ὑπεράρχιος ἀρχὴ), the good-imparting for what is hidden according to the divine law, and, to speak simply, the life of that which lives and the being of that which exists, source and cause of every life and being, producing and sustaining all beings in being through its goodness.[54]

It is not the case, then, that Dionysius removes causality of God. And as I will argue both below and in chapter 4, nor could he.[55]

This in itself is no trivial point, especially given that so many interpreters of the Dionysian corpus seem to think that Dionysius denies *absolutely everything* of God, causality included. But I am after a bigger fish here: if Dionysius does not remove causality in general from God, then Dionysius also cannot remove the divine names themselves in particular from God—for it is as the divine names themselves that God is the cause of all. This "fish" is not only philosophically sound; it is also textually compelling. For at no place in the Dionysian corpus does Dionysius indicate that God is not some *auto*-prefixed divine name.[56] And when Dionysius does remove divine names from God in *Mystical Theology* 5, what he removes are only the properties that the divine names themselves source, *not the divine names themselves*. This is so for three reasons. Syntactically, these terms are not *auto*-prefixed (as divine names themselves often are). Semantically, these terms are not only referred to as "beings" (and therefore cannot refer to divine names themselves, which are *hyper* being) but also of the same logical type as the perceptible symbols that are removed in the preceding chapter (which, unlike divine names, do not possess a causal respect). And logically, as mentioned above, if divine names themselves are removed from God then causality itself is removed from God; but causality itself is not removed from God; so the divine names themselves cannot be removed from God.

---

54. *DN* 1.3, 589C.

55. And as I'll also argue in chapter 4, it hardly matters here if causation is "vertical" rather than "horizontal" (as Perl's *Theophany* [17–19] seems to say).

56. As I mentioned in note 18 of chapter 1, Dionysius does sometimes *auto* prefix the *hyper*-prefixed divine names. But, as I explained in section III of chapter 1, this is just to speak about a respect in which God pre-contains the divine names themselves prior to them being substanced from out of God.

Negating Negation

And since the divine names themselves pre-contain the properties that they source, these too cannot be removed from God. It is therefore the case that when Dionysius removes divine names from God, what he is in fact removing is only the properties that the divine names source—not the divine names themselves, nor their pre-contained effects. Thus the ambiguity of *hyperochē* cannot be resolved by demoting all connotations of preeminence to a ("lower") divine-name causality that is ultimately washed away in a sea of ("higher") undifferentiated thearchic transcendence.[57] Instead, *hyperochē* should be disambiguated by distinguishing between, on the one hand, the properties that the divine names source to participating beings, and, on the other hand, the pre-contained divine names-themselves and their effects: whereas God utterly transcends the divine names *qua* properties, God preeminently possesses the divine names *qua* causes and their pre-contained effects. To interpret *apophatic* predicate-terms *hyperochically* is therefore to see that although God does not possess the properties that the divine names source, these properties are nevertheless pre-contained in the divine names themselves (in a *hyper*-unified, *hyper*-existent manner), which are themselves pre-contained in God (in a *hyper*-unified, *hyper*-existent manner). And this parenthetical phrase cannot be stressed enough: divine names themselves and their pre-contained effects are *hyper-unified* and *hyper-existent*. Thus when Dionysius tells us that he denies *all beings* of the cause of all, we can take him at his word: neither divine names themselves nor their pre-contained effects are things of being.

I will have a little more to say about this last point in the next section. For now, I would like to draw this section to a close by briefly considering what it means to interpret the predicate-terms other than divine names in a *hyperochic* manner (particularly those that occur in *MT* 4–5). In the case of perceptible symbols, the process seems to be twofold: first, the literal meaning is removed to reveal the metaphorical meaning (e.g., God is not literally a rock but is steadfast); next, the metaphorical meaning is removed to reveal a divine name itself and its pre-contained effect (e.g., God does not participate in the property of steadfastness but is the divine name *rest-itself* as well as its pre-contained effects).[58] In the case of Trinitarian properties,

---

57. Consider also that just as a number of passages attribute the *hyper*-names to the *hyper*-being God, so a number of passages attribute positive superabundant preeminence to the *hyper*-being God. See especially, *DN* 1.3, 589ABC; *DN* 1.5, 593BCD; *DN* 13.3, 980BCD; *EP* 5, 1073A–1076A. See also the passages that attribute the *hypernames* to God listed in notes 52 and 54 of chapter 1.

58. Also consider that since perceptible symbols are made possible by, among other

the process is probably simpler: the properties of being a father, son, and spirit are removed with respect to being to reveal the *hyper*-being persons of the Trinity. And in the case of the properties pertaining to knowing and speaking about God, what is removed is ways of knowing and speaking about God with respect to being and what is revealed is ways of knowing and speaking about God that transcend being (e.g., *hyper-nous* knowing and *hyper-logos* saying)—or so I shall argue in chapter 4.

IV. Confirmation: The Grammar of *Aphairesis* and the Unity of Dionysian Negation

I believe that this disambiguation makes good sense of much of the evidence presented thus far in this book—*apophatic* interpretation is *hyperochic* not *steretic*, *hyperochē* registers both inapplicability and preeminence, the Dionysian God is the cause of all, divine names themselves are divine causal powers, divine names themselves are pre-contained in God, divine names themselves are *hyper*-unified and *hyper*-existent, divine names themselves are not removed from God, the properties that divine names themselves source are pre-contained in the divine names themselves in a *hyper*-unified manner, and so on. I also believe that this disambiguation makes good sense of much of the evidence presented in the chapters yet to come—in particular that which concerns *hyper-nous* knowing of the *hyper-ousia* God. But here I will argue that this disambiguation makes good sense of both the grammatical-logical form of *aphairetic* removal as well as the way in which *aphairetic* removal and *apophatic* interpretation fit together.

As indicated above (section I), the logical form of Dionysian negation is narrow-scope predicate-term negation, which, according to Aristotle fails to obey the law of the excluded middle just in case either the referring expression is vacuous or the predicate expression is a category mistake. This means that if mind is a category mistake of God, then there is no contradiction when Dionysius asserts at the beginning of *Mystical Theology* 4 that *God is not mind-less* and then later asserts in *Mystical Theology* 5 that *God is not mind*. But it means more, since it is not the middle but the *non*-middle that

---

things, the *paradeigmata/logoi* (of the divine name *being-itself*), which cause the corporeal things that become the vehicles of the perceptible symbols, then it is these *paradeigmata/logoi* that are also revealed in the *apophatic* interpretation of the perceptible symbols.

Negating Negation

Dionysius excludes.[59] Both mind and mind-less are false of God since God is *hyper* or *hyperochē* mind.

As demonstrated in the previous section, one way of understanding *hyperochē* mind is as the divine name *mind-itself* as well as its pre-contained effects. Now I add that another way of understanding *hyperochē* mind is as *mind hyper being* (or *hyper-being mind*, or *hyper-mind mind*, or *mind hyper-mind*—Dionysius uses all such combinations). Here God is neither mind nor mind-less since these properties are things of being that are a category mistake of a *hyper*-being God; but God is *hyper* or *hyperochē* mind as *hyper*-being mind, mind in a *hyper*-unified and *hyper*-existent manner. And of course these are just two ways of understanding the same "thing": on the one hand, God is neither mind nor mind-less since the property of mind is something of being, which is therefore a category mistake of a *hyper*-being God; on the other hand, God is *hyper* or *hyperochē* mind as the divine name *mind-itself* and its pre-contained effects, both of which "exist" *hyper* being.

It is not surprising, then, to find Dionysius not only making frequent and key use of the adverb *hyperbeingly* and the formula *hyper-dn dn and dn hyper-dn* (e.g., *hyper-being being, goodness hyper-good*) but also objecting to the application of things of being both to the divine names themselves and to the persons of the Trinity.

> But God, *hyper*-established *hyper* mind and being, not known and not being in general, exists *hyper*-beingly and is known *hyper*-mind.[60]
>
> For example, this is unified and common to the henarchic Trinity with respect to the divine unity *hyper*-beingness: the *hyper*-being subsistence, the *hyper*-divine divinity, the *hyper*-good goodness, the identity beyond all of the whole identity beyond all, the *hyper*

---

59. Horn, explicating the position of Otto Jespersen, provides the following example of an excluded non-middle: If someone believes that *War and Peace* is an excellent book, she may in certain circumstances deny both that *War and Peace* is a good book (since it is more than just good) and that *War and Peace* is not a good book (since it is not a bad book) (*A Natural History of Negation*, 204). See Horn's treatment of scalar predication (ibid., 204–67). And note that Horn believes scalar predicates are pragmatically, not semantically, ambiguous—i.e., in certain contexts they can be used to mean "exactly p" rather than "at least p" (ibid., 243, 250, 266–67).

60. *EP* 1, 1065A. For more uses of *hyperbeingly*, see the following: *DN* 1.3, 589C; *DN* 2.10, 648CD; *DN* 2.11, 649BCD; *DN* 4.7, 704B; *DN* 5.8, 824AB; *DN* 9.8, 916B; *DN* 11.6, 953C; *DN* 13.3, 980BC; *DN* 13.3, 980D–981A; *CH* 7.4, 212D; *CH* 9.4, 261D; *MT* 1.2, 1000A; *EP* 4, 1072AB.

henarchic unity, the unspeakable, the much-speaking, the unknowable, the all-intelligible, the positing of all, the removal of all, the *hyper* all positing and removal, the remaining and foundation of the henarchic substances in one another (if I may so speak), wholly *hyper*-unified, and in no part comingled [...].[61]

It is neither lawful nor desirable to speak or conceive something of beings about the divine peace and rest—whatever it is—which the holy Justus calls unspeakable and unmoved in every known procession, how it rests and is tranquil, how it is in itself and within itself and is wholly *hyper*-unified with its wholeness, and how it does not abandon its unity in going into itself and multiplying itself, but proceeds to all, remaining wholly within through a *hyper*-throwing of unity *hyper*-having all. But having referred to it as unspeakable and unknowable, as beyond all being, let us investigate its intellectual and spoken participation, as far as possible, to men and us, who are inferior to many good men.[62]

How, you say, is Jesus, who is beyond (ἐπέκεινα) everything, placed in the same class with all humans? For he is not called a human here as being the cause of humans, but rather as being himself truly human in entire being. But we do not define Jesus humanly, for [he is] not only a human—[since he is] not *hyper*-being if [he is] only a human—but rather [we define him as being] truly a human [out of his] preeminent love of humans, a *hyper*-being who took on the being of humanity. But the *hyper*-being is always nothing less than *hyper*-full with being; indeed in this superiority, and coming into being truly, invested with being *hyper* being, he does the work of humans *hyper* humans.[63]

These passages show us not only that the triune God and the divine names "exist" in a *hyper*-being manner but also that it is a mistake to apply the things of being not only to the *hyper*-being triune God but also to the divine names themselves. (Of course, as I have argued above, there really is not a distinction between these two—the *hyper*-being God *is* the divine names themselves.) This is not to say that God or the divine names are

---

61. *DN* 2.4, 641A. For more uses of *hyper-dn dn* formulas, see the following: *DN* 1.1, 588B; *DN* 1.3, 589C; *DN* 2.11, 649C; *DN* 4.7, 704A; *DN* 5.1, 816B.

62. *DN* 11.1, 949AB. For more objections to the application of things of being to that which is *hyper* being, see the following: *DN* 2.7, 645AB; *DN* 7.1, 865C–868A; *DN* 7.3, 869C–872A; *DN* 13.3, 981A; *MT* 1.1, 997B–1000A; *MT* 1.2, 1000AB; *CH* 2.3, 140D–141A; *CH* 13.4, 261C; *MT* 2, 1025AB; *EP* 1, 1065AB; *EP* 5, 1073A–1076A.

63. *EP* 4, 1072AB.

Negating Negation

"being in the highest degree." It is, though, to say that God and God's divine names "are" in some manner, a *hyper*-being manner.[64] And it is also to say that what is removed from God is only the things of being. To interpret *apophatically* is to remove the things of being in order to reveal that which is *hyper* being.

Table 2: The Logic of Apophasis

Hyper-being revelation	God is *hyper*-mind, mind *hyper*-being, mind-itself
Being removal	God is not mind in the highest degree God is not mind in some partial respect God is not mind-less

What then of *aphairetic* removal? If it serves only to remove predicate-terms, whereas *apophatic* logic interprets predicate-terms both preeminently and transcendentally, are *aphairesis* and *apophasis* at odds with one another? Some have charged that this is in fact the case—that *apophasis* discloses a superabundantly preeminent God, one that possess an excessive measure of all things, whereas *aphairesis* points to an utterly removed God, one that transcends all things.[65] But there are several reasons for rejecting this claim.

One initially telling sign of the compatibility of *aphairesis* and *apophasis* in the Dionysian corpus is the fact that both terms appear in one (and only one) passage in the Dionysian corpus, *Mystical Theology* 1.2 (which also happens to be the only passage in the *Mystical Theology* in which *apophasis* makes its two appearances).

> It is necessary is to posit (τιθέναι) and to affirm (καταφάσκειν) all the positings (θέσεις) of beings of it as cause of all, and more fittingly to negate (ἀποφάσκειν) all of them as *hyper*-be-ing *hyper* all.

---

64. Does the Dionysian God have a *hyper-being hyparxis*? Although *DN* 1.5, 593C does identify the *hyper*-being thearchy as *hyper-hyparxis*, it also later identifies it as the *hyparxis* of goodness and *hypostasis* of the whole. Add to this, the fact that *DN* 2.4, 641B predicates the Trinity as *hyper*-being *hyparxis*, that *DN* 9.8, 916B says that God subsists (*hyparchein*) in a *hyper*-beingly unmoved manner, and that *DN* 10.3, 940A says that God subsists (*hyparchonta*) before time. Perhaps what David Bradshaw claims about Plotinus' One applies as well to the triune thearchy of Dionysius: "The One's being *epekeina ousias* does not rule out that it is supreme *ousia*, in the more exalted sense that it exists in full actuality and is the source of *ousia* in other things" (*Aristotle East and West*, 91). For a different reading of *hyperousios ousia*, see Jones' "An Absolutely Simply God?"

65. Raoul Mortley claimed that Plotinian *aphairesis* implies a transcendence of utter removal and separation, whereas Procline *apophasis* suggests a less disjunctive transcendence of preeminence and superiority (*The Way of Negation*, 30–31).

And do not think that the negations (ἀποφάσεις) are opposed to the affirmations (καταφάσεσιν), but rather that that which is *hyper* all removal (ἀφαίρεσιν) and positing (θέσιν) is far superior, *hyper* privations (στερήσεις).[66]

This passage is sometimes interpreted so as to make it seem that *apophasis* either equates to *aphairesis of all* or constitutes the negation and transcendence of *aphairesis*.[67] But Dionysius here draws an explicit distinction between *apophasis* and *sterēsis* as well as between *apophasis* and *kataphasis* (a positive predicate-term)—not between *apophasis* and *aphairesis*. Dionysius indicates that *apophatic* terms are not semantically opposed to *kataphatic* terms and therefore are not *steretic* in nature, not that *apophasis* either equates to the *aphairesis* of all or culminates the *aphairesis* of all (by negating *aphairesis* itself), for it is God, not *apophasis*, that is here identified as *hyper* all *aphairesis* and *thesis*.[68] *Apophasis* is therefore properly contrasted, on the one hand, *syntactically* with *kataphasis* as the difference between a negative predicate-term and a positive predicate-term and, on the other hand, *semantically* with *sterēsis* as the difference between a negative predicate-term that signifies excess and a negative predicate-term that signifies lack. And *aphairesis* is properly contrasted with *thesis* as the difference between a method that removes properties from God and a method that posits properties of God.[69]

66. *MT* 1.2, 1000B.

67. These are the interpretations of *apophasis* offered by John N. Jones and Janet Williams, respectively. Jones maintains that whereas *individual aphairesis* negates individual predicates from God one by one, both *aphairesis of all being* and *apophasis*—terms that Jones calls "synonymous" and "correlated" ("Sculpting God," 366, 369)—negate all predicates of God at once. Thus, Jones calls *apophasis* a "second-order rule for the employment of first-order names," one that stipulates the impossibility of knowing and saying anything about God (ibid., 368). Somewhat similarly, Williams believes that *apophasis* is not a general synonym for negation but rather "refers specifically to the denial that human language can contain the fulness of divine meaning" ("The Apophatic Theology," 167). Thus, *apophasis* refers only to the "last part" of the way of "negation," the negation of the dialectic of *thesis* and *aphairesis* at the conclusion of the *Mystical Theology* (ibid., 168).

68. See chapter 4 for my interpretation of *hyper aphairesis*.

69. Two notes about this chart are necessary. First, although Dionysius makes no explicit distinction between the assertion of a negative predicate (e.g., God is un-wise/not-wise) and the denial of a positive predicate (e.g., God is not wise), the interpretation of *aphairesis* above as narrow-scope predicate-term negation necessitates such a distinction: *aphairesis* would therefore encompass only the assertion of a negative predicate (i.e., narrow-scope predicate-term negation), whereas *thesis* would include not only the assertion of a positive predicate but also the denial of a positive predicate (i.e., wide-scope

Negating Negation

Table 3: Terms of Affirmation and Negation in the Dionysian Corpus

	Method	Logic
Positive	*Thesis*: the positing of a positive (*kataphatic*) predicate-term of God (e.g., God is wise)	*Kataphasis*: a positive predicate-term (e.g., wise)
Negative	*Aphairesis*: the removal of a negative (*apophatic*) predicate-term from God (e.g., God is not-wise)	*Apophasis*: a negative predicate-term of excess (e.g., not-wise *qua hyper* wise) *Sterēsis*: a negative predicate-term of lack (e.g., not-wise *qua* lacking wisdom)

Nevertheless, as this table illustrates, the *aphairetic* removal of properties from God employs negative predicate-terms, which, as Dionysius says elsewhere, must be interpreted *apophatically* (when predicated of God). *Aphairesis* and *apophasis* therefore not only fit together but also require one another. *Apophasis* interprets that which *aphairesis* removes.

This would mean that *aphairesis* does more than just remove the properties of being from God; it also reveals *hyper*-being preeminence. And indeed Dionysius seems to say just this in at least three different ways. First, Dionysius' sculpture metaphor from *Mystical Theology* 2 (see section I above) indicates not only that *aphairesis* flat out removes properties of God but also that even after "all things" have been removed from God, a finished sculpture remains. As in the case of *apophasis*, the best way to make sense of this apparent paradox is to distinguish between that which is according to being and that which transcends being: *aphairesis* removes predicate-terms with respect to being in order to reveal their *hyper*-being excess. Second, Dionysius' discussion of the two ways of approaching God at *Divine Names* 7.3 combines *aphairesis* and *hyperochē* in one and the same way (contrasting it to the way of causation).

---

predicate denial). (This may be the reason why Dionysius says in the above passage from *MT* 1.2 that it is necessary both to posit [*thesis*] and to affirm [*kataphasis*] of God all the predicates of being—i.e., to clarify that he is speaking here only about the assertion of positive predicates and not also the denial of positive predicates.) Second, although Dionysius usually removes *apophatic* predicates from God, he also sometimes removes what seem to be *sterētic* predicates from God, e.g., in the first line from *MT* 4 where Dionysius declares that God is not-being-less, not-life-less, not-reason-less, and not-mind-less.

> It is never true to say that we know God in its nature since this is unknown and *hyper*-raised (ὑπεραῖρον) all reason and intellect; but rather out of the order of all beings as projected out of it and as having some likenesses and similarities to its divine paradigms, we approach, as far as we have power, to that which is beyond (ἐπέκεινα) all by a way and order both in the removal (ἀφαιρέσει) and *hyper*-having (ὑπεροχῇ) of all and in the cause of all. Therefore God is known in all and apart (χωρὶς) from all.[70]

Here Dionysius says that one of the two ways of approaching God not only removes properties of God but also interprets these removed properties *hyperochically* (rather than *steretically*). Here Dionysius says that *aphairesis* itself states preeminence. Thus Dionysius effectively says that removed properties should be interpreted *apophatically*. Thirdly, Dionysius twice conjoins the terms *aphairesis* and *hyperochē* together in the phrase *hyperochē aphairesis*.

> It is permissible for no one who is a lover of the truth *hyper* all truth to hymn the thearchic *hyper*-beingness—whatever is the *hyper*-subsistence (ὑπερύπαρξις) of the *hyper*-goodness—as word, power, mind, life, or being, but as *hyper-havingly* removed (ὑπεροχικῶς ἀφῃρημένην) from all condition, motion, life, imagination, opinion, name, word, thinking, intellection, being, rest, foundation, unity, limit, non-limit, and whatever else has being.[71]

> As we showed in the *Theological Outlines* with many examples from the sacred writings, the things unified of the whole divinity are the *hyper*-good, the *hyper*-divine, the *hyper*-being, the *hyper*-life, and the *hyper*-wise and whatever else is of the *hyper*-having removal (τῆς ὑπεροχικῆς ἐστιν ἀφαιρέσεως) [...].[72]

---

70. *DN* 7.3, 869D–872A.

71. *DN* 1.5, 593C.

72. *DN* 2.3, 640B. See also *DN* 4.3, 697A, which contains the term *hyperochē*, alpha privative prefixed divine names, and the phrase *aphairesis of all*.

> If the Good is *hyper* all beings, as it is, the formless produces-form. And in it alone non-being (ἀνούσιον) is *hyper*-throwing (ὑπερβολή) being, non-life (ἄζωον) is *hyper*-having (ὑπερέχουσα) life, and non-intellect (ἄνουν) is *hyper*-raising (ὑπεραίρουσα) wisdom, and whatever is in the Good is of the hyper-having (ὑπεροχικῆς) form-production of that which is formless. And, if it is lawful to say, non being (μὴ ὂν) itself desires the Good *hyper* all beings, and strives somehow to be in the Good, and is truly *hyper*-being with respect to the removal of all (τὴν πάντων ἀφαίρεσιν).

Also consider the following passages that join *hyperochē* and *exairō*: *DN* 2.7, 645B; *DN* 2.8, 645C; *DN* 8.1, 889C; *DN* 12.4, 972AB; *CH* 3.2 165C. Interestingly, the phrase

Negating Negation

In these passages Dionysius indicates that *aphairesis* states *hyperochic* pre-eminence. To remove from God condition, motion, and life is to interpret these properties *hyperochically*, just as to name God as *hyper*-good, *hyper*-divine, and *hyper*-being is implicitly to remove these names (in their non *hyper*-prefixed form) with respect to being. To *aphairetically* remove in a *hyperochic* manner is therefore to remove *apophatically*.

So although it is true that Dionysian negation is constituted by two different principal terms, *aphairesis* and *apophasis* function together to yield a single cohesive picture of negation. *Aphairesis* is a method of removing properties from God through predicate-term negation, whereas *apophasis* is a logic of interpreting negative predicate-terms *hyperochically* rather than *steretically*. Dionysian negation removes the ordinary (*being*) senses of properties in order to reveal their extraordinary (*hyper-being*) meanings, both as the divine names themselves and as their pre-contained, *hyper*-unified effects.

---

hyperochē apophasis also appears once in the corpus (*EP* 4, 1072B—see above), but seems redundant on the interpretation of *apophasis* above (i.e., since *apophasis* already states excess). Finally, note that the remaining five uses of *aphairesis*—*DN* 8.3, 892B; *DN* 8.5, 893A; *MT* 1.1, 1000A; *EH* 3, 425A; *EH* 4.III.3, 477A—neither add nor subtract anything from the analysis of *aphairesis* in this chapter.

Chapter 3

Ranks Are Not Bypassed;
Rites Are Not Negated

THE LAST TWO CHAPTERS looked at one half of the Dionysian corpus; this chapter turns to the other. This is to say its concern is not with the procession from God, the divine names that source intelligible properties to participating beings, but with the return to God, the hierarchical ("sacredly-ordered") ranks and hierurgical ("sacredly-worked") rituals that mediate and effect deification-union for practicing beings.[1] But this said, this chapter will also consider the whole of the Dionysian corpus. For insofar as the *Divine Names* and *Mystical Theology* not only describe the divine-name procession from God but also prescribe a performative practice for returning to God through the removal of divine names (and perceptible symbols), this chapter argues that such a practice serves as a preparation

---

1. *Hierurgy* ("sacred work") is Dionysius' preferred term for what is usually (in late Neoplatonism) called *theurgy* ("divine work")—divinely-established, ritualized practices that effect union with higher planes of reality; see *EH* 3.III.4, 429D and *EH* 3.III.12, 441C; see also Klitenic, "Theurgy"; Louth, "Pagan Theurgy"; and Rorem, *Biblical and Liturgical Symbols*. *Theurgy* is instead usually reserved for the divine acts of God (Jesus) that the hierurgical rituals imitate. But as with most things Dionysian, this usage is not always precise. *Theurgy* is sometimes employed to refer to any work that is divine in nature, whether performed by God (Jesus) or humans (see *EH* 2.II.7, 396D and *EH* 4.III.12, 484D; see also Struck, "Pagan and Christian Theurgies"; and Shaw, "Neoplatonic Theurgy"). And *hierurgy* is sometimes used to refer only to the sacramental rites of baptism, eucharist, and myron consecration, but other times used to refer more broadly to any "sacred work" undertaken by humans (in particular the non-sacramental rites of clerical ordination, monastic tonsure, and the rite for the dead). (Myron consecration refers to ritual anointing with sacred oil.)

for and technique within the liturgical rituals of the *Ecclesiastical Hierarchy*. Negative theology is not the means by which hierarchical ranks and hierurgical rituals are negated or abandoned; they are a means by which they are affirmed and accomplished.

Those that interpret the Dionysian corpus through the lens of apophatic abandonment see things differently, arguing that apophasis, in effect, trumps hierarchy and hierurgy—that the hierarchical ranks of angels and humans and the hierurgical rituals of baptism, eucharist, and myron consecration are an unnecessary or insufficient means of return. The "unnecessary" version of the argument insists that apophatic ascent, which culminates in union with God, bypasses all hierarchies, which serve not as ladders leading up to God but as beacons of divine glory.[2] More radically, it proposes that Dionysian hierarchies and hierurgies are, even for Dionysius, just "useful means," one among many different soteriologically efficacious but literally false religious paths.[3] The "insufficient" version of the argument is a bit more nuanced, maintaining that although hierarchical ranks and hierurgical rituals are necessary to deification-union, they ultimately must be surpassed.[4] Here, things go something as follows: the Dionysian corpus offers but one path of return, that of symbolic interpretation; just as the *Divine Names* and *Mystical Theology* advance a method for interpreting "symbols" for God, so do the *Celestial Hierarchy* and *Ecclesiastical Hierarchy* for the angels and liturgy. But, continues this argument, the Dionysian path of return culminates in the absolute negation of all symbols whatsoever; thus whereas the *Celestial Hierarchy* and *Ecclesiastical Hierarchy* interpret symbols for the angels and liturgy by "negating" their perceptible form to recover their intelligible content, the *Mystical Theology* "interprets" all symbols by negating not only their perceptible form but also their intelligible content. Thus, concludes this argument, although hierarchical ranks and hierurgical rituals play a necessary initial role in the process of return—al-

---

2. Here I have in mind the arguments of Andrew Louth (*Denys*, 108, 105). Note, though, that Louth does recognize the fundamentally "liturgical" nature of both the Dionysian corpus and Dionysian theology (ibid., 29–31); for more on this, see notes 73 and 87 below.

3. Here I refer once again to Denys Turner and John Hick, particularly the latter, for whom all "divine names"—a category that seems to include all religious beliefs and practices whatsoever—are just "useful means." See note 1 in chapter 1 and note 4 in chapter 2.

4. Here I'm thinking of the work of Paul Rorem, in particular his books (*Biblical and Liturgical Symbols, Pseudo-Dionysius*), but also some of his articles ("The Place of *The Mystical Theology*," "The Uplifting Spirituality," and "Moses as the Paradigm"). See section III below for more on Rorem's arguments and evidence.

Ranks Are Not Bypassed; Rites Are Not Negated

beit more as interpreted than as performed—that role is one that requires their eventual negation, "not in further interpretation but in final rejection and abandonment."[5]

All this is apophatic abandonment—attempts to minimize the necessity and ultimacy of the hierarchies and hierurgies for return due to the conviction that if God is absolutely ineffable, then nothing can be literally true with respect to God, not even the hierurgical rituals that are revealed by and effect uplifting through the hierarchical ranks. Such rituals and ranks must therefore be just one among many different possible routes of access to God. And even if they are personally or communally useful, they must ultimately be kicked away like so many Wittgensteinian ladders that not only serve purely provisional purposes but also thwart higher spiritual aspirations.

Although such a Dionysius may well be in step with our times, he is at odds with his own writings. This chapter speaks on behalf of those writings, showing how they do not abandon all things hierarchical and hierurgical to apophasis, but rather regard negation as a means of properly preparing for and performing the rituals. In doing so, this chapter offers four distinct arguments. First, for every hierarchical rank of being after the first rank of angels, union with God is hierarchically mediated by, and therefore spiritually inferior to, the superior ranks of hierarchical beings. Second, for every ecclesiastical rank of being (i.e., humans), deification-union requires not only an understanding of all relevant symbols but also their actual ritual-communal practice (at least in cases where these symbols are liturgical-hierurgical in nature, as they are for humans). Third, proper understanding of liturgical symbols does not involve their negation but the recovery of their intelligible-spiritual meaning from their perceptible form. Fourth, if the two "halves" of the Dionysian corpus do fit together, they do so in such a way that aphairetic removal serves and supports hierurgical ritual rather than rejecting and abandoning it. And so, this chapter speaks on behalf of not only a "positively different" Dionysian corpus but also a positively different Dionysian God—a God who bestows hierarchical ranks, hierurgical rituals, and hierarchical-hierurgical symbols for the proportionate deification-union of humans; a God who calls for uplifting by these ranks, practice of these rituals, and interpretation of these symbols; a God who desires not the utter negation of these ranks, rituals, and symbols, but their proper religious use and interpretation.

5. Rorem, *Pseudo-Dionysius*, 206; see also 210–13.

I. Deification-Union is Hierarchically Mediated

In one sentence, the first and only sentence from *Celestial Hierarchy* 3.1, Dionysius tells us just about everything that we need to know about hierarchy.

> According to me, hierarchy is sacred order (τάξις) and science (ἐπιστήμη) and activity (ἐνέργεια), being assimilated to the godform as much as possible and being lifted up to the god-imitation in proportion to the enlightenments divinely given to it, while the god-becoming beauty—as simple, good, and source of initiation— is completely pure of every dissimilarity, giving its proper light to each according to worth, and perfecting in most divine sacrament (τελετῇ) each of those being harmoniously perfected according to the precise form.[6]

Here lie four key characteristics of hierarchy: (1) hierarchies are constituted by sacred orders, sciences, and activities; (2) they function to purify, illuminate, and perfect their members; (3) they do so to the end of uplifting to and assimilation with God; (4) and they achieve these functions to these ends in proportion to the hierarchical position or capacity of their members. I will venture no further than these four claims in this section, seeking to demonstrate the necessity of hierarchical mediation for deification-union.

A hierarchy is constituted by a sacred order (*taxis*), science (*epistēmē*), and activity (*energeia*). This is not as unhelpful as it may at first seem. Each hierarchy is a sacred order insofar as it possesses both a general triadic structure and a specific hierarchical type (celestial, human, or legal); a sacred science insofar as it enables a certain means of intellecting (*noēsis*) divine matters (immaterial, ecclesiastical-symbolic, or legal-symbolic, respectively); and a sacred activity insofar as it employs a certain set of unifying-deifying practices (contemplative, Christic-sacramental, or Mosaic-legalistic, respectively).[7]

---

6. *CH* 3.1, 164D. Note that two slightly different definitions of hierarchy can be found at *EH* 1.1, 369–372A and *EH* 1.3, 373C.

7. *EH* 5.I.2, 501A–504A.

Ranks Are Not Bypassed; Rites Are Not Negated

Table 4: Hierarchical Orders, Sciences, and Activities

	Sacred Order	Sacred Science	Sacred Activity
Celestial Hierarchy	*1st rank:* seraphim, cherubim, thrones *2nd rank:* dominions, powers, authorities *3rd rank:* archons, archangels, angels	Immaterial (unsymbolic) intellection	Contemplative (unritualistic) practice
Human Hierarchy	*1st rank:* baptism, eucharist, myron *2nd rank:* hierarchs, priests, deacons *3rd rank:* monks, sacred people, those undergoing purification	Intellection through material-ecclesiastical symbols	Ritualistic practice and interpretation of christological sacraments
Legal Hierarchy	*1st rank:* law of the sacred tabernacle *2nd rank:* Moses and priests *3rd rank:* people	Intellection through material-legal symbols	Ritualistic practice and interpretation of Mosaic Law

Thus the celestial hierarchy is composed of three ranks (*diakosmeis*) of angels, each of which is populated by three distinct orders (*taxeis*): a superior rank of the orders of seraphim, cherubim, and thrones; an intermediate rank of the orders of dominions, powers, and authorities; and an inferior rank of the orders of archons, archangels, and angels.[8] And the celestial hierarchy intellects divine matters directly, thereby requiring no perceptible symbols or material rituals.[9] The human hierarchy,[10] by contrast, is heterogeneous

---

8. *CH* 6.2, 200D–201A. As Sheldon-Williams observed, Dionysius is not entirely consistent in his application of the terms *ranks* (*diakosmeis*) and *orders* (*taxeis*) ("The Ecclesiastical Hierarchy," 295–96).

9. *EH* 1.4, 376B.

10. If, as is widely believed, the titles and subtitles of the Dionysian corpus are later editorial additions, then it is the case that Dionysius never refers to the "ecclesiastical hierarchy" as such, preferring instead to call it, usually, "our hierarchy" and, less frequently, "human hierarchies" or "the hierarchy among us" or "our most pious hierarchy" or "the orders of the ranks here and now" (Rorem, *Biblical and Liturgical Symbols*, 28 n. 6). But since *ecclesiastical hierarchy* is the widely accepted name of the hierarchy described in

in nature, composed of one rank of ecclesiastical rituals and two ranks of ecclesiastical roles—the first rank is constituted by the sacramental rituals of baptism, eucharist, and myron consecration,[11] whereas the remaining two ranks are populated by a superior clerical rank of hierarchs, priests, and deacons, and an inferior lay rank of monks, sacred people, and those being purified (the last of which is further trichotomized into the sub-orders of catechumens, penitents, and possessed). Unlike the superior celestial hierarchy, the human hierarchy intellects divine matters through perceptible symbols and material rituals; but unlike the inferior legal hierarchy, these christological-sacramental symbols and rituals are entirely "precise" and therefore completely "appropriate" to this end.[12] Finally, the legal hierarchy—which, with the coming of Jesus, gets supplanted by the ecclesiastical hierarchy[13]—permits a merely faint and obscure intellection of divine matters through the symbols and rituals of the Mosaic "law of the sacred tabernacle."[14]

As Dionysian scholars have long noted, there are some obvious problems with the parallelism employed here. Whereas the celestial hierarchy is composed of three ranks of three orders of beings, the ecclesiastical and legal hierarchies are populated by both beings and sacraments. Thus when Dionysius tries to trace the blueprint of the ecclesiastical hierarchy—three types of sacraments, three types of beings who initiate, three types of beings who are initiated—onto the other hierarchies, he not only distorts the celestial hierarchy (which has no sacraments, at least not in the *Celestial Hierarchy*[15]) but also overcomplicates the legal hierarchy (which appears

---

the treatise *Ecclesiastical Hierarchy*, I will employ it interchangeably with *our hierarchy* and *human hierarchy*.

11. Although the *Ecclesiastical Hierarchy* explicates six ecclesiastical rituals in total, only these three are called sacraments (*teletē*) and numbered among the first rank of the human hierarchy. (The other three, non-sacramental rituals are clerical ordination, monastic tonsure, and the rite for the dead.) But, again, this usage is not precise, as Dionysius refers to the deifying-unifying practices of both the celestial and legal hierarchies as sacramental in *EH* 5.I.2.

12. *EH* 2.III.6, 401C; *EH* 2.III.1, 397AB; *EH* 2.III.7, 404B. For more on the precision and appropriateness of the ecclesiastical symbols-rituals, see section III.

13. *EH* 5.I.2, 501C.

14. Whether such intellection is possible at all is debatable. My contention is that it is, albeit faintly: *EH* 5.I.2 asserts that the sacrament of the legal hierarchy is elevation to spiritual worship and that the initiated of the legal hierarchy are those being conducted to a more perfect initiation of the symbols of the law.

15. In the *Ecclesiastical Hierarchy* Dionysius calls the sacrament of the celestial hierarchy "immaterial knowledge of God and divine things" (*EH* 1.I.501A). But there is no

Ranks Are Not Bypassed; Rites Are Not Negated

not to have distinct orders within its ranks).[16] And the same holds true of the hierarchical functions of purification, illumination, and perfection: Dionysius would like it to be the case that the three orders (sacraments) of the first rank are the agents of perfection, illumination, and purification, respectively; that the three orders (initiators) of the second rank are the administrators of these agents of perfection, illumination, and purification, respectively; and that the three orders (initiated) of the third rank are administered respectively by these agents of perfection, illumination, and purification. But this not only assumes that the celestial and legal hierarchies share the same type of "sacred order" as the human hierarchy, but also fudges at least one detail of the human hierarchy—viz., baptism serves both to purify and illuminate, whereas both myron consecration and eucharist serve to perfect.[17] As one Dionysian scholar has noted, it is therefore the case that Dionysius' "claims for a single structure common to all three hierarchies are rather forced."[18] (As an aside, let me again say here that the lengths to which Dionysius goes in order to "force" triplicate structures in the hierarchies is reason to look for triplicate structures among the divine names—see chapter 2, section II.) Nevertheless, it is also the case that just as hierarchies possesses the constituents of order, science, and activity, they likewise possess the functions of purification, illumination, and perfection. Moreover, as the above passage from *Celestial Hierarchy* 3.1 suggests, these functions and constituents are correlated. Purification removes the divine dissimilarity that comes from being out of hierarchical order; illumination imparts enlightenment and thereby enables scientific intellection of divine matters; and perfection bestows divine imitation and union through the correct performance and intellection of a hierarchy's hierurgical practices.[19] These features, then, are common to every hierarchy: the constituents

---

evidence of this in the *Celestial Hierarchy*. Moreover, its addition to the celestial hierarchy upsets its triadic-triadic organization, giving it an unseemly total of ten types of entities.

16. *EH* 5.I.1, 501A; *EH* 5.I.2, 501ABCD; *EH* 5.III.8, 516A.

17. *EH* 5.I.3, 504BC; *EH* 3.I, 425AB. As Dionysius freely admits, it is also a stretch to say that any member of the celestial hierarchy is undergoing purification (*EH* 6.III.6; see also *CH* 7.2, 208A–209A).

18. Rorem, *Biblical and Liturgical Symbols*, 29.

19. *CH* 3.2, 165BC; *CH* 3.3, 165D–168A. Note that these three constituents and functions of hierarchy also correspond to the Neoplatonic triad of remaining, proceeding, and reverting: hierarchical order or purity is the static remaining of hierarchy, hierarchical science or illumination is the dynamic procession of enlightenment down through the hierarchical ranks, and hierarchical activity or perfection is the uplifting reversion of souls through the hierarchical ranks. For more on purification, illumination, and

of sacred order, science, and activity; and the functions of purification, illumination, and perfection.

These constituents and functions are for the sake of the ultimate ends of hierarchy—return, uplifting, salvation, assimilation, divinization, union. Although there are some differences between these terms that will be noted below (section IV), for now allow them to stand as different terms for the same general Neoplatonic process of return (*epistrophē*), the process by which humans ascend from lower to higher, inferior to superior, diverse to simple.[20] This goal, as Dionysius makes clear in the passages below, can only be realized through hierarchy. Thus both *Celestial Hierarchy* 3.2 and *Ecclesiastical Hierarchy* 2.I inform us that the goal of hierarchy is assimilation and union with God as much as possible. And, to this, *Ecclesiastical Hierarchy* 2.I adds that humans will only be assimilated and unified with God by their love and hierurgical practice of the commandments.

> And so the aim of hierarchy is the assimilation (ἀφομοίωσις) and union (ἕνωσις) with God, as much as possible, having God leading all sacred knowledge and activity, and steadfastly seeing and having impressed the divine comeliness of God as much as possible, and perfecting the divine image of each member as most clear and spotless mirrors, receptive of the source-light and thearchic ray and sacredly filled with the given radiance, and ungrudgingly spreading this light again in sequence in accordance with the thearchic law.[21]
>
> Therefore, we have sacredly said that this is the goal of our hierarchy: our assimilation (ἀφομοίωσίς) and union (ἕνωσις) with God as much as possible. But, as the divine Scriptures teach, we will only

---

perfection in general, see the following: *CH* 7.2, 208A–209A; *CH* 7.3, 209CD; *CH* 10.3, 273C; *EH* 5.I.3, 504AB–5.I.7, 509A; *EH* 6, 532A–533A; *EH* 6, 537ABC. As several Dionysian scholars have noted, all three are dominated by an intellective element. In the words of two such scholars, purification frees the intelligence of everything other than God, illumination reveals God, transmitting the science of God and divine things, and perfection is characterized by the ability to contemplate the sacred mysteries (see, for example, Wear and Dillon, *Dionysius the Areopagite*, 62). Still, this is not to say that such contemplation is effective apart from the actual practice of the sacraments.

20. Rorem, *Biblical and Liturgical Symbols*, 99. In fact, the last passage quoted in this paragraph practically equates *salvation, divinization, assimilation,* and *union* (*EH* 1.3, 373D–376A; see also *EH* 2.II.1, 393A); and a great number of passages use *return* and *uplifting* interchangeably (e.g., *CH* 9.2, 260B and *CH* 15.1, 333B).

21. *CH* 3.2, 165A. In addition to the passages below, see the following for the importance of hierarchy to salvation-union: *CH* 1.2, 121ABC; *CH* 1.3, 121C–124A; *CH* 7.2, 208A.

> be made this by the affections and hierurgies (ἱερουργίαις) of the most august commandments.[22]

Similarly, both *Ecclesiastical Hierarchy* 1.4 and *Ecclesiastical Hierarchy* 1.3 tell us that hierarchy is a gift from God to rational and intelligible beings for their salvation and deification (the latter of which involves an assimilation and unification with God as far as possible). And *Ecclesiastical Hierarchy* 1.3 adds that this salvation is possible in no other way than by the deification of the saved through the assimilation and unification with God (as far as possible).

> And so, let us say that the thearchic beatitude, the divine by nature, the source of deification (θεώσεως), from which those deified are deified, gave, by divine goodness, the gift of hierarchy to all rational and intelligent beings for their salvation and deification (θεώσει).[23]

> The will of this most thearchic beatitude beyond all, this threefold monad and really being, which is inscrutable to us but known to itself, is the rational salvation of beings like us and *hyper* us. But this salvation cannot otherwise happen except that those who are being saved are being deified. And this deification (θέωσις) is the assimilation (ἀφομοίωσίς) and unification (ἕνωσις) with God so far as possible. And this is the common end of every hierarchy—the immediate love of God and divine things, hierurgified (ἱερουργουμένη) in an inspirited and uniform manner; and prior to this, the complete and unswerving removal of things contrary, the knowledge of beings as they really are, the vision and science of sacred truth, the inspirited participation in the uniform perfection, the banquet of contemplation of the One itself as far as possible, which nourishes intelligibly and deifies all who are lifted up toward it.[24]

Hierarchy, we might therefore say, is both the necessary and sufficient condition of deification-union. As I will argue in the remainder of this section, this is to say that there is no deification-union that is not hierarchical—no deification-union that either bypasses or is disproportionate to hierarchical order. And as I will argue in the following two sections, this is also to say that deification-union requires nothing more than hierarchy—nothing more than the correct practice and interpretation of the hierarchical-hierurgical rites, not their negation and transcendence.

22. *EH* 2.I, 392A.
23. *EH* 1.4, 376B.
24. *EH* 1.3, 373D–376A.

Negating Negation

There is no deification-union that bypasses correct hierarchical order (i.e., purification). Such order is, quite simply, one in which superior hierarchical members preside over, pass down enlightenment to, and uplift inferior hierarchical members. Each member of the celestial hierarchy must be uplifted by an adjacently superior member of the celestial hierarchy (with the sole exception of the highest members of the celestial hierarchy, the seraphim, which are uplifted directly by Jesus).[25] And each member of the human hierarchy must be uplifted by a superior member of the human hierarchy (with the sole exception of the highest members of the human hierarchy, the hierarchs, who are uplifted by the lowest member of the celestial hierarchy, the angels).[26] Thus *Celestial Hierarchy* 9.2 says that the first rank of angels uplifts the second, which in turn uplifts the third, all so that "uplifting and reversion and communion and union to God might be according to order."

> One must consider, as has been said, that the superior rank, as drawing near in the manner of the first rank to that which is hidden, hiddenly hierachizes the second, while the second, which is composed of holy dominions and powers and authorities, leads the hierarchy of the archons and archangels and angels more clearly than the first hierarchy but more hiddenly than that after it, and the revealing rank of archons and archangels and angels presides through one another over the human hierarchies, so that the uplifting and reversion and communion and union to God might be according to order, and indeed also so that the procession from God [might be] beneficently given to all the hierarchies and communally manifested with most sacred order.[27]

---

25. For uplifting within the celestial hierarchy, see the following: *CH* 5, 196C; *CH* 7.3, 209AB; *CH* 8.1, 204B; *CH* 8.2, 240C–241D; *CH* 9.2, 257CD; *CH* 10.1, 272D–273A; *CH* 10.2, 273AB; *CH* 13.3, 301A–304B; *CH* 13.4, 305B–308B; *CH* 15.6, 333C–336B; *EH* 5.I.2, 501AB; *EH* 6.III.6, 537BC; *DN* 11.1, 949A. For uplifting of the angels by Jesus, see the following: *CH* 7.3, 209BCD; *EH* 1.1, 372AB. For passages that discuss Jesus' various hierarchical roles, see the following: *CH* 4.4, 181D; *CH* 7.3, 209B; *EH* 1.1, 372AB; *EH* 1.2, 373B; *EH* 5.I.5, 505B. Note also that the entire process of uplifting is enabled by God (*CH* 1.2, 121ABC; *EH* 1.3, 373C–376A).

26. For uplifting within the human hierarchy, see the following: *EH* 1.2, 372C–373B; *EH* 1.5, 376D; *EH* 2.III.3, 400B; *EH* 2.III.4, 400C; *EH* 3.III.12, 441C–444B; *EH* 6.III.1, 533C; *EP* 8.1, 1089A. And for uplifting of humans by angels, see the following: *CH* 4.3, 180C–181A; *CH* 4.4, 181BC; *CH* 5, 196C; *CH* 7.4, 212ABCD; *CH* 8.2, 241C; *CH* 9.2, 257C–260B; *CH* 10.1, 273A; *CH* 10.2, 273AB; *CH* 13.3, 301C; *CH* 13.4, 304B–308B; *EH* 1.2, 373A; *DN* 4.1, 696A; *DN* 4.2, 696C.

27. *CH* 9.2, 260AB. See also the passages two notes above.

Ranks Are Not Bypassed; Rites Are Not Negated

And *Ecclesiastical Hierarchy* 1.2 applies this basic mechanism to the human hierarchy, telling how the human hierarch passes down his deification to inferior members of the hierarchy.

> Nevertheless, it is necessary to say this, that both that hierarchy and every hierarchy hymned now by us has one and the same power throughout the whole of its hierarchical operation; and that the hierarch himself, according to his nature and aptitude and rank, is initiated in divine things, and is deified, and imparts to the subordinates, according to the merits of each, a share of the sacred deification received by him from God; and that the subordinates follow their superiors, who lift up the inferiors toward that which is in front, some of whom go forward and lead others on as far as possible; and that through this inspirited and hierarchical harmony, each participates in the truly beautiful and wise and good, so far as possible.[28]

And *Celestial Hierarchy* 10.1 shows how the third rank of the angels uplifts the human hierarchy to God in accordance with the law of well-ordered hierarchical regularity.

> We have concluded, then, that the most primordial rank of the minds around God, hierarchicalized by the perfecting illumination through its immediate elevation to it, is purified and illuminated and perfected by a gift of light from the thearchy that is both more hidden and more manifest—more hidden, as more intelligible, more simplifying, and more unifying; more manifest, as first gift, first manifestation, more complete, and more clearly poured out from it. And from this [first rank] again, in due degree, the second, and from the second, the third, and from the third, our hierarchy, is hierarchically uplifted, in divine harmony and proportion, to the *hyper*-source source and consummation of all good order in accordance with the law itself of the well-ordered source of order.[29]

---

28. *EH* 1.2, 372C–373A. See also the passages two notes above.

29. *CH* 10.1, 272D–273A. See also the passage three notes above. Note that the first order of celestial beings is here said to be "purified and illuminated and perfected by a gift of light from the thearchy that is both more hidden and more manifest"—the former, since it is more intelligible, simplifying, and unifying; the latter, since it is a first gift that is more completely and clearly poured out. Note also that the prior passage from *CH* 9.2 suggests that, whereas the first order of celestial beings "hiddenly hierarchalizes" the second, the second hierarchicalizes the third in a manner that is less hidden. I don't think this is to say that there is "a dialectic of hiddenness and revelation in the celestial hierarchy" (as one anonymous reviewer suggested), at least not if this implies an inverse

Negating Negation

Not only is there no deification-union outside of correct hierarchical order; there is also no deification-union that is not proportionate to correct hierarchical order. The angelic hierarchy in general enjoys a deification-union superior to that of the human hierarchy. And only the first rank of the angelic hierarchy—the seraphim, cherubim, and thrones—participate immediately in God; all other hierarchical beings can only return to God through intermediary beings in the hierarchy. Accordingly, *Celestial Hierarchy* 6.2 says that the first rank of angels is united to God more closely and immediately than any other being.

> Theology has designated the whole heavenly beings as nine with nine revealed names; our divine sacred-initiator divides them into three threefold-orders. He says that first is that which is always around God, declared by tradition to be united closely and immediately to him before all the others. For he says that the revelation of the Holy Scriptures declares that the most holy thrones as well as the many-eyed and many-winged hosts, which are named cherubim and seraphim in the Hebrew tongue, are established immediately around God with a nearness superior to all. And so our illustrious guide spoke of this threefold order as one and of equal rank and really first hierarchy, than which there is not another more godlike or immediately proximate to the earliest illuminations of the thearchy. But he says that which is composed of the authorities, and lordships, and powers is second; and, as regards

---

relationship between hiddenness and manifestation. For the first order of celestial beings receives a gift of divine light that is *both more hidden and more manifest*, the former since it is more simple and unified, the latter since it is more complete and clear. It stands to reason, then, that as the gift of light continues to be poured out it becomes both less hidden (i.e., less simple and unified) and less manifest (i.e., less complete and clear). Regardless of the merit of this interpretation, I can't say that I see how any such dialectic creates difficulties for my overall hypotheses. It's still the case (1) that union with God is hierarchically mediated, (2) that union with God by humans requires correct understanding and practice of the appropriate perceptible-liturgical symbols, (3) that correct understanding of perceptible-liturgical symbols requires recovery of their intelligible-spiritual meaning rather than their wholesale negation, (4) and that *aphairetic* removal (probably) serves and supports *hierurgical* ritual as a means by which the hierarch remains unified even while distributing the pluralized symbols of the liturgy. In fact, if "hidden" = more simple and unified, and if "manifest" = more complete and clear, then the hierarch here, like the first order of celestial beings above, is "purified and illuminated and perfected by a gift of light from the thearchy that is both more hidden and more manifest" (albeit only as mediated by the celestial hierarchy and therefore not in as hidden and manifest a manner as the celestial hierarchy).

the last of the heavenly hierarchies, the order of the angels and archangels and principalities is third.[30]

And *Ecclesiastical Hierarchy* 1.2 indicates that the human hierarchy in general enjoys a participation in God that is inferior to that of the celestial hierarchy.

> But the beings and orders *hyper* us, of whom we have already made sacred mention, are incorporeal, and their hierarchy is intelligible and *hyper*-cosmic, but let us view our hierarchy, comfortably to ourselves, abounding in the variety of perceptible symbols, by which we are hierarchically lifted up, in proportion to our capacity, toward the uniform deification, God and divine virtue. They, as minds, intellect according to the laws for them, but we are lifted up by perceptible images toward divine contemplations as much as possible. And to speak truly, there is one to whom all the uniform aspire, but they do not participate uniformly of this that is one and the same, but as the divine measure distributes to each according to merited inheritance.[31]

And *Celestial Hierarchy* 8.2 maintains that it is divinely ordained by law that inferiors participate in God through superiors and therefore less perfectly.

> For, as those who are skillful in our sacred sacraments say, the directly revealed fullness of divine things is more perfecting than the divine contemplations imparted through others, and so, I think, the immediate participation of the angelic ranks firstly elevated to God is more direct than that of those perfected through a mediator. Hence, by our hierarchical tradition, the first minds are named perfecting and illuminating and purifying powers of their subordinates, who are uplifted through them to the *hyper*-being source of all, and come to participate, as far as permissible to them, in the purifications and illuminations and perfections of the source of perfection in accordance with the divine law. For this has been divinely ordained by law absolutely by the divine source of order: through the first, the second participate in the thearchic illuminations. You will find that this has been declared frequently by the theologians.[32]

---

30. *CH* 6.2, 200D–201A. In addition to the passage below, see the following: *CH* 4.2, 180A; *CH* 5, 196C; all of *CH* 7; *CH* 10.1, 272D; *CH* 12.2, 292C–293A; *CH* 13.3, 301D–304A; *EH* 1.2, 372C–373B; *EH* 3.III.3, 432CD; *EH* 4.III.5, 480BC; *EH* 5.I.2, 501AB; *EH* 6.III.6, 537BC.

31. *EH* 1.2, 373AB.

32. *CH* 8.2, 240CD. For Eric Perl, hierarchical participation in God is nevertheless

Negating Negation

In fact, Dionysius repeatedly tells the reader that all of this—the necessity of hierarchical uplifting, the importance of hierarchical position, the degree of hierarchical union—is divine law.

> But the theology wisely teaches this also—that it came to us through angels, as though the divine regulation were laying down this rule, that through the first, the second are brought to the divine things. For not only with regard to the superior and inferior minds, but even for those of the same rank, this law has been established by the *hyper*-being order-source, that within each hierarchy there are first and middle and last orders and powers, and that the more divine are initiators and conductors of the less to the divine access and illumination and communion.[33]

> It is the all-sacred law of the thearchy that through the first, the second are uplifted to its most divine light. Do we not see the perceptible substances of the elements first approaching that which is more akin to themselves and through these diffusing their own energy to others? Naturally, then, the source and foundation of all good order, both visible and invisible, permits its theurgifying rays to approach the more godlike first and through them, as more translucent minds that are more properly adapted to the reception and transmission of light, to shine out and proportionately illumine their subordinates. And so it is of these, the first contemplators of God, to teach ungrudgingly and in due measure the divine visions reverently gazed upon by themselves to those of second rank, and to initiate them in hierarchical matters (since they have been abundantly initiated with a perfecting science in all divine matters relating to their own hierarchy and have received the perfecting power of initiation), and to impart sacred gifts according to fitness (since they scientifically and wholly participate in the hierarchic perfection).[34]

By divine law, then, there is no deification-union without hierarchic mediation—no deification-union that bypasses hierarchic uplifting, no deification-union that is disproportionate to hierarchic position.

"direct" insofar as "hierarchical structure is itself the very means and revelation of God's immediate creative omnipresence" ("Hierarchy and Participation," 16; see also "Symbol, Sacrament, and Hierarchy," 345). This makes good sense to me.

33. *CH* 4.3, 181A. See also *DN* 4.1, 696A; *CH* 3.2, 165A; *CH* 8.2, 240D; *CH* 10.1, 273A.

34. *EH* 5.I.4, 504C–505A.

II. Deification-Union is Hierurgically Effected

Given that hierarchical beings are in correct hierarchical order (i.e., purified), they are able not only to receive divine revelation from their superiors (i.e., to be enlightened) but also to practice and contemplate it (i.e., to be perfected). For members of the human (ecclesiastical) hierarchy, this revelation includes both the sacred words (*hierologia*) and sacred works (*hierourgia*) of Scripture as well as a "more immaterial initiation" that is not written down but rather is passed on "from mind to mind."[35] Although this more immaterial initiation concerns the inner intelligible-spiritual meaning of the sacred words and sacred works, it is crucial not to overlook the fact that the sacred works and sacred words must be ritually performed.[36] Thus *Ecclesiastical Hierarchy* 3.III.12 announces that imitation of God is only possible by "renewing" the divine works or works of God (theurgies) in the sacred words (hierologies) and sacred works (hierurgies) of the human hierarchy.

> But how could the imitation of God otherwise become ours unless the remembrance of the most sacred theurgies (θεουργιῶν) were constantly renewed by the hierarchic hierologies (ἱερολογίαις) and hierurgies (ἱερουργίαις)?[37]

And *Ecclesiastical Hierarchy* 2.I again reiterates that assimilation and unification with God are only possible by love for and sacred workings (hierurgies) of the commandments.

---

35. *EH* 1.4, 376BC. See also *EH* 3.III.12, 441C and *EH* 5.III.7, 513C. Rorem treats this "more immaterial initiation" as the *hierurgical* practices themselves; a consideration of other uses of *hierology, hierurgy, theology*, and *theology*, however, suggests that this "more immaterial initiation" is the intelligible-spiritual meaning of the sacred words and sacred works (which is not itself contained in the writing of Scripture).

36. For passages that address the importance of the interpretation of perceptible symbols of ecclesiastical hierarchy, see the following: *EH* 1.2, 373AB; *EH* 1.4, 376BC; *EH* 1.5, 376D–377A; *EH* 5.I.2, 501D; *EH* 5.I.3, 504ABC; *EH* 5.I.6, 505D–508A; *EP* 9.1, 1104BC. For passages that address the importance of the interpretation of perceptible symbols of celestial hierarchy to uplifting, see the following: *CH* 1.2, 121ABC; *CH* 1.3, 121C–124A; *CH* 2.1, 136D–137A; *CH* 2.2, 140AB; *CH* 2.3, 141ABC; *CH* 2.4, 144BC; *CH* 2.5, 145AB; *CH* 4.1, 177C; *CH* 7.2, 208A; *CH* 13.1, 382; *CH* 4.2, 180B; *CH* 7.4, 212CD. For passages that address the importance of hierurgical practice, see the many excerpts and notes of this section as well as *EH* 2.III.1, 397AB; *EH* 3.III.7, 433C, 436B; *EH* 4.III.3, 467D–477B; *EH* 6.I.1, 532B; *EH* 6.I.2, 532BC.

37. *EH* 3.III.12, 441C.

Negating Negation

> Therefore, we have sacredly said that this is the goal of our hierarchy: our assimilation (ἀφομοίωσίς) and union (ἕνωσις) with God as much as possible. But, as the divine Scriptures teach, we will only be made this by the affections and hierurgies (ἱερουργίαις) of the most august commandments.[38]

What are these sacred words and sacred works? Although they seem to include any and all religious utterances and actions, Dionysius reserves a place of privilege for the ritualized utterances and actions of the liturgy, and in particular for the sacramental rites of baptism, eucharist, and myron consecration.[39] For it is these sacraments, as *Ecclesiastical Hierarchy* 5.I.3 indicates, that between them possess the threefold power of purification-illumination-perfection, and it is the rites of eucharist and myron consecration that in particular effect unifying uplifting to and blessed communion with the thearchy.

> And so, the threefold power of the holy hierurgy (ἱερουργίας) of the sacraments (τελετῶν) is hymned, since the sacred divine-birth is shown in the Scriptures to be a purification and enlightening illumination and the sacraments (τελετῆς) of synaxis and myron [are shown] to be a perfecting knowledge and science of the theurgies (θεουργιῶν), through which the unifying uplifting toward the thearchy and most blessed communion are sacredly perfected.[40]

---

38. *EH* 2.I, 392A.

39. See note 11 of this chapter for the distinction between sacramental and non-sacramental rites. For passages that use *hierurgy* for the sacramental rites in general or some sacramental rite in particular, see *EH* 2.I, 392A; *EH* 2.III.6, 401C; *EH* 3.III.7, 436BC; *EH* 3.III.10, 440A; *EH* 3.III.12, 441C–444A; *EH* 4.III.1, 473B; *EH* 4.III.2, 476B; *EH* 4.III.12, 485A; *EH* 5.I.1, 500D; *EH* 5.I.2, 501D; *EH* 5.I.3, 504A. For passages that use *hierurgy* indiscriminately of all the liturgical rites of the human hierarchy, see *EH* 1.4, 376C; *EH* 3.III.4, 429D; *EH* 3.III.12, 441C; *EH* 5.I.5, 505B; *EH* 5.I.6, 505D–508B; *EH* 5.III.7, 513CD; *EH* 6.I.1, 532A; *EH* 6.I.2, 532B; *EH* 6.I.3, 532D. For passages that use *hierurgy* for the individual ritualized actions of a liturgical rite, see *EH* 3.I, 425B; *EH* 3.III.6, 432C; *EH* 3.III.8, 437A. For a use of *hierurgy* for the rites of the legal hierarchy, see *EH* 5.I.2, 501C. And for even more uses of *hierurgy*, see notes 43 and 45 below. Somewhat similarly, *hierlogos* is sometimes used to refer to sacred utterances, writings or reasons in general (*EH* 1.5, 377A; *EH* 2.1, 392A; *EH* 2.II.6, 396B; *EH* 3.III.4, 432A; *EH* 3.III.5, 432A; *EH* 5.III.7, 513C; *DN* 3.3, 684B; *DN* 4.12, 709B) and other times used to refer to the ritualized utterances or uttering of the rites (*EH* 2.II.4, 393C; *EH* 3.II, 425B; *EH* 3.III.4, 429C, 432A; *EH* 3.III.6, 432C; *EH* 3.III.12, 441C; *EH* 4.II, 473A; *EH* 4.III.3, 476D; *EH* 6.II, 533AB; *EH* 6.III.1, 533C).

40. *EH* 5.I.3, 504BC. In addition to the following note, see also *EH* 2.III.8, 404D; *EH* 3.III.13, 444CD; *EH* 6.I.3, 532B; *EH* 6.III.5, 536BCD.

Ranks Are Not Bypassed; Rites Are Not Negated

Moreover, it is the ritualized utterances and actions of the sacramental rite of eucharist that are exalted above all. For, as *Ecclesiastical Hierarchy* 3.I declares, although every sacrament grants communion and union with the One, only eucharist perfects and completes the others, effecting a gathering to the One and completing a communion with God for those who participate in it.

> First, let us sacredly consider why that which is common to the other hierarchical sacraments (τελεταῖς) is pre-eminently attributed to this one [i.e., eucharist] beyond the rest, and why it uniquely receives the name of communion and synaxis when each holy-perfecting operation collects our divided lives into uniform deification and gives communion and union with the One by the godlike folding-together of our differences. But we say that the perfection that lies in the participation of the other hierarchical symbols comes from the thearchic and perfecting gifts of it [i.e., eucharist]. It is almost impossible for any hierarchical sacrament (τελετὴν) to be perfected without the most divine eucharist as crowning-point of the things perfected (τελετῶν) in each, hierurgizing (ἱερουργούσης) the gathering of the person initiated to the One, and completing his communion with God through the god-given gift of the perfecting mysteries.[41]

But as some of the above passages indicate, the Dionysian corpus uses *hierurgy* to refer to more than just the liturgical rites themselves; the verbal form of *hierurgy* in particular (*hierourgeō*) tends to refer instead to either the bodily-ritualized performance of these rites (as a sacred working of the sacred works) or the deifying-unifying effects achieved by this practice (as what is sacredly worked by the sacred works). (Similarly, *hierologeō* usually refers to the ritualized uttering of ritual utterances.[42]) This former sense (ritualized performance of the rites) is displayed in, among other passages, the following excerpts from *Ecclesiastical Hierarchy* 2.I and 3.II.

> Therefore, it is sacredly said to us that this is the goal of our hierarchy: our assimilating (ἀφομοίωσίς) and unifying (ἕνωσις) with God as much as possible. But, as Scripture teaches, we will only be

---

41. *EH* 3.I, 424C–425A. About this passage Eric Perl asserts: "There is no suggestion here that the sacraments merely 'show' us this communion; Dionysios explicitly asserts that they themselves effect it" ("Hierarchy and Participation," 31).

42. *EH* 2.II.4, 393C; *EH* 3.III.4, 432A; *EH* 6.II, 533B; *EH* 6.III.1, 533C.

> made this by the affections and hierurgies (ἱερουργίαις) of the most august commandments.⁴³
>
> When the hierarch has hymned the sacred theurgies (θεουργίας), he hierurgizes (ἱερουργεῖ) the most divine things and holds up to view the things hymned, reverently brought forth through the symbols [. . .].⁴⁴

And this latter sense of *hierurgy* (deifying-unifying effects of the rites) is reflected in, among other passages, the following excerpts from *Ecclesiastical Hierarchy* 3.I and 3.III.7.

> It is almost impossible for any hierarchical mystery to be celebrated without the most divine eucharist at the crowning-point of the rites celebrated in each. It hierurgizes (ἱερουργούσης) the gathering of the initiated into the One and completes his communion with God through the god-given gift of the perfecting mysteries.⁴⁵
>
> Then the all-holy sacred-workers (ἱερουργοί) and loving-seers of the all-holy things, reverently contemplating the most holy sacrament (τελετὴν), hymn in a universal hymn-singing the good-working and good-giving principle by which the wholesome sacraments (τελεταί), which were revealed to us, sacredly-work (ἱερουργοῦσαι) the sacred deification (θέωσιν) of the initiated (τελουμένων).⁴⁶

These passages show, yet again, that the liturgical rituals must be bodily practiced and that when they are, they effect (degrees of) deification-unification in their practitioners.

Of course this is not to say that liturgical rituals do not also need to be "cognitively" interpreted. (This is the "more immaterial initiation" that is not written down but rather is passed on "from mind to mind" by the hierarchs.) But there's no indication that such interpretation obviates bodily

---

43. *EH* 2.I, 392A. For passages that use *hierurgy* to refer to the performance of sacred works, see (in addition to the passage in the next note) the following: *CH* 3.2, 165B; *CH* 7.1, 205B; *CH* 13.3, 300C; *EH* 3.III.5, 432A; *EH* 3.III.7, 436A; *EH* 3.III.8, 437A; *EH* 3.III.10, 437D, 440B; *EH* 3.III.11, 440C; *EH* 3.III.12, 444A; *EH* 4.III.4, 477BC; *EH* 5.I.6, 505D; *EH* 5.III.6, 513B; *EH* 5.III.8, 516AB; *EH* 6.I.3, 532B, 533A.

44. *EH* 3.II, 425D.

45. *EH* 3.I, 424D. For passages the use *hierurgy* to refer to the effects of the sacred works, see (in addition to the passage in the next note) the following: *EH* 1.3, 376A; *EH* 4.I, 472D; *EH* 5.I.6, 508A; *EH* 5.III.8, 516AB; *EH* 6.I.3, 533A; *EH* 7.III.9, 565C.

46. *EH* 3.III.7, 436C. Note that this passage also uses *hierourgos* to refer to a sacred worker (priest); for more such uses, see *CH* 13.2, 300B.

practice (at least not for embodied humans[47]). Nor is there any indication that the interpretation of the liturgical symbols/rites calls for their negation. Rather, such interpretation intuits unified intelligible-spiritual meaning out of diversified perceptible symbols. (This is also true of the celestial hierarchies—see, for example, *CH* 1.3 and *CH* 2.2.) Thus *Ecclesiastical Hierarchy* 2.III.2 calls the perceptible symbols of the hierurgical rites "representations of intelligible things to which they lead and show the way."

> Let this be an introductory soul-uplifting for the uninitiated, setting apart, as is right, hierarchical and unified things from the majority, and apportioning the harmonious uplifting to the orders in due measure, while we, having ascended in sacred gradations to the sources of these performed sacraments, and having been sacredly initiated in them, will recognize of what stamps they are the reliefs and of what invisible things they are the images. For, as is clearly established in the treatise *On the Intelligible and the Perceptible*, the perceptibly sacred things are representations of intelligible things to which they lead and show the way, while the intelligible things are source and science of the hierarchical things that are perceptible.[48]

And *Ecclesiastical Hierarchy* 3.III.2 exhorts the reader to uncover the symbolic veils of the eucharist in order to contemplate their intellectual archetypes.

> Leaving behind, as I said, those things beautifully depicted on the gateways of the innermost sanctuaries as sufficient for those who are imperfect at contemplation, let us pass on from the effects to the causes with respect to our sacred synaxis. And with Jesus lighting the way, we shall view the fitting contemplation of the intelligible things, which vividly shines forth with the blessed beauty of the archetypes. But, oh most divine and sacred sacrament, uncovering the veils of the dark mysteries that envelop you in symbols, show yourself more clearly, and fill our intellectual visions with uncovered and filling light.[49]

---

47. Certain passages (e.g., *DN* 1.4, 592BC) indicate that symbolic interpretation will no longer be necessary when humans become "incorruptible and immortal." Does this apply to ritualized sacred work too? Insofar as the celestial hierarchy is said to have sacramental-initiatory practices (*EH* 5.I.2), I tend to think not.

48. *EH* 2.III.2, 397C.

49. *EH* 3.III.2, 428C.

Negating Negation

Note that this intelligible-spiritual meaning concerns not the apophatic indeterminacy of the thearchy but the saving work of Jesus. In this sense it is correct to say that hierurgy, the "sacred work" performed by humans, constitutes a ritual enactment of theurgy, the "divine work" performed by God (especially in the incarnation of Jesus Christ).[50] Accordingly, *Ecclesiastical Hierarchy* 3.III.13 tells us that the hierarch draws out Jesus Christ in the perceptible elements of the eucharist.

> The hierarch reveals these things in the sacredly performed sacraments, bringing the veiled gifts to light by dividing their unity into multiplicity and making the participants sharers in them in the highest union of the distributed things with those who receive them. For he delineates in these perceptible things our intelligible life in images, bringing to view out of the divine hiddenness Jesus Christ, who philanthropically put on our human nature in the all-perfect and unconfused incarnation, came to our divided condition without change from his essential unity, and called the human race into participation with himself and his own good gifts through this philanthropy of good-work, provided that we are united to his most divine life by our assimilation to it as far as possible and, in this, have been truly perfected sharers with God and divine things.[51]

And *Ecclesiastical Hierarchy* 2.III.7 reveals the inner meaning of the triple immersion in the rite of baptism as the three-day entombment of Jesus.

> And consider attentively with me how most appropriately the symbols hold the sacred things. For since death is for us not an annihilation of being, as others think, but the separation of things united, leading to that which is invisible for us—the soul becomes invisible through the deprivation of the body, while the body loses the form of human by being covered in the earth or some other kind of bodily change—the entire covering by water is appropriately taken as an image of the death and darkness of the tomb. And so the symbolical teaching mystically-uplifts [i.e., teaches] that the man sacredly baptized imitates, in so far as divine imitation is possible for humans, by the triple immersion in the water the thearchic death of the life-giving Jesus, who spent three days and nights in the tomb, and in whom according to the mystical and secret tradition of the Scriptures the prince of this world found nothing.[52]

50. See note 1 of this chapter.

51. *EH* 3.III.13, 444CD. In addition to the passage below, see the following: *EH* 3.III.7, 436D; *EH* 3.III.12, 441C–444B.

52. *EH* 2.III.7, 404BC.

It is therefore by virtue of both correct intellection of Jesus' divine work (*theurgy*) and correct reenactment of this divine work in the sacred work (*hierurgy*) of the liturgical rites that humans are saved, divinized, assimilated, and unified. Two points deserve reiteration: first, hierurgical practice-interpretation is a component of the ecclesiastical hierarchy; second, hierurgical interpretation involves the recovery of intelligible-spiritual content. Thus my claim remains—hierarchy is the necessary and sufficient condition of deification-union: the practice-interpretation of the hierurgical rites (which is a component of hierarchical uplifting) is both necessary to deification-union and, as it is not supplemented by anything extra-hierarchical or supplanted by negation, sufficient to deification-union as well.

III. Hierarchies and Hierurgies Are Not Negated

Despite this textual evidence, generalists usually assume and specialists sometimes argue that apophatic negation trumps hierarchical mediation and hierurgical practice—that all hierarchical symbols, together with their spiritual-intelligible denotations, are ultimately negated and transcended in the return to God. I would therefore like to spend a little more time with this claim, offering a couple more textual and logical arguments against it.[53]

First, and perhaps most importantly, nowhere in the Dionysian corpus is it said that the conceptual content signified by the hierarchical symbols should be flatly negated. As we saw in the preceding chapter, the *Mystical Theology* neither explicitly removes such content from God nor gives any implicit indication that it should be removed from God.[54] (Nor, for that

---

53. My arguments here will be directed against the position of Paul Rorem. (See the next two notes for some particularly relevant aspects of this position.) But I've also often heard generalist philosophers of religion articulate this view (in conference presentations).

54. Rorem maintains that chapter 3 of the *Mystical Theology* serves as both "a methodological parenthesis which surveys the entire corpus and enterprise" and "a brief summary or even the climax of Dionysian thought" (*Biblical and Liturgical Symbols*, 130; *Pseudo-Dionysius*, 183). He therefore believes that the aphairetic removals of chapters 4 and 5 of the *Mystical Theology* apply also to the symbols of the celestial and ecclesiastical hierarchies (*Pseudo-Dionysius*, 206). Thus, like perceptible symbols and intelligible names for God, perceptible symbols for the celestial and ecclesiastical hierarchies should first be interpreted and then be negated. And since the liturgical symbols are less incongruous than the celestial symbols, the interpretation-negation of the former should precede that of the latter. And since all these symbols are perceptible in nature, their negation should precede that of the intelligible divine names. According to Rorem,

Negating Negation

matter, does it explicitly or implicitly remove the perceptible form of the hierarchical symbols—more on this in the next paragraph.) The same is true of *Celestial Hierarchy* 2, a chapter that is sometimes said to imply that all hierarchical symbols must ultimately be completely negated.[55] Although *Celestial Hierarchy* 2 does make comparisons of negation (*apophasis*[56]) and symbolic dissimilarity, it neither states nor suggests that the conceptual content denoted by the hierarchical symbols should be negated. The first of these passages, *Celestial Hierarchy* 2.3, simply makes the point that just as negations are more fitting of the transcendent God than affirmations, so dissimilar symbols are more fitting of the immaterial angels than similar symbols. But this is the case simply because both are effective at showing what their referents are not—just as God is not anything of being (intelligible), so the angels are not anything of body (perceptible).

> Indeed the mystical traditions of the revealed Scriptures sometimes hymn the sacred blessedness of the *hyper*-being thearchy as word and mind and being, to show of it the divine-suitable expression and wisdom and really being subsistence and true cause of the subsistence of being, and represent it as light and hail it as life. While such sacred representations are more sacred, and seem in a certain way to be superior to the material forms, they still fall short of the thearchic likeness in reality (for it is *hyper* all being and life, characterized by nothing of light, incomparably leaving behind the similarity to it of every *logos* and mind). But other times God is *hyper*-cosmically hymned in negative (ἀποφατικαῖς) revelations by the Scriptures themselves, named invisible, infinite, ungraspable, and that which signifies not what it is but what it is not. For this, I think, is more appropriate to it, since, as the secret and sacred tradition has instructed, we speak truly of it as not being according to things of being, but we do not know of its incomprehensible and ineffable *hyper*-being and indeterminacy. Therefore, since the negations (ἀποφάσεις) are true

---

the sequence of negation, therefore, goes something as follows: *MT* 4, *CH*, *EH*, *MT* 5 (*Biblical and Liturgical Symbols*, 128–30; *Pseudo-Dionysius*, 207–10). (Note, though, that Rorem resists "pressing too hard for a formal sequence" [*Pseudo-Dionysius*, 210].)

55. Rorem believes that chapter 2 of the *Celestial Hierarchy* serves as "a methodological prologue to the rest of the treatise and to all Dionysian exegesis and reflection on theological language" (*Pseudo-Dionysius*, 56). He therefore believes that it offers a hermeneutic that applies to all predication of divine things (celestial and ecclesiastical symbols as well as divine symbols and names), a hermeneutic that strips away "dissimilarities" to reveal "similarities" (ibid., 54, 56).

56. Note that only the term *apophasis* is used here (at *CH* 2.3, 140D–141A and *CH* 2.5, 145A); *aphairesis* is nowhere present.

Ranks Are Not Bypassed; Rites Are Not Negated

of the divine while the affirmations are unfitting to the hiddenness of the inexpressible things, the manifestation through dissimilar shapings is more fitting to the invisible.[57]

The second of these passages, *Celestial Hierarchy* 2.5, begins by saying that just as gross perceptible symbols are used of the angels, so they are also used of God. But this does not entail that the intelligible content signified by these angelic symbols should be negated (in a way that is similar to the way in which divine names are aphairetically removed from God).

> We shall find the mystic theologians applying these things not only to the illuminations of the heavenly orders, but also sometimes to the thearchic revelations themselves. At one time, indeed, they hymn the thearchic revelations under exalted imagery as sun of righteousness, as morning star rising sacredly in the mind, and as light illuminating undisguisedly and noetically; and at other times, through things in our midst, as fire shining harmlessly, and as water furnishing a fullness of life, and, to speak symbolically, flowing into the belly and bubbling forth rivers that flow irresistibly; and at still other times, from things most remote, as sweet-smelling ointment, and as corner-foundation stone. But they also clothe it in the peculiar nature of wild beasts, identifying it with a lion and a panther, and saying that it is a leopard and a rushing bear. But I will also add that which seems to be more dishonorable than all and most incongruous, that those skillful in divine things have shown it to us as representing itself under the form of a worm.[58]

Finally *Celestial Hierarchy* 2.5 goes on to say that divine things are honored both by true negations and unlike comparisons insofar as both drive the intellect beyond the perceptible symbols to their *hyper*-cosmic upliftings. But, once again, this does not indicate that in the case of the celestial beings or ecclesiastical rituals, these *hyper*-cosmic upliftings themselves are "unlike" and should therefore be negated.

> So all the theosophists and interpreters of the hidden inspiration undefiledly separate the "Holy of Holies" from the uninitiated and unholy and honor the dissimilar sacred-shape, so that the divine things are not accessible to the profane and those longing to see the divine imagery do not remain in the shapes as true, and so that the divine things should be honored by the true negations (ταῖς

57. *CH* 2.3, 140D–141A.
58. *CH* 2.5, 144C–145A.

Negating Negation

ἀληθέσιν ἀποφάσεσι) and by the comparisons with the last things, which are diverse from their proper resemblance. Hence, for the aforesaid reasons, there is nothing absurd if they depict even the heavenly beings under incongruous dissimilar similitudes. For probably not even we should have come to an investigation from aporia, to an uplifting through the precise examination of the sacred things, unless the deformity of the descriptions representing the angels had shocked us, not permitting our mind to linger in the discordant representations, but rousing us to reject the material proclivities and accustoming us to elevate ourselves through things that are seen to their *hyper*-cosmic upliftings.[59]

It is just not true, therefore, that "the principle of negation is hard at work in the opening chapters of *The Celestial Hierarchy*"[60]—not, anyway, as negation of the conceptual content denoted by the perceptible symbols of the celestial and ecclesiastical hierarchies. Nor is such a principle of negation hard at work anywhere else in the Dionysian corpus.

In fact, the Dionysian corpus gives no reason to believe that even the perceptible symbols of the ecclesiastical hierarchy (i.e., liturgical symbols) should be subjected to negation. (Here, as I will show below, there is a distinct difference between liturgical symbols and angelic symbols.) Quite the contrary, Dionysius' exposition of these symbols not only fails to qualify them as "dissimilar" but also refers to those pertaining to the sacrament of baptism in particular as "exact images" of their conceptual content, as containing "nothing unbecoming or irreverent" with respect to that content, and as "very appropriately" holding sacred things.[61]

> You see the exact images of these things in the hierarchically performed sacraments.[62]

> Indeed, this sacrament of the sacred divine-birth contains nothing unbecoming or irreverent in the symbols, nor of the perceptible images, but rather [contains] enigmas of contemplation worthy of God, imparting form to natural and humanly-suitable images.[63]

---

59. *CH* 2.5, 145AB.

60. Rorem, *Pseudo-Dionysius*, 207.

61. Rorem points this out, then goes on to claim that the discussion of perceptible symbols in *Celestial Hierarchy* 1–3 nevertheless applies to the symbols/rites of the ecclesiastical hierarchy (*Biblical and Liturgical Symbols*, 95–96; *Pseudo-Dionysius*, 99, 207). I've argued against this claim above and will continue to argue against it below.

62. *EH* 2.III.6, 401C.

63. *EH* 2.III.1, 397AB.

And consider attentively with me how most appropriately the symbols hold the sacred things.[64]

This evidence cannot be explained away by insisting that since Dionysius speaks of perceptible symbols in general as "dissimilar similarities" (in *Celestial Hierarchy* 2), the *Ecclesiastical Hierarchy's* symbols for the hierurgical rites must be dissimilar in exactly the same way as those of the celestial hierarchy. For this neither solves the problem as to why Dionysius speaks about these liturgical symbols as exact, absolutely becoming, and most appropriate, nor does it confront the larger issue as to why the *Ecclesiastical Hierarchy* as a whole simply does not indicate that its symbols are incongruous or dissimilar. Of course it is true that the symbols of the *Ecclesiastical Hierarchy*, just like those of the *Celestial Hierarchy*, must be interpreted in such a way that one intellects their spiritual-conceptual content though their perceptible form (a conceptual content that in the case of the liturgical symbols concerns the divine work of Jesus). But Dionysius maintains that these symbols are most worthy and becoming in this task, revealing their conceptual content exactly and appropriately. They are therefore strikingly different from the perceptible symbols for the angels, which Dionysius often indicates are manifestly absurd, particularly insofar as they depict the immaterial-intelligible angels in the forms of animals and therefore risk leading the interpreter astray.[65] So if liturgical symbols are "dissimilar," they are so only in that they symbolize conceptual content, not in that they are grossly dissimilar from that content. More to point, to say the spiritual-conceptual content of liturgical symbols must be intellected through their perceptible form is not to say that either this content or this form should be negated and transcended.

Speaking of which, although I know perfectly well what it means to interpret conceptual content through liturgical symbols, I am not sure that I know what it means to outright negate liturgical symbols. It cannot mean to negate the actual liturgical practices for then they could not be practiced. And it also does not make much sense to negate the conceptual content symbolized by these practices. Of what is this content a negation? God? This would make textual sense given that *Mystical Theology* 5 negates intelligible divine names of God. But it does not make logical sense to say that God is not, for example, the three-day entombment (which is symbolized

---

64. *EH* 2.III.7, 404B.

65. *CH* 2.1, 137A; *CH* 2.2, 137CD; *CH* 2.3, 141AB. The same can be said for many of the perceptible symbols for God; see, for example, *EP* 9.1.

by the triple immersion in the sacrament of baptism).[66] Should this conceptual content then simply be pronounced false, as in "It is not the case that God (in Jesus) was entombed for three days"? But this is patently false for Dionysius and, moreover, is in no way indicated in the Dionysian corpus. In short, it is in no way clear what it means to negate the conceptual content of liturgical practices. (And this difficulty applies also to the beings of the celestial and ecclesiastical hierarchies. Are we supposed to negate the beings of these hierarchies? Their titles? Their hierarchical order? The fact that superior members uplift inferior members? The fact that the former enjoy an assimilation-union superior to the latter? And are we supposed to negate these of God [which makes no logical sense]? Or pronounce them false [which has no textual support]?)

Finally, the claim that all perceptible symbols are both dissimilar/inadequate and similar/adequate is incompatible with the leading claim of apophatic abandonment—that the Dionysian God is absolutely ineffable and unknowable. This is so since, on the one hand, if any perceptible symbol is partly similar/adequate to the Dionysian God, then that God cannot be absolutely ineffable and unknowable; and, on the other hand, if the Dionysian God is absolutely ineffable and unknowable, then no perceptible symbol can be partially similar/adequate to that God. Here, the proponent of apophatic abandonment usually wants things both ways: symbols are both relatively similar/adequate and ultimately dissimilar/inadequate—relatively true such that they can be arranged on an "appropriateness" scale, yet ultimately false of an utterly ineffable God. But as the next chapter will argue, such a position simply is not coherent: if nothing is literally true of an absolutely ineffable and unknowable God, then nothing can be more or less metaphorically or relatively true of that God; and if things can be more or less metaphorically or relatively true of God, then God cannot be absolutely ineffable and unknowable.

In sum: there is little textual support for the claim that Dionysius negates and surpasses the celestial and ecclesiastical hierarchies; indeed, little rational plausibility to the claim that the celestial and ecclesiastical hierarchies even *could* be negated and surpassed.

---

66. Note that it is obviously the case that the triple immersion is not itself the three-day entombment but rather only a symbol for it. But this claim isn't nearly strong enough for the ends of the apophatic abandonment, which requires the negation not only of all perceptible symbols or signifiers but also of all intelligible contents or signifieds.

IV. "Negation" Serves as Theological Preparation for or Ritual Component of Hierurgy

But what then is one to make of the *Mystical Theology*'s removal of perceptible symbols and divine names? If hierarchical order and hierurgical ritual are necessary to deification-union, and if hierarchies and hierurgies are not negated and transcended, then what role, if any, does aphairetic removal play in the hierarchical-hierurgical process of deification-union? Dionysius does not say. Nowhere in the corpus does he explicitly relate the relative roles of aphairetic removal and hierurgical ritual with respect to deification-union—not even, as argued above, in *Celestial Hierarchy* 2 or *Mystical Theology* 3. Nevertheless, textual evidence suggests that if these two "halves" of the corpus do fit together, they do so insofar as aphairetic removal serves and supports hierurgical ritual rather than negating and transcending it.

One way in which the aphairetic removals of the *Mystical Theology*—in concert with the thetic positions of the *Theological Outlines*, *Divine Names*, and *Symbolic Theology*—serve and support the hierurgical rituals is by providing the theological preparation that is essential to the proper working of the rituals. Bear in mind here that for Dionysius, it is necessary both to bodily practice the liturgical rites and to cognitively interpret the liturgical symbols because correct interpretation of the liturgical symbols is a function of the degree to which spiritual-conceptual meaning is intellected through them. Also remember that these spiritual-conceptual meanings concern divine matters *hyper* being (such as, in particular, the incarnation of Jesus). Accordingly, the degree that one has received theological instruction about such matters—about the Trinitarian thearchy from the *Theological Outlines*, about the divine names from the *Divine Names*, about the perceptible symbols from the *Symbolic Theology*, and about the way in which the triune thearchy transcends the things of being/mind in the *Mystical Theology*—one is able to interpret correctly the liturgical symbols and therefore to perform correctly the liturgical rites (and thereby achieve greater degrees of deification-union). This is the "more immaterial initiation" that is not written down in the Scriptures *per se* but rather is passed down from "mind to mind."[67] This is the perfected meaning of the liturgical rites/symbols that the hierarch teaches to (some of) the laity.[68]

---

67. See note 35 above.

68. See especially *EH* 5.I.6, 505D–508A, which reports that the priests are to send to

Negating Negation

Thus we can understand the *Mystical Theology* to be just what it says it is—theology (in the full sense of the word).[69] Indeed the *Mystical Theology* is not only called a theology; it also reads like theology: the opening prayer asks the Trinity to serve as a guide to the highest summit of mystical "Scripture" (*logiōn*) where the mysteries of theology are veiled; the following address advises Timothy to leave behind everything perceivable and conceivable in his study of divine matters; and the subsequent section speaks of positing and removal as *theology* and *gospel*.[70] Moreover, as *Epistle* 9.1 informs us, one aspect of the double theological tradition is "ineffable and mystical" as well as "symbolical and sacramental," serving to establish the practitioner of the symbolic sacraments in God "through the un-taught mystagogy."[71] This appears to be just what these ("un-taught" or "un-written"[72]) theological treatises did—prepared practitioners for the liturgy by mystically uplifting them to "ineffable" theological knowledge so that they might better be able to interpret spiritual-conceptual content in the liturgical symbols, thereby more securely establishing them in God.[73]

---

the hierarchs all those who desire a deeper understanding of the hierurgical rites; and *EH* 1.3, 376A, which states that among the things that precede practice of the sacred work (*hierurgy*) are both "knowledge of beings as they are in themselves" and "the vision and science of sacred truth."

69. Consider here that "theology" was at this time a *logos* not only of *theos* but of everything divine, including, importantly, the liturgical rites (Golitizin, "Dionysius Areopagita," 194). Thus Golitizin notes that the first four entries for *theology* in Lampe's *Patristic Greek Lexicon* are as follows: "(1) God, especially as in the inner life of the Trinity; (2) the experience of God in Trinity, i.e., the mystical (in the modern sense) encounter, also the beatific vision; (3) divine praise, liturgy, as in the worship of: (a) angels, and (b) the church; and (4) the Scripture" (ibid., 194). Only at "the very bottom of a long list of meanings," says Golitizin, does the entry "rational discourse about divine things" appear (ibid., 194).

70. *MT* 1.1, 997A; *MT* 1.1, 997B; *MT* 1.3, 1000BC.

71. *EP* 9.1, 1105D.

72. For Dionysius, this is to say that they are not part of the written Scripture (*logion*); rather they are passed down "from mind to mind." They are taught; just not in written Scripture.

73. It is in this respect we might think of the *Mystical Theology* as something like a "celebrant's handbook" that elucidates the inner meaning or nature of what is accomplished in the liturgy (Louth, *Denys*, 104). But this is not altogether correct: if these theological treatises (including, but not limited to, the *Mystical Theology*) are a "celebrant's handbook," then they are one that elucidates the inner meaning or nature of the liturgical symbols, not the inner meaning of nature of that which is accomplished in the liturgy (particularly if, by this, Louth means an experience of divine union).

Ranks Are Not Bypassed; Rites Are Not Negated

Also relevant, therefore, is the type of union that aphairetic removal is said to achieve. It is worth noting that most of the terms used for the process of return do not appear in the *Mystical Theology*: *return* or *reversion* (*epistrophē*), *salvation* (*sōtēria*), *divinization* (*theōsis*), and *assimilation* (*aphomoiōsis*) are entirely absent; *uplifting* (*anagōgē*) is used just once; and *union* (*henōsis*) makes only three appearances.[74] Even more important, though, is the fact that these three uses of *union* indicate that aphairesis effects union with the illuminating divine rays, not with God or the members of the Trinity. The first use of *union*—which also contains the only use of *uplifting* in the *Mystical Theology*—exhorts Timothy to leave behind all sensible and intelligible things in his earnest study of mystical sights so that he may be uplifted to union with the *hyper*-being ray of the divine darkness.

---

74. As I explained above (in section I), the differences between these terms are minimal and thus not particularly relevant to my overall arguments. (Moreover, they are often used interchangeably, especially the first two [*return, uplifting*—see *CH* 9.2, 260B and *CH* 15.1, 333B] and the last four [*salvation, divinization, assimilation, unification*—see *EH* 1.3, 376A and *EH* 2.II.1, 393A].) Nevertheless, for the sake of full disclosure, I present here what I have found to be the individual applications of these terms in the Dionysian corpus. Although *return* or *reversion* (*epistrophē*) just is the general process by which humans ascend from lower to higher, inferior to superior, diverse to simple, the other terms concern aspects of this process. *Uplifting* (*anagōgē*) involves the reception and intellection of divine enlightenment and therefore tends to be used for either the general process by which superiors raise up inferiors or the specific process by which intelligible content is interpreted out of perceptible symbols (Rorem, *Biblical and Liturgical Symbols*, 54–58, 99–116). *Salvation* (*sōtēria*)—which begins in the sacrament of baptism and is completed upon death, and which is granted by the saving work of Jesus and through the hierarchies—pertains in particular to the preservation of proper hierarchical order (*EH* 2.II.4, 393C; *EH* 2.III.4, 400D; *EH* 3.III.6, 432C; *EH* 7.1, 553A; *EH* 7.9, 565C; *CH* 4.4, 181BD; *EH* 1.4, 376B; *DN* 8.9, 896D–897A). *Divinization* (*theōsis*) refers to a perfected understanding of symbols that is made possible by hierarchical mediation, hierurgical performance, and ethical observance (*CH* 1.3, 124A; *EH* 1.2, 373A; *EH* 1.4, 386B; *EH* 3, 424C; *EH* 3.III.7, 436C; *EH* 3.III.7, 433C.). *Assimilation* (*aphomoiōsis*), which is hierarchically-hierurgically effected, is just the process of being made like, or making oneself like, God or Jesus or the angels (*CH* 3.1, 164D; *CH* 3.2, 165B; *EH* 2.I, 392A; *EH* 3.III.12, 444A; *CH* 1.3, 124A; *CH* 8.2, 241C; *EH* 1.1, 372A; *EH* 2.I, 392A; *EH* 2.II.1, 393A; *EH* 3.III.11, 441C; *EH* 3.III.13, 444D). And *union* (*henōsis*) comes in different varieties, the most important of which, for present purposes, are, on the one hand, a union with the divine rays through an aphairetic-ecstatic ascent and, on the other hand, a union with the triune thearchy by means of hierarchical-hierurgical practices (see the notes of this paragraph). (Two other important types of union are union with others [*DN* 8.5, 892C; *DN* 11.2, 949CD; *DN* 11.2, 952A] and final union at death [*DN* 1.4, 592BC; *EH* 3.III.9, 437BC; see also *EH* 7.I.1, 553B; *EH* 7.III.5, 560C; *EH* 7.III.9, 565C].)

Negating Negation

> This is my prayer; and you, dear Timothy, in the earnest study of mystical sights, leave behind sensible and intellectual activities, all sensible and intelligible things, all non-beings and beings, and unknowingly strive upward, as far as possible, toward the union (ἕνωσιν) of that which is *hyper* all being and knowledge. By an undivided and absolute *ecstasis* of yourself and everything, shedding (ἀφελὼν) all and freed from all, you will be purely uplifted (ἀναχθήσῃ) to the *hyper*-being ray (ἀκτῖνα) of the divine darkness.[75]

The second use of *union* reports that upon entering the mystical darkness of unknowing, Moses is "united surpassingly to the completely unknown by an inactivity of all knowledge, knowing *hyper* mind by knowing nothing."

> And then he [Moses] is released from what sees and is seen and enters into the truly mystical darkness (γνόφον) of unknowing, in which he shuts out every knowing apprehension and comes into the wholly intangible and invisible, being entirely of that which is beyond everything and nothing, neither himself nor another, united surpassingly (κατὰ τὸ κρεῖττον ἑνούμενος) to the completely unknown by an inactivity of all knowledge, knowing *hyper* mind by knowing nothing.[76]

And the third use of *union* speaks of aphairetic discourse itself as "wholly united to the unspeakable."

> But now, ascending from what is below to that which lies above, [the *logos*] is shortened according to the measure of ascent and, after all ascent, is wholly soundless (ἄφωνος) and wholly united (ἑνωθήσεται) to the unspeakable (ἀφθέγκτῳ).[77]

What is described in these passages is an epistemic union with "ineffable" and "unknowable" divine knowledge—knowledge that is ineffable and unknowable since it lies above being and mind but nevertheless can be "known" and "said" by humans due to the revelatory illumination of the divine rays,[78] the hierarchical transmission of this illumination by the angels,

---

75. *MT* 1.1, 997B–1000A.

76. *MT* 1.3, 1001A. For more on the phrase *kata to kreitton*, see note 30 of chapter 4.

77. *MT* 3, 1033C. See also the following passages from the *Divine Names*: *DN* 1.4, 592C–593A; *DN* 1.5, 593BC; *DN* 4.9, 705AB; *DN* 4.11 708D; *DN* 7.3, 872AB; *DN* 11.2, 949CD.

78. The register of terms in the critical edition of the Dionysian corpus lists thirty-one occurrences of *ray* (*aktis*), the vast majority of which associate the divine ray/s with divine illumination: *DN* 1.1, 588A; *DN* 1.2, 588C, 589A; *DN* 1.4, 592C, 592D; *DN* 3.1, 680C [two occurrences]; *DN* 4.1, 693B; *DN* 4.4, 697B, 697D [two occurrences]; *DN* 4.6,

and the transcendence of ordinary human powers of cognition in a state of *hyper-nous* knowing. (More on ineffability and unknowability as well as *hyper-nous* knowing in chapter 4.) This stands in notable contrast with the type of union effected by the hierurgical rituals—an ontological union with the triune thearchy: *Ecclesiastical Hierarchy* 3.I states that each hierarchical sacrament "collects our divided lives into uniform deification and gives communion and union *with the One*";[79] *Ecclesiastical Hierarchy* 1.3 indicates that the goal of every hierarchy is that those who are being saved are also being deified by "the assimilation and unification *with God* in so far as possible";[80] *Ecclesiastical Hierarchy* 3.III.12 specifies that the hierurgy of communion makes us one *with Jesus*;[81] and *Ecclesiastical Hierarchy* 2.III.8 says that sacrament of baptism brings union *with the* thearchic *Spirit*.[82] It seems therefore that aphairesis in particular and the theological treatises in general played a preparatory epistemic role with respect to practice of the liturgical rites, which themselves effected an ontological union with the triune thearchy.

But this is probably not the only role that the theological treatises played with respect to the hierurgical rites—for it would have been crucial for their theological knowledge to have been ritually actualized so that the liturgical symbols could have been correctly interpreted during the performance of the hierurgical rites. More succinctly, aphairesis most likely also functioned as a ritual technique. Thus we might also understand aphairetic removal and thetic positing to be just what the *Mystical Theology* says they are—a hymning of God (particularly since hymns were, for late

---

701A; *DN* 4.7, 701C; *DN* 4.11, 708D; *DN* 7.3, 872B; *CH* 1.2, 121B [two occurrences]; *CH* 3.2, 165A; *CH* 9.3, 260D; *CH* 13.3, 301A, 301C; *CH* 15.8, 337A; *EH* 2.III.3, 397D; *EH* 4.III.2, 476B; *EH* 5.I.4, 504D; *EH* 6.III.6, 537C; *EH* 7.III.9, 569A; *MT* 1.1, 1000A; *MT* 1.3, 1000D; *EP* 8.1, 1085C; *EP* 10, 1120A. But note that since it is the divine names that are responsible for all processions from the triune thearchy, and since the divine rays are spoken of as illuminative processions from the triune thearchy, the epistemic union with the divine rays might also involve an ontological union with the divine names (in their processional respects).

79. *EH* 3.I, 424CD.

80. *EH* 1.3, 373D–376A.

81. *EH* 3.III.12, 444B.

82. *EH* 2.III.8, 404C. In addition to the passages above, see the following: *CH* 3.2, 165A; *CH* 9.2, 260B; *EH* 2.I, 392A; *EH* 2.II.1, 393A; *EH* 3.I, 424C–425A; *EH* 3.III.3, 429AB; *EH* 3.III.8, 437A; *EH* 3.III.10, 440AB; *EH* 3.III.13, 444CD; *DN* 3.1, 680A–680D. Also see Wear and Dillon (*Dionysius the Areopagite*, 117–29) for more on, and a different ranking of, the types of union in the Dionysian corpus.

Negating Negation

Neoplatonists and especially Proclus, a theurgic device).[83] As such, these "hymns" were probably not publicly and audibly sung;[84] rather, they were the private and inaudible means by which liturgical participants—and especially the hierarch[85]—"ascended" from the necessarily pluralized symbols of the rituals to the unified conceptions that these symbols signified, thereby remaining conceptually unified while participating in the materially pluralized symbols of the hierurgical rituals.

Interesting in this respect is the language of rising from last things to first things,[86] which appears both in the methodological chapters on aphairesis in the *Mystical Theology* and in the explanation of several of the hierurgical rites.[87] On the one hand, chapters 2 and 3 of the *Mystical Theology* refer to systematic aphairetic removal as an ascent from last things to first things.

> It is necessary, I think, to hymn the removals (τὰς ἀφαιρέσεις) oppositely from the positings; for we posit these beginning from the first things (πρωτίστων) and descending (κατιόντες) through the middle things (μέσων) to the last things (ἔσχατα); but then we remove everything (τὰ πάντα ἀφαιροῦμεν) making the search for the highest principles (ἀρχικώτατα) from the last things (ἐσχάτων), so that we may unhiddenly know this unknowing that is covered by all the knowledge among all beings, and we may see this *hyper-being* darkness that is hidden by all the light among beings.[88]

---

83. *MT* 2, 1025AB; *MT* 3, 1032D–1033B; see also *DN* 1.3, 589BC; *DN* 1.5, 593BC. On hymns as theurgic devices, see Van den Berg, *Proclus' Hymns*.

84. It is, though, interesting to consider the overall unitive effect that public-audible hymns are said to have in Dionysius' description of the liturgy. See, for example, *EH* 2.II.4, *EH* 2.II.7, *EH* 3.III.4–5, and *EH* 4.III.3. And see also Dionysius' descriptions of the hymns sung by the first rank of angels in *CH* 7.4 and *CH* 13.4.

85. See *EH* 5.III.7 for a depiction of the hierarch's complete knowledge of the sacred and divine words and works.

86. According to Thomas Campbell's note to his translation of this passage, Josef Stiglmayr pointed out that "this expression is as foreign to Christian usage as it is favored by Neoplatonic writers" (129 n. 64).

87. Also consider that Dionysius' use of Moses as mystic exemplar in *Mystical Theology* 1.3 not only depicts Moses' mystical ascent within a liturgical literary context (as has been recognized by a good many Dionysian scholars) but also occurs within the textual context of a characterization of the aphairesis as ascent from last things to first things (at *MT* 1.2). Note that Andrew Louth has also caught many of these similarities (*Denys*, 101), including also the use of liturgical language in the description of Hierotheus' ecstatic experience in *DN* 3.2 (102).

88. *MT* 2, 1025B.

Ranks Are Not Bypassed; Rites Are Not Negated

> But why in short, you say, having posited the divine positings from the first thing (πρωτίστου), do we begin the divine removal (τῆς θείας ἀφαιρέσεως) from the last things (ἐσχάτων)? Because when positing that which is *hyper* all positing it is necessary to posit the attributive affirmation from the more akin to it; but when removing that which is *hyper* all removal (τὸ ὑπὲρ πᾶσαν ἀφαίρεσιν ἀφαιροῦντας) it is necessary to remove (ἀφαιρεῖν) from the farthest away from it. Is it not life and goodness more than air and stone? And not drunkenness and not anger more than not speaking and not intellecting?[89]

On the other hand, chapters 2 and 3 of the *Ecclesiastical Hierarchy* tell us that the hierarch rises, at the conclusion of the sacrament of baptism, "from his occupation with secondary matters to the contemplation of primary things (*prōtōn*)"; and is raised, at the conclusion of the sacrament of eucharist, "to the holy principles (*archas*) of the sacraments in blessed and intellectual visions."[90] And chapter 3 of the *Ecclesiastical Hierarchy* also indicates that such rising occurs both when the hierarch instructs others about the sacramental symbols of the eucharist and when the hierarch ritualistically proceeds to the sacramental symbols of the eucharist.

> In the same godlike manner, the divine hierarch, if he benevolently imparts his unique science of the hierarchy to his subordinates by using the multiplicities of the divine enigmas, he is, again, as absolutely free from inferior things, undiminishedly restored to the proper source, and, having made his intellectual journey to the One, he clearly sees the uniform *logoi* of the performed sacraments (τελουμένων), making the more divine return to the primary things (πρῶτα) the goal of the philanthropic procession to the secondary things (δεύτερα).[91]

> [. . .] and benevolently proceeding to the secondary things (δεύτερα), he will be resistless and free as absolutely uniform; and unitarily returning (ἐπιστρεφόμενος) again to the One, he will make his return without spot and blemish as preserving the fullness and wholeness of the divine likeness. Thus, the hierarch is unified (ἑνοῦται) to divine things and, after he has hymned the holy theurgies (θεουργίας), he hierurgizes (ἱερουργεῖ) the most divine things and brings to view that which has been hymned.[92]

---

89. *MT* 3, 1033CD.
90. *EH* 2.II.8, 397A; *EH* 3.II, 428A.
91. *EH* 3.III.3, 429AB.
92. *EH* 3.III.10, 440AB.

Negating Negation

And so aphairesis might have also served as a ritual technique that aided in the interpretation of the liturgical rites, particularly with respect to spiritual-conceptual content that concerned divine matters *hyper*-being.

This is not to say that the liturgical symbols were flatly negated by such an aphairetic technique. Aphairetic removal is not a culminating rejection or abandonment of liturgical rites or their symbols. Rather, it is part of the general hermeneutical "ascension" from the pluralized symbols of the liturgy to their spiritual-conceptual meanings—meanings that concern, ultimately, the nature and action of the *hyper*-being triune thearchy (particularly in the person of Jesus), and are therefore illuminated, most effectively, by the technique of aphairetic removal. Insofar as it plays a role in the liturgy, then, aphairetic removal plays the role of ritualistically actualizing theological knowledge about the *hyper*-unified and *hyper*-existent triune thearchy. Please note, yet again, that this interpretive process does not end in sheer indeterminacy, but in the triune thearchy in general and the divine works of the incarnated Christ in particular; that this interpretive process does not discard the liturgical symbols, but uses them as a "precise" and "exact" conduits to their spiritual-conceptual meanings; and that this interpretive process does not supplant the liturgical rites, but rather perfects them so that they might more completely effect union with the triune thearchy.

And so, aphairesis might have served not only as theological preparation for the hierurgical rites but also as a ritual component of the hierurgical rites. Admittedly, these hypotheses are, well, hypothetical.[93] For, again, the Dionysian corpus just does not say what role, if any, aphairetic ascent plays with respect to hierurgical ritual. But for the sake of my larger argument, this hardly matters. For it is sufficient merely to show that the Dionysian corpus neither states nor suggests that hierurgical rites should be apophatically abandoned and transcended. And this I have done.

93. Resolving the status of negative theology in Prolcine theology might provide more perspective on the relationship between the *Mystical Theology* and the *Ecclesiastical Hierarchy*. Although Proclus ranked the theurgic power of "faith" above the divine philosophy of "truth" (*Platonic Theology* I.112.25–113.6; see also *Platonic Theology* IV.28.22–29.5; *Platonic Theology* IV.31.6–16), it is debatable both whether Procline theurgy can be divided into "low" (immaterial) and "high" (immaterial) types and whether "high" theurgy is or includes negative theology. For a brief discussion of this first debate as well as the claim that like Procline theurgy, Dionysian *hierurgy* surpasses both low-material (discursive) *theoria* and high-immaterial (hyper-noetic) *theoria*, see Klitenic, "Theurgy in Proclus," 86–87. And for a brief account of the second debate (as well as the claim that unlike Procline theurgy, which is at the highest level the practice of negative theology, Dionysian materialistic-symbolic *hierurgical* practices "elevate the laity to absolute Unity"), see Burns, "Proclus," 118, 128.

Chapter 4

The Ineffable God
Is Not Ineffable

Let us review what has been said about the Dionysian God. The Dionysian God is the cause of all. It is so by means of its divine names. These divine names preexist in, are given substance from, and therefore just *are* God in pluralized yet *hyper*-unified form. These divine names source intelligible properties to participating beings, enabling them not only to be the general and particular types of hierarchical beings that they are but also to be unified in a manner appropriate to their hierarchical rank. These divine names are therefore of a very specific number and order.

When these divine names are removed from God, they are so as the properties that they source, not as the divine names themselves. God remains the divine names themselves—indeed, *must* remain the divine names themselves. For if God did not pre-contain and process the divine names, there would be *no* beings, *no* hierarchies, *no* cosmos. And since God pre-contains the divine names themselves, which themselves pre-contain the properties they source, God also pre-contains these properties in a manner that is both *hyper*-existent and *hyper*-unified.

God is also the source of hierarchical order, hierological illumination, and hierurgical practice. Hierarchical order not only divides intellectual and rational beings into a superior angelic hierarchy and an inferior human hierarchy but also organizes each of these hierarchies into orders and ranks of superior and inferior members. Hierological illumination utilizes this hierarchical order as a means of passing down divine revelation, thereby enabling illumination about divine things. And hierurgical practice provides the methods by which rational beings in particular can effect salvation, divinization, and union.

Given that Dionysius says all this about the Dionysian God, how can the Dionysian God be absolutely and unqualifiedly ineffable and unknowable? Here proponents of apophatic abandon offer two types of arguments, the first of which is primarily logical; the second, textual. The first, logical argument goes something like this: if thought and being are interconnected such that thought always has being as its object, and if Dionysius denies that God is a being, then Dionysius must necessarily deny all thinking and speaking of God. Since God is not a being, God simply cannot be thought. And this impossibility is not due to some human limitation; it is logical in nature. Moreover, this impossibility applies to all forms of thought or cognition or intellection—there is no manner whatsoever in which that which is not a being may be "thought."[1]

---

1. Here I have in mind the arguments of Eric Perl, all of which are contained in the following quotation from his *Theophany*.

> Dionysius' God, like the One of Plotinus, is transcendent, not in a vague, unspecified sense, but in the very precise metaphysical sense that he is not at all included within the whole of reality, of things that are, as any member of it. If he has no "name," this is because he is not anything at all. God is not merely beyond "human thought" or "finite thought," as if there were some "other" sort of thought that could reach him, or as if his incomprehensibility were simply due to a limitation on our part, but is beyond thought as such, because thought is always directed to beings, and hence to that which is finite and derivative. When we hear that God is beyond being, we inevitably imagine some thing, a "superessentiality," lying above or outside of being. But this fails to realize the meaning of "beyond being," because it still thinks of God as something, some being. Rather, we must recognize that for Dionysius, as for Plotinus, God is simply not anything, not "there" at all. If our thought cannot attain to God, this is not because of our weakness but because there is no "there" there, no being, no thing that is God. Understanding Dionysius within the Neoplatonic tradition to which he belongs, we must take him at his word and not seek to mitigate the force of his negations by interpreting his thought in the light of later theories which attempt to allow for "infinite being" and thus break with the fundamental Neoplatonic principle that to be is to be intelligible and therefore to be finite. (13)

Perl's argument is persuasive, though only in the abstract. Contrary to this abstraction, I'll show in this chapter that if we "take him at his word," we'll find that Dionysius in fact *doesn't* maintain that God is altogether beyond all thought. (And if we read Dionysius in the context of Neoplatonism, we'll find analogues not only to such *hyper-nous knowing* but also to a hypostasis that exceeds being-life-mind.) In fact, I think Perl gives away his argument on the next two pages, first by quoting Dionysius' claim that the removals of the *Mystical Theology* are made of "the cause of all things" (ibid., 14), then by trying to distinguish between a God that is no-thing and no God at all (ibid., 15). If the Dionysian

The Ineffable God Is Not Ineffable

The second, textual arguments for the unqualified ineffability and unknowability of God instead looks to those passages in the Dionysian corpus that supposedly indicate the unqualified ineffability of God. It notes that *Mystical Theology* 4–5 negates not only perceptible symbols and divine names of God but also, in the end, affirmation (*thesis*) and denial (*aphairesis*) themselves. It registers Dionysius' frequent pronouncements of ineffability and unknowability as well as Dionysius' occasional claims of *hyper*-ineffability and *hyper*-unknowability. It points to those passages that speak of the cessation of intellectual and verbal activities that both engender and accompany a state of union with God. And it sometimes even looks to Dionysius' explication of perceptible symbols in an effort to show that all theological language is both metaphorical and conventional in nature, and therefore literally false of an ineffable and unknowable God.[2]

But this first argument, although logically sound, disregards a host of contrary evidence in the Dionysian corpus itself. And this second argument, whereas textually rooted, reads much too crudely the nuances of Dionysius' notions of ineffability and unknowability. Simply put, the ineffable and unknowable God of Dionysius is not (absolutely) ineffable and unknowable. Dionysius' concepts of ineffability and unknowability are not our concepts of ineffability and unknowability; they are not the concepts of *absolute* or *unqualified* ineffability and unknowability. Rather, in saying that something is ineffable and unknowable—and note that the Dionysian corpus indicates that much more than just the *hyper*-being God is ineffable and unknowable to humans—Dionysius would have us understand it to be completely ineffable and unknowable by "ordinary" cognitive means, but partially effable and knowable as divinely revealed, hierarchically disseminated, and *hyper-noetically* understood.

This is to say, first of all, that unknowable and ineffable things must be both divinely revealed and hierarchically transmitted; humans are naturally unable to know and speak about divine things. But it is also to say, secondly, that unknowable and ineffable things can be "known" in a state of knowing that transcends the natural rational-intellectual powers

---

God is the cause of all, then it cannot be an indeterminate nothing that is absolutely and unqualifiedly ineffable, even if it is beyond being. And if the Dionysian God can be discriminated from nothing at all, then it is a particular kind of "no-thing" that can be so effed, even if woefully inadequately.

2. Here I'm thinking once again of the arguments of Denys Turner and John Hick, particularly the latter, for whom the Dionysian God is absolutely and unqualifiedly ineffable. See note 1 of chapter 1 and note 4 of chapter 2.

of humans, a state *hyper-nous knowing* or *unknowing knowing* that makes it possible to "know" things that transcend being and mind. These are my two principal arguments against the arguments above. They will occupy the bulk of this chapter. But between these arguments I will insert a corollary: if unknowable and ineffable things may be known *hyper nous* as divinely revealed, then the celestial beings, beings that are better equipped to transcend intellectual cognition and receive divine revelation, are better able to know that which is unknowable and say that which is ineffable. And after the second of these arguments, I will append three logically-based arguments against the notion of absolute ineffability-unknowability: first, an absolutely ineffable and unknowable God cannot be all the things that Dionysius says it is, indeed cannot even be the cause of all; second, an absolutely ineffable and unknowable God cannot be predicated either by the divine names in an ordered sequence or by the perceptible symbols in a metaphorical manner; third, that which is ineffable and unknowable can only be known and said to be such from a perspective from which it is not ineffable and unknowable. Thus the Dionysian corpus neither actually applies ineffability and unknowability to God in an absolute and unqualified manner, not logically *could* apply ineffability and unknowability to God in an absolute and unqualified manner. And thus the Dionysian God is not that from which all things are apophatically abandoned, but that which can be known *hyper*-mind and said *hyper*-speech.

I. The Unknowable and Ineffable God is Known as Divinely Revealed

A good many of the passages that speak of God as ineffable or unknowable explicitly state not only that such ineffability-unknowability is due, at least in part, to human limitation but also that it can be—indeed, is—overcome through divine revelation. This is a common motif in the opening chapter of the *Divine Names*, a chapter that is often said to concern the problem of naming an utterly ineffable and unknowable God. Instead, Dionysius indicates right from the get-go not only that ineffable-unknowable things may be known through divine revelation but also that they are so known in a state of union that surpasses our ordinary rational and intellectual powers.

> And now, O blessed one, after the *Theological Outlines* I will proceed to the explication of the divine names as far as I am able. And now let the law of the Scriptures, which limits us beforehand, bind

> us fast to the truth of what is said about God, "not in persuasive words of human wisdom, but in demonstration" of the Spirit-moved "power" of the theologians, by which we are unspeakably (ἀφθέγκτως) and unknowingly (ἀγνώστως) conjoined to unspeakable things (ἀφθέγκτοις) and unknowable things (ἀγνώστοις) through a union (ἕνωσιν) that is superior (κατὰ τὴν κρείττονα) to our rational and intellectual power and activity.[3]

A few things here seem clear. Dionysius asks that his explication of the divine names be bound fast to the truth of what is said about God by the theologians. (The theologians are, of course, the authors of the revealed sacred Scriptures, whether biblical or extra-biblical.) What is said about God by the theologians is not said in persuasive words of human wisdom but through a power that is set in motion by the Spirit. This power enables humans to be unspeakably and unknowably joined to unspeakable and unknowable things in a manner that is superior to our rational and intellectual power and activity. And these unspeakable and unknowable things concern Dionysius' explication of the divine names themselves. Now one could argue that the "unspeakable and unknowable things" should not be identified with the "truth of what is said about God" with respect to the divine names. But a good reason would then need to be supplied as to why this absent term, and not the present precedent *divine names*, is co-referential with the phrase *unspeakable and unknowable things*. One could also argue that if these so-called unspeakable and unknowable things are the divine names, then they are not really unspeakable and unknowable, that Dionysius is here employing hyperbole. But this would be to twist the plain words of the text, imposing on it our own presuppositions about what it is supposed to say. Instead, it makes far more sense to interpret this passage as suggested above: ineffable-unknowable things—here, the truth of God with respect to the divine names—may be known through divine revelation in a state of union that surpasses the normal rational-intellectual powers of humans. Moreover, the rest of this section, as well as the sections to follow, confirm this interpretation.

Thus the second paragraph of *Divine Names* 1.1 picks up and develops these themes.

> Therefore, in general one must dare neither to say nor, indeed, to conceive anything about the *hyper*-being and hidden divinity over and above that which has been divinely revealed to us in the

---

3. *DN* 1.1, 585B–588A.

Negating Negation

> sacred Scriptures. For one must attribute the *hyper*-being science (ἐπιστήμην) to the *hyper*-beingness unknowing (which is *hyper* speech and mind and being), looking up to this great height as much as the ray of the thearchic Scriptures gives itself, drawn together to the higher splendors by temperance and piety for the divine things. For if one must trust the all-wise and most-true theology, the divine things are revealed and contemplated, according to the analogy of each of the minds, of the thearchic goodness, which divinely distributes the immeasurable (as that which cannot be contained) in saving justice of those things that are measured.[4]

Here we are first told that the *hyper*-being and hidden divinity has been revealed in the sacred Scriptures, but that we are not to say or conceive anything about it over and above this revelation.[5] Then we are told that we must attribute to this *hyper*-beingness unknowing, which is *hyper* speech and mind and being, a *hyper*-being science (*epistēmē*). Clearly, then, the fact that God is a *hyper*-being and hidden divinity, a *hyper*-beingness unknowing *hyper* logos and intellect and being is not the end of the story for human knowability and effability about God. For this *hyper*-being and hidden divinity is revealed in the sacred Scriptures, which are a *hyper*-being "science" of divine things. And it is revealed, as the last sentence tells us, in accordance with the analogical position of our intellect. This last sentence offers a corollary to the basic claim that humans bring natural limitations to the knowing and saying of God—angels, on account of their superior intellects, bring far fewer such limitations. But I would like to pass over this corollary for now so as to stay on track: although humans cannot know the *hyper*-being God *through their natural rational-intellectual powers*, they can know God *in divine revelation* by means of power that exceeds these powers.

This is confirmed again in the final paragraph of *Divine Names* 1.1: the fact that God is not knowable through rational-intellectual means does not mean the God is entirely unknowable.

> For just as intelligible things are incomprehensible and unseen to the senses, and uncompounded and unformed things [are incomprehensible and unseen] to that in shape and form, and the intangible and unstructured formlessness of bodiless things

---

4. *DN* 1.1, 588A.

5. A strange admonition from an author who routinely says extra-biblical things about God! Then again, "the sacred Scriptures" (*logion*) most likely includes much more than the Bible for Dionysius.

The Ineffable God Is Not Ineffable

> [are incomprehensible and unseen] to that which is formed according to the structure of bodies, then, according to the same analogy of truth, the *hyper*-being infinite lies above beings and the *hyper* mind unity lies above minds. The One *hyper* thought is unthinkable (ἀδιανόητόν) to all thinking, the Good *hyper* speech is ineffable (ἄρρητόν) to all speech, *henad* uniting every *henad* and *hyper*-being being and un-intelligible (ἀνόητος) intellect and ineffable (ἄρρητος) speech, speechlessness (ἀλογία) and intellectlessness (ἀνοησία) and namelessness (ἀνωνυμία) and being according to nothing of being and cause of all being, but itself not being as beyond all being so that it alone could properly and scientifically (ἐπιστητῶς) manifest itself about itself.[6]

Here we are told that just as intelligible things are incomprehensible to the senses, so the *hyper*-being infinite and *hyper*-mind unity is incomprehensible to beings and minds. Note that this is not at all to say that that which is *hyper*-being and *hyper*-mind is absolutely incomprehensible. Rather, we are invited here to carry out the analogy: just as that which is intelligible is incomprehensible to the senses yet comprehensible to the intellect, so that which is *hyper* being and mind is incomprehensible to the intellect yet comprehensible to that which transcends being and mind. Thus, as the second sentence tells us, even though God is unthinkable to all thinking and ineffable to all speech, God is nevertheless "unit uniting every unit," "*hyper*-being being," "unintelligible intellect," and "ineffable speech." These are not merely paradoxical, intellect-befuddling utterances. They point to a manner in which God "is," is "known," and is "said" beyond the manner of being, knowledge, and speech. As this sentence continues, although God is nothing according to being—speechlessness, intellectlessness, namelessness—God nevertheless both is the "cause of all being" and does "properly and scientifically manifest itself about itself." And, to tie in some earlier threads, this revelation overcomes human limitation, permitting *hyper*-mind knowledge of the *hyper*-being God.

All three of these themes—the limitation of the rational-intellectual powers of humans, the overcoming of these limitations in divine revelation and through a *hyper-nous* state of knowing—continue on into *Divine Names* 1.2 and 1.3. In fact, the opening sentence of the first paragraph of *Divine Names* 1.2 is almost verbatim the first sentence of the second paragraph of *Divine Names* 1.1—an admonition not to say or conceive anything about the *hyper*-being and hidden divinity beyond what has been

6. *DN* 1.1, 588B.

Negating Negation

revealed about it in the sacred Scriptures. After this, we are told, first, that the science (*epistēmē*) and contemplation of it is inaccessible to all beings since it is *hyper*-beingly lifted out of all; and then, that the theologians therefore hymn God with alpha-prefixed predicate-terms such as invisible, incomprehensible, unsearchable, and inscrutable. Once again, we ought not proof-text by lifting these later two sentences out of the context of the opening sentence (as well as the rest of the corpus—especially those sections that tell us what it means to interpret alpha-prefixed terms *apophatically qua hyperochically*). It is not the case that God is simply and utterly inaccessible and incomprehensible; rather, we are told that this *hyper*-being and hidden divinity is divinely revealed to us in the sacred Scriptures. Here is the paragraph in full.

> And so, about this, as has been said, one must dare neither to say nor, clearly, to conceive anything about the *hyper*-being and hidden divinity beyond what has been divinely revealed to us in the sacred Scriptures. For even as it has benevolently (ἀγαθοπρεπῶς) taught about itself in the Scriptures, the science (ἐπιστήμη) and contemplation of it—whatever it is—is inaccessible to all beings as it is *hyper*-beingly lifted-out of all. You will find that many of the theologians have hymned it not only as invisible (ἀόρατον) and incomprehensible (ἀπερίληπτον) but also as unsearchable (ἀνεξερεύνητον) and inscrutable (ἀνεξιχνίαστον) since there is no track of anyone who has penetrated into its hidden infinity.[7]

The second and final paragraph of *Divine Names* 1.2 then goes on to speak about how the *hyper*-being founding ray is revealed to and enlightens beings in analogical proportion to their ontological position. Here is it in full.

> Indeed the Good is not entirely unshared by any one being, but rather, abidingly in itself, it benevolently reveals the *hyper*-being founding ray to the analogical illumination of each being and draws up to the desired contemplation and communion and likeness of it those sacred intellects who, as far as is permitted, sacred-fittingly strive after it, neither powerlessly boastful toward that which is higher than the harmoniously given theophany, nor slipping away toward the lower out of the declination to the worse, but rather steadfastly and unswervingly stretched forth toward the ray that

---

7. *DN* 1.2, 588C.

illumines them and prudently and piously raised up with sacred reverence by the proportioned love of the permitted illuminations.[8]

And finally *Divine Names* 1.3 speaks to the state of "cognition" in which divine revelation may be understood. When we honor the ineffable thearchic hiddenness *hyper* mind and being with a "non-searching and sacred reverence of mind" and a "temperate silence," we are lifted up to the bright lights that *hyper*-cosmically illumine us in the sacred Scriptures. Thus do we understand God's divine names. Here is the section in full.

> Following these thearchic yokes that govern the entire holy ranks of the *hyper*-celestial orders, and honoring both the thearchic hiddenness *hyper* mind and being with a non-searching and sacred reverence of mind and that which is ineffable with a temperate silence, we are then lifted up to the bright lights that illumine us in the sacred Scriptures. And we are guided by them toward the thearchic hymnings, through which we are *hyper*-cosmically illuminated and molded to the sacred hymns, so as both to see the thearchic lights fittingly given to us by them and to hymn the good-giving source of every sacred manifestation of light, as it itself has taught about itself in the sacred Scriptures. [It taught,] for example, that it is cause and source and being and life of all, a recalling and resurrecting of those who have fallen away from it, a renewal and re-formation of those who are slipping away toward the destruction of the divine form, a sacred foundation of those who are tossed about in an unholy perplexity, a steadfastness for those who continue to stand, a guiding hand that is stretched out for those who are being led back to it, an illumination for those who are being illumined, a source of perfection for those who being perfected, a source of divinity for those who are being divinized, a simplicity for those who are being simplified, a unity for those who being unified, the *hyper*-beingly *hyper*-source source of every source, the good-imparting for what is hidden according to the divine law, and, to speak simply, the life of that which lives and the being of that which exists, source and cause of every life and being, producing and sustaining all beings in being through its goodness.[9]

Again, divine illumination overcomes a natural human weakness.

For obvious reasons, I am not going to be able to sustain this paragraph-by-paragraph exposition for the entirety of the first chapter of the

8. *DN* 1.2, 588C–589A.
9. *DN* 1.3, 589ABC.

Negating Negation

Divine Names. Still, to avoid the accusation of dodging some possibly confuting passages in *Divine Names* 1.4 and 1.5, I would like to spend some time there before passing on to a second set of arguments. (After *Divine Names* 1.5 there are not any terribly relevant passages to the argument at hand.) In *Divine Names* 1.4, after first informing us that every hymning of the theologians sets in order the divine names, and then taking us on quick tour of some of the more important divine names, Dionysius tells the reader that although we must now be lifted up to the intelligible through the sensible, this will not be the case after death. We will then participate in God's intellectual gift of light with a passionless and immaterial mind and in God's *hyper-nous* unity through the unknown and blessed radiations of the divine rays. We will then be more like the angelic minds, perhaps even equal to them.

> But then, when we have become indestructible and immortal and have reached the Christ-like and most blessed lot, "we shall be," according to the Scripture, "always with the Lord," filled with the visible theophany of God in all-holy contemplations, which will illumine us in most brilliant splendors as the disciples in that most divine transfiguration, participating of his intellectual gift of light in a passionless and immaterial mind and of the *hyper nous* unity through the unknown and blessed radiations of the *hyper*-light rays. For in a more divine imitation of the *hyper*-celestial minds, we shall be, as the truth of the Scriptures say, "equal to the angels and sons of God, being sons of the resurrection."[10]

And the second and final paragraph of *Divine Names* 1.4 continues this theme, though this time explaining that even now we might be lifted up from the sensible to the intelligible, and then, though a cessation of our intellectual activities, to the *hyper*-being ray.

> And now, to the best of our ability, we use symbols fitting symbols to the divine things, and we are analogically lifted up from these to the simple and unified truth of the intellectual divine visions, and after our every intellection of the divine-ideas, ceasing our intellectual activities, we thrust ourselves, to the best of our ability, towards the *hyper*-being ray, in which all the boundaries of all knowledge *hyper*-ineffably pre-existed (προΰφέστηκεν), which it is possible neither to conceive nor to speak nor to contemplate in any way since it is lifted-out from all and *hyper*-unknowing, *hyper*-beingly pre-containing (προειληφυῖαν) within itself the

10. *DN* 1.4, 592BC.

The Ineffable God Is Not Ineffable

whole completions of every essential knowledge and power, while established above all, even the *hyper*-celestial minds, by its absolute power. For if all knowledge is of beings and has its limits in beings, then that beyond every being is lifted-out of all knowledge.[11]

It is the latter half of the first sentence above that is often seized upon by those who champion the absolute ineffability and unknowability of the Dionysian God, for here we are told that the boundaries of all knowledge *hyper*-ineffably pre-existed in the *hyper*-being ray, that this *hyper*-being ray is inconceivable and unspeakable in any way, that it is lifted-out from all and *hyper*-unknowing, and that it is established above all, even the *hyper*-celestial minds. But we ought not lose our heads here. On the one hand, Dionysius has repeatedly told us, from the very beginning of the *Divine Names*, that the sacred Scriptures reveal to us "unspeakable things and unknowable things," the "*hyper*-being and hidden divinity," the "*hyper*-being infinite," the "*hyper* mind unity," the "*hyper*-being founding ray," and the "thearchic hiddenness *hyper* intellect and being." And on the other hand, the final sentence of *Divine Names* 1.4 clearly indicates that the knowledge of which Dionysius is here speaking is a knowledge *of beings*. So to say that God is not knowable or speakable "in any way" does not rule out ways of knowing that are not of being. For such "ways of knowing" are not, technically speaking, ways of knowing. This must be the case if we are to make sense of all the preceding passages that speak of some sort of extraordinary way of knowing divine things—the "union that is superior to our rational and intellectual power and activity" and "*hyper*-being science" of *Divine Names* 1.1, the "non-searching and sacred reverence of mind" and "temperate silence" of *Divine Names* 1.3, and the "passionless and immaterial mind" and "*hyper nous* unity in the unknown and blessed radiations of the *hyper*-light rays" of *Divine Names* 1.4. And as we will soon see, this must also be the case if we are to make sense of all the references to *hyper-nous knowing* or *unknown knowing* elsewhere in the corpus. Such a knowing is, again, technically speaking, not a knowing since, as Dionysius tells us above, all knowledge is of beings. Thus it is a knowing that is not a knowing, a knowing beyond mind. Still, it is a noetic something that makes possible revelatory access to the *hyper*-being God.

These arguments also apply to those ostensibly confuting passages of *Divine Names* 1.5. Here Dionysius begins by asking how we can examine

---

11. *DN* 1.4, 592C–593A.

Negating Negation

the divine names if God is superior to every expression and every knowledge and is altogether established *hyper* mind and being.

> And clearly, if it is superior to every expression and every knowledge and is altogether established *hyper* mind and being—being an embracing and gathering and anticipating of all—and it is altogether incomprehensible to all, and there is no sensation, imagination, opinion, name, expression, touch, and science of it, how is the treatise *On Divine Names* to be examined by us, having shown the *hyper*-being divinity to be incomprehensible and *hyper*-name?[12]

Again, though, we cannot read such passages out of context. It cannot be the case that the *hyper*-being God is entirely unknowable and ineffable, since we have already been told that this *hyper*-being God is revealed to us in the sacred Scriptures, which may be understood by us through a divine illumination that is superior to our rational-intellectual powers. Rather, God is unknowable and ineffable only (!) with respect to being and mind.

These qualifications also apply to the second paragraph of *Divine Names* 1.5, a passage that is reminiscent of the earlier admonitions against saying and conceiving anything about God and therefore carries with it the implicit qualification *apart from what the sacred Scriptures tell us about God*.

> But we said this very thing when we set forth the *Theological Outlines*: it is possible neither to say nor to conceive the One, the unknown, the *hyper*-being, the Good itself, which is, I say, the triadic *henad*, the same God, the same Good. But even the angel-befitting unions of the holy powers, which it is necessary to speak of as either emissions or receptions of the *hyper*-unknowing and *hyper*-appearing goodness, are ineffable and unknowable, and they are contained only in those angels that are deemed worthy of the *hyper* angelic knowledge.[13]

Note that this passage says that we may not say or conceive anything not only about the *hyper*-being Trinity of the *Theological Outlines* but also about the divine names of the *Divine Names*. These "angel-fitting unities of the holy powers," which are "emissions or receptions from the *hyper*-unknowing and *hyper*-appearing goodness," are also ineffable and unknowable. And yet, they are, as Dionysius has repeatedly said above,

12. *DN* 1.5, 593AB.
13. *DN* 1.5, 593B.

revealed in the sacred Scriptures. Moreover, they are, as Dionysius tells us here, contained in those angels that are deemed worthy of *hyper*-angelic knowledge. In other words, the unknowable can be known, just not through ordinary rational-intellectual powers, and it can be known in greater degree by superior beings, which then are responsible for passing down this revealed "knowledge." Thus the next paragraph tells us that the angels, who are unified to the divine names in the cessation of all intelligent activity yet illumined truly and *hyper*-naturally in this union, hymn God through the removal of all beings (a hymn that they have revealed to humans, a hymn that not only removes the things of being but also reveals the "things" *hyper* being).[14] And the following and final paragraph tells us that if we are lovers of the truth *hyper* truth, we too will wish to preeminently remove the things of being from the thearchic *hyper*-beingness, yet also to hymn the providence of the thearchy from all that is caused.[15] Thus it is the case that none of these passages from *Divine Names* 1.4 and 1.5 confutes the overall message of the first chapter of the *Divine Names*: the unknowable and ineffable God may be *hyper*-noetically known through divine revelation as the divine names.

II. The Ineffable and Unknowable God Is Better Known by Angels Than by Humans

As both mentioned above by me and indicated above in several of the passages from the first chapter of the *Divine Names*, one corollary to the claim that human beings are limited in their natural ability to know and speak about God is the fact that angelic beings are not quite as limited. This is registered throughout the Dionysian corpus, though perhaps most clearly in *Celestial Hierarchy* 7, a chapter devoted to an explication of the first rank of angels.[16] Before getting into the subject of angelic knowing in this chapter, however, I would like briefly to mention that the subject of knowing angels is also *apropos*, for, as passages like *Celestial Hierarchy* 6.1 indicate, even knowledge of the angels is impossible for humans apart from divine revelation.

---

14. *DN* 1.5, 593BCD.

15. *DN* 1.5, 593D.

16. See also chapter 13 of the *Celestial Hierarchy* and *Ecclesiastical Hierarchy* 4.III.5–10.

Negating Negation

> How many and of what kind are the orders of the *hyper*-celestial beings, and how each achieves perfection, I say, only the deifying source of their perfection distinctly knows; besides this, they know their own proper powers and illuminations and their sacred and *hyper*-cosmic good-order. For it is impossible that we should know the mysteries of the *hyper*-celestial minds and their most holy perfections, except, someone might say, insofar as the thearchy has initiated us through them as knowing well their own condition. We, then, will say nothing in a self-moved manner; but whatever angelic visions have been contemplated by the sacred theologians, we who are initiated in these will set forth as best we can.[17]

This is to say, once again, that the natural limits of human knowledge—apart from divine revelation or initiation—extends to more than just the *hyper*-being God, including also, per the section above, the number and order of the divine names and, per the passage above, the mysteries and perfections of the celestial beings.[18] And this is in turn to say, once again, that what Dionysius means by unknowable and ineffable must be something different from what we (post)moderns mean by unknowable and ineffable since Dionysius claims to know (as divinely revealed) and deigns to say (as divinely empowered) quite a bit about the divine names and the celestial beings. And this is also true of the thearchy itself: the unknowable and ineffable Dionysian God is not unknowable and ineffable, at least not absolutely and enduringly so.

Now for angelic knowing. *Celestial Hierarchy* 7 begins its examination of the first rank of angels (seraphim, cherubim, thrones) by explicating their names. The name of the cherubim deserves special note since it denotes a knowledge and vision of God, a capacity for receiving the highest gift of light and contemplating the thearchic majesty, and a state of being filled with the wisdom-making gift and sharing such wisdom with subordinate celestial beings.

> And the appellation of the cherubim denotes their knowledge and their vision of God, their capacity for receiving the highest gift of light, their capacity for contemplating the thearchic majesty in primordial power, their being filled with the wisdom-making gift,

---

17. *CH* 6.1, 200C.

18. Two other significant subject matter that are said to be ineffable include the nature and activity of Jesus (*DN* 1.4, 592A; *DN* 2.6, 644C; *DN* 2.9, 648A; *DN* 2.10, 648D, 649A; *EH* 4.III.10, 484A; *EP* 3, 1069B) and hierurgical processes and experiences (*DN* 3.3, 684B; *EH* 2.I, 392B; *EH* 2.III.8, 404D).

and their ungrudging sharing with the secondaries in abundance of the given wisdom.[19]

Celestial Hierarchy 7.2 next goes on to speak about the respects in which the first rank of angels can be considered pure, contemplative, and perfected. Particularly notable are the latter two, as contemplation is equated with a satiation with the *hyper*-being and thrice-manifested contemplation of the maker and source of beauty, and perfection is associated with the highest science (*epistēmē*) of the divine-work (*theurgy*) possible in angels.

> And so we must think of them as pure, not as having been freed from unholy stains and blemishes, nor as unreceptive of earthly fantasies, but as far exalted above every weakness and every inferior holiness according to the highest purity, established above the most godlike powers, and firmly adhering to their own self-moved and same-moved rank according to their unchanging love of God, knowing no declivity at all to inferior things, but having as their own godlike identity an eternally unfailing, unmoved, and completely unmixed foundation. And again [we must think of them] as contemplative, not as contemplators of perceptible or intelligible symbols, nor as being uplifted to the divine by the variety of contemplations of the sacredly-written, but as being filled with every immaterial knowledge of sublime light and satiated, as permissible, with the *hyper*-being and thrice-manifested contemplation of the beauty-making and source of beauty; and in like manner, they who are deemed worthy of the communion with Jesus do not pictorially stamp the theurgizing similitude in divinely-formed images but rather by really drawing near to him in first participation of the knowledge of his theurgizing illuminations; and indeed the God-imitation is given to them in the highest possible degree and they participate, so far as is allowable to them, of his theurgizing and philanthropic virtues in primordial power. And likewise [we must think of them] as perfected, not as illumined with an analytic science of sacred variety, but as filled with a first and preeminent deification according to the highest science of the theurgy possible in angels. For not through other holy beings, but rather hierarchicalized from the thearchy itself by the immediate elevation to it in the power and rank preeminent of all, they are established near the all-holy without any wavering, and are led in contemplation to the immaterial and intelligible majesty as far as permissible, and are initiated into the scientific methods

---

19. *CH* 7.1, 205C. Bear in mind, though, that all this of course applies also to the other orders of the first rank of angels, i.e., the seraphim and thrones.

of the theurgies, as being first and around God, hierarchicalized in the highest degree from the source of perfection itself.[20]

Celestial Hierarchy 7.3 then reminds the reader that although the lower ranks of angels are enlightened by the superior ranks of angels, the very first rank of angels is enlightened by Jesus himself, and thereby perfected by their participation in the first-given knowledge (*gnōsis*) and science.

> And so, the first hierarchy of the heavenly minds, being hierarchicalized by the source of perfection itself, is purified and enlightened and perfected by being lifted up immediately to it, and is thereby filled by it, according to degree, with the most all-hallowed purification of the boundless light of the pre-perfect perfection-working, unmixed with any weaknesses, filled with primal light, perfected by participation of the first-given knowledge and science.[21]

And finally *Celestial Hierarchy*, before discussing the divine hymns of the first rank of angels, summarizes the findings of the chapter, reiterating that the first rank of angels knows many divine things preeminently and participates in the divine science and knowledge as much as is permitted.

> This, then, according to my science, is the first rank of the heavenly beings that "encircle God" and stand immediately around God and dance simply and incessantly around God's eternal knowledge in the highest ever-moving stability of angels, purely seeing many and blessed contemplations, illuminated with simple and immediate splendors, filled with divine nourishment that is many by the first-given flowing but one by the unvariegated and unifying oneness of the thearchic banquet, deemed worthy of much participation and cooperation with God through assimilation to him as far as possible of their beautiful habits and energies, preeminently (ὑπερκειμένως) knowing many divine things, and participating in thearchic science and knowledge as much as is permitted.[22]

Now it is important to emphasize that the first rank of angels does not completely know the *hyper*-being God; rather they know God only as much as is permissible or lawful. But that hardly matters for the purposes of my argument. For even if the first rank of angels know (and "say" to their subordinates) only a very little about the Dionysian God—and I think the

---

20. *CH* 7.2, 208B–209A.
21. *CH* 7.3, 209C.
22. *CH* 7.4, 209D–212A.

passages above suggest that the first rank of angels knows (and says) more than just this—it is still the case that the Dionysian God is not *completely* unknowable and ineffable. And if this is the case, then what Dionysius means by *unknowable* and *ineffable* is something other than what we (post) moderns mean by these terms.

Indeed, Dionysius must—for, again, what is included among the unknowable and ineffable is more than just the *hyper*-being God; it is also, for humans, the divine names and the celestial hierarchy. And these latter things, plainly, *can* be known and said by humans (even if not completely). Thus I propose that by *ineffable* and *unknowable* Dionysius means something like this:

> not at all sayable and knowable through ordinary rational-intellectual means, yet partially sayable and knowable as divinely revealed, hierarchically transmitted, and extra-intellectually understood.

It is the last part of this formula, the state of *hyper-nous* knowing, that I turn to now.

III. The Unknowable and Ineffable God Is Known *Hyper* Mind (and Said *Hyper Logos*)

Defenders of apophatic abandonment will be quick to counter that even if certain divine matters are divinely revealed and hierarchically disseminated, it is still the case that the transcendent God is absolutely ineffable and unknowable. And if not the first chapter of the *Divine Names*, they will most likely call upon the *Mystical Theology* as witness. So even though I believe I have provided sufficient evidence above that even the *hyper*-being God is not absolutely ineffable and unknowable, I will devote some attention below to demonstrating this in the *Mystical Theology*. Here, as mentioned above, my focus will be on the state of *hyper-nous* knowing rather than the process of divine revelation (though these of course go hand-in-hand).

What is particularly convenient about the *Mystical Theology* is that within the span of this short treatise Dionysius shows off just about every one of the rhetorical techniques by which he expresses (relative) divine inexpressibility and unknowability. Of course, this includes Dionysius' removal from God of perceptible and intelligible predicate-terms in the last two chapters of the treatise. But it also includes more direct means, such as both the assertion of negative predicate-terms pertaining to effability and

Negating Negation

knowability (e.g., *ineffability, unspeakability, unnamability, unthinkability, unintelligibility, unknowability*) and the denial or *hyper*-predication of these terms' positive counterparts.[23] Beyond this, Dionysius thrice denies or *hyper*-predicates the very methods by which predicate-terms are applied to or removed from God (i.e., *thesis* and *aphairesis*), for example at the very conclusion of the *Mystical Theology*.

> There is neither positing nor removal (ἀφαίρεσις) of it at all. Making positings and removals (ἀφαιρέσεις) of what comes after it, we neither posit nor remove (ἀφαιροῦμεν) of it, since the perfect and singular cause of all is *hyper* all positing, and the preeminent absolutely free of all and beyond the whole is *hyper* all removal (ὑπὲρ πᾶσαν ἀφαίρεσιν).[24]

And Dionysius also draws quite extensively on metaphors of clouded darkness and mountain summits as symbols of divine unknowability and ineffability,[25] most notably in the first chapter, which opens with a prayer for divine guidance to the "highest summit of mystical Scripture" where "mysteries of theology are veiled by the *hyper*-light darkness of hidden silence,"[26] and which closes by exemplifying Moses as one who has made such as ascent.

> And then he [Moses] is released from what sees and is seen and enters into the truly mystical darkness (γνόφον) of unknowing, in which he shuts out every knowing apprehension and comes into the wholly intangible and invisible, being entirely of that which is beyond everything and nothing, neither himself nor another, united surpassingly (κατὰ τὸ κρεῖττον) to the completely

---

23. See especially *MT* 3, 1033BC and *MT* 5, 1045D–1048B. The critical edition of the Dionyaisn corpus lists six occurrences of *nameless* (*anōnymia, anōnymos*), eleven occurrences of *unspeakable* (*aphthegktos*), and twenty-one occurrences of *ineffable* (*arrētos*). Thesaurus Linguae Graecae confirms these and also finds twenty-seven occurrences of *logos-less* (*alogos*). Note that although most occurrences of *alogos* are better translated as reasonless; some clearly convey a sense of unspeakability, ineffability, or unassertability.

24. *MT* 5, 1048A–1048B. There are two other occurrences of *hyper positing and removal* in the *Mystical Theology* (*MT* 1.2, 1000B; *MT* 3, 1033CD) and one more elsewhere (*DN* 2.4, 641B).

25. The former draws on the basic metaphor *unknowing is up*, which has its experiential basis in the fact that it is easier to see and grasp objects that are close to the ground; the latter draws on the metaphor *unknowing is darkness*, an extension of the primary metaphor *knowing is seeing* (Lakoff and Johnson, *Metaphors We Live By*, 53–54).

26. *MT* 1.1, 997AB. See Perczel, "Pseudo-Dionysius," which argues that *summit* (*koryphēn*) here refers to Jesus Christ.

The Ineffable God Is Not Ineffable

unknown by an inactivity of all knowledge, knowing *hyper* mind by knowing nothing.[27]

Finally, and also in the opening prayer of the *Mystical Theology*, Dionysius once employs the construction *hyper-unknowable*, using it to attribute the enshrouded summit of mystical Scripture. (Elsewhere Dionysius also employs the construction *hyper-ineffable*.[28])

> Trinity *hyper*-being and *hyper*-divine and *hyper*-good, overseer of Christians in divine wisdom, guide us to the *hyper*-unknown (ὑπεράγνωστον) and *hyper*-brilliant highest summit of mystical Scripture; there the simple, absolute, and unchanged mysteries of theology are veiled by the *hyper*-light darkness of hidden silence, *hyper*-illuminating the *hyper*-most-appearing in the darkest and *hyper*-filling the sightless minds with *hyper*-beauty beauties in the wholly imperceptible and invisible.[29]

All this is taken as evidence for the unqualified ineffability and unknowability of God.

But Dionysius also has quite a lot to say about God in the *Mystical Theology*. God is addressed as Trinity and predicated with *hyper*-names such as *hyper*-being and *hyper*-divine and *hyper*-good; God is assumed to be able to respond to petitions to assist in the ascent to his enshrouded summit (where the mysteries of theology reside); God is said to be both many-*logos* and un-*logos*; and God is flatly asserted to be more like certain (intelligible) names (e.g., life, goodness, speaking, thinking) than other (perceptible) names (e.g., air, stone, drunkenness, anger). And so it is once again the case that what Dionysius means by *ineffability* and *unknowability*

---

27. *MT* 1.3, 1001A. Again see Perczel, "Pseudo-Dionysius," which argues that Dionysius here one-ups Proclus, asserting that Moses, having completed the full Procline ascent to the *hypothetical logoi*, goes even further into the divine darkness, to the *unhypothetical principle of all things* (ibid., 521–24). More uses of darkness and height as metaphors for divine unknowability in the *Mystical Theology* can be found at *MT* 1.2, 1000A; *MT* 1.3, 1000CD; *MT* 2, 1025AB; *MT* 3, 1033BC. See below for an analysis of these metaphors.

28. The register of the critical edition of the Dionysian corpus lists four instances of *hyper*-unknowable (*hyperagnōstos—DN* 1.4, 592D; *DN* 1.5, 593B; *DN* 2.4, 640D; *MT* 1.1, 997A) as well as four instances of *hyper*-ineffable (*hyperarrētos—DN* 1.4, 592D; *DN* 2.4, 640D; *CH* 13.4, 304C; *EP* 7.2, 1080C). (And Thesaurus Linguae Graecae reveals an additional occurrence of *hyperagnotatēs* at *CH* 10.3, 273C.) Wear and Dillon single out *hyperarrētos* as peculiar to the Dionysian corpus (*Dionysius the Areopagite*, 11). But Griffith indicates that it appears in Damascius too ("Neo-Platonism and Christianity," 240). Note that Dionysius never says that God is *hyper not-removal* or *hyper not-positing*.

29. *MT* 1.1, 997AB.

Negating Negation

seems not to be what we (philosophers) mean by these terms, that the Dionysian rhetorical techniques listed above serve to show that God is ineffable and unknowable in certain respects only, that the Dionysian God is not unqualifiedly ineffable and unknowable.

Key in this case is the state of *hyper-nous knowing* and the way in which it lifts the restriction of ordinary states of knowing to objects of being. Several passages in the *Mystical Theology* speak rather clearly of this state of transcendent knowing. The above-quoted final sentence of chapter 1, wherein Moses is exemplified as one who has made the ascent to the enshrouded divine summit, speaks of a state of "knowing *hyper* mind by knowing nothing."

> And then he [Moses] is released from what sees and is seen and enters into the truly mystical darkness of unknowing, in which he shuts out every knowing apprehension and becomes wholly intangible and invisible, being entirely of that which is beyond everything and nothing, neither himself nor another, united surpassingly (κατὰ τὸ κρεῖττον) to the completely unknown by an inactivity of all knowledge, knowing *hyper* mind by knowing nothing.[30]

The final sentence of chapter 2 refers to knowing unhiddenly the "unknowing that is covered by all the knowledge among beings."

> It is necessary, I think, to hymn the removals oppositely from the positings; for we posit these beginning from the first things and descending through the middle things to the last things; but then we remove everything making the search for the highest principles from the last things, so that we may unhiddenly know this unknowing that is covered by all the knowledge among all beings, and we may see this *hyper*-being darkness that is hidden by all the light among beings.[31]

And the first sentence of *Mystical Theology* 2 asks to come to a *hyper*-light darkness in which true knowledge of the unknowable God is acquired by not-knowing to know not to know that which is *hyper* knowledge.

---

30. *MT* 1.3, 1001A. See Golitzin's discussion (in "Suddenly Christ") of the phrase *kata to kreitton* (which I've translated as "surpassingly," but is more literally rendered as "according to what is greater"). And see Vannest (*Le Mystère de Dieu*), Rist ("Mysticism and Transcendence"), and de Andia (*Henosis*), all of whom identify this with a certain *hyper nous* faculty in humans (which Dionysius refers to as *henosis*).

31. *MT* 2, 1025B.

The Ineffable God Is Not Ineffable

> We pray to come to this *hyper*-light darkness, and through not-seeing and not-knowing to see and to know not to see and to know that which is *hyper* sight and knowledge itself—for this is truly seeing and knowing—and [we pray] to hymn *hyper*-beingly the *hyper*-being through the removal of all beings [. . .].[32]

Two things are notable about these passages: first, the state of knowing depicted in them is one that suspends and transcends ordinary knowing; second, the object of knowing depicted in them is one that is beyond the ordinary objects of being.[33] Thus the first passage refers to a knowing *hyper nous* that knows nothing (of being) through an inactivity of knowledge (of being); the second, to an unhidden knowing that is covered by all the knowledge among beings; and the third, to both an unknowing knowing of that which is *hyper* knowledge and a *hyper*-being hymning of the *hyper*-being through the removal of all beings. Thus it appears that the *hyper*-being God can be known in a manner *hyper nous* through the removal of all beings (which, as I argued in chapter 2, are the properties that the divine names source, not the divine names themselves).

And it is not just in the *Mystical Theology* that this state of transcendent knowing figures prominently. It appears in the very first paragraph of the *Divine Names*, a passage that was examined in detail above (section I).

> And now, O blessed one, after the *Theological Outlines* I will proceed to the explication of the divine names as far as I am able. And now let the law of the Scriptures, which limits us beforehand, bind us fast to the truth of what is said about God, "not in persuasive words of human wisdom, but in demonstration" of the Spirit-moved "power" of the theologians, by which we are unspeakably (ἀφθέγκτως) and unknowingly (ἀγνώστως) conjoined to unspeakable things (ἀφθέγκτοις) and unknowable things (ἀγνώστοις) through a union (ἕνωσιν) that is superior (κατὰ τὴν κρείττονα) to our rational and intellectual power and activity.[34]

And it later makes some notable appearances within Dionysius' explication of the divine name *wisdom* in the seventh chapter of the *Divine Names*—particularly in *Divine Names* 7.1, which mentions a unity that is raised above the nature of *nous* by which *nous* is joined to what is beyond it, but

---

32. *MT* 2, 1025A.

33. For passages that speak to the restriction of knowing to the things of being, see note 62 in chapter 2.

34. *DN* 1.1, 585B–588A.

Negating Negation

also in *Divine Names* 7.3, which refers to the most divine knowledge of God as a *hyper-nous* union with the *hyper*-brilliant rays that is engendered by a standing away from all beings.

> But, as I have said in other places, we are deceived into following the divine and ineffable *logos* according to appearance when we take things *hyper* us in a manner that is familiar to us, become entangled in that which is habitual to the sensory perceptions, and set divine things next to that which is according to us. It is necessary to know that our mind has the power to intellect, through which it views intellectual things, but it also has the unity (ἕνωσιν) raised above (ὑπεραίρουσαν) the nature of mind, through which it is joined to that which is beyond itself. And so we must intellect divine things according to this [unity], not according to ourselves, but by standing our whole selves outside of our whole selves and becoming wholly of God, for it is better to be of God and not of ourselves. For thus divine things will be given to those who come to be with God.[35]

> And there is, further, the most divine knowledge of God, which is known through unknowing during the union (ἕνωσιν) *hyper* mind, when the mind, having stood apart from all beings, then having given up even itself, is united (ἑνωθῇ) to the *hyper*-brilliant rays, there illumined by the inscrutable depth of wisdom.[36]

And transcendent knowing also receives a couple of explicit treatments in the *Epistles*, the first of which states that our knowledge of that which is *hyper* everything known is a *hyper-nous* knowledge that escapes those with knowledge *of being*, and the fourth of which adds that those who divinely see *hyper nous* will correctly interpret affirmations about Jesus as having the power of preeminent negation.

> Darkness disappears in the light, the more so, the more light; unknowing is removed by knowledge, the more so, the more knowledge. Having understood this preeminently (ὑπεροχικῶς) rather than by privation (στέρησιν), you will declare *hyper*-truthfully that the unknowing of God escapes those having existing light and knowledge of beings, and that God's transcendent darkness is hidden from all light and concealed from all knowledge. And if someone, seeing God, has understood what has been seen, that person has not seen God but rather something of God's that has being and is known. But God, established above *hyper* mind and being,

---

35. *DN* 7.1, 865C–868A.
36. *DN* 7.3, 872AB; see also *DN* 7.4, 872D.

The Ineffable God Is Not Ineffable

not known and not being in general, exists *hyper*-beingly and is known *hyper*-mind. And the surpassingly complete unknowing is a knowledge of that which is *hyper* everything known.[37]

Why should one go through the remaining things, which are numerous? Through them the one who sees divinely will know *hyper* mind that the affirmations about Jesus' love for humanity have the power of preeminent negation (ὑπεροχικῆς ἀποφάσεως). So we may say briefly, he was not human, not as non human, but as from humans being beyond humans and as *hyper* human having truly become human, and, as for the rest, not having done the things of God as God, nor the things of humans as human, but administering for us a new theandric activity as God having become human.[38]

And this is not all. This state of transcendent knowing is also metaphorically depicted as one of luminous or *hyper*-light darkness.[39] On a number of occasions Dionysius very clearly declares that darkness should not be understood as a privation of light. Darkness, rather, is a preeminence of light. *Epistle* 5, for example, identifies divine darkness with unapproachable light and preeminent brightness.

The divine darkness is the "unapproachable light" in which it is said God lives, being invisible through its preeminent (ὑπερέχουσαν) brightness, and being unapproachable through its excess of *hyper*-being streaming of light. In it enter all who are worthy of knowing and seeing God—not by knowing and seeing God, but by really coming to be in that which is *hyper* sight and knowledge, knowing that God is after all perceptible and intelligible things, and saying prophetically, "Knowledge of you is too wonderful for me; it is too high; I cannot attain it." Thus the divine Paul is said to have known God as *hyper* all intellection and knowledge. Thus he says that his ways are inscrutable, "his judgments are unsearchable," his gifts are indescribable, and his peace exceeds (ὑπερέχουσαν) "all understanding," for he found that which is *hyper* all and knew *hyper* understanding that it is beyond (ἐπέκεινα) all as the cause of all.[40]

---

37. *EP* 1, 1065AB.

38. *EP* 4, 1072BC.

39. Peter Kügler's otherwise interesting treatment of divine darkness ("The Meaning of Mystical 'Darkness'") entirely misses this crucial point. So does Denys Turner's analysis of "brilliant darkness" as a "self-subverting utterance" (*The Darkness of God*, 22).

40. *EP* 5, 1073A–1076A.

Negating Negation

And *Mystical Theology* 1.1 not only petitions the Trinity to guide Christians to the highest summit of mystical Scripture that is both *hyper*-unknown and *hyper*-brilliant but also implores Timothy to be uplifted to the *hyper*-being ray of the divine darkness.

> Trinity *hyper*-being and *hyper*-divine and *hyper*-good, overseer of Christians in divine wisdom, guide us to the *hyper*-unknown (ὑπεράγνωστον) and *hyper*-brilliant (ὑπερφαῆ) highest summit of mystical Scripture; there the simple, absolute, and unchanged mysteries of theology are veiled by the *hyper*-light darkness (ὑπέρφωτον γνόφον) of hidden silence, *hyper*-illuminating the *hyper*-most-appearing in the darkest (ἐν τῳ σκοτεινοτάτῳ τὸ ὑπερφανέστατον ὑπερλάμποντα) and overfilling the sightless minds with *hyper*-beauty beauties in the wholly imperceptible and invisible. This is my prayer; and you, dear Timothy, in the earnest study of mystical sights, leave behind sensible and intellectual activities, all sensible and intelligible things, all non-beings and beings, and unknowingly strive upward, as far as possible, toward the unity of that which is *hyper* all being and knowledge. By an undivided and absolute *ecstasis* of yourself and everything, shedding all and freed from all, you will be purely uplifted to the *hyper*-being ray of the divine darkness (τὸν ὑπερούσιον τοῦ θείου σκότους ἀκτῖνα).[41]

And *Mystical Theology* 2 opens with a prayer to come to the *hyper*-light darkness.

> We pray to come to this *hyper*-light darkness (ὑπέρφωτον γνόφον), and through not-seeing and not-knowing to see and to know not to see and to know that which is *hyper* sight and knowledge itself—for this is truly seeing and knowing [. . .].[42]

These luminous-darkness constructions are not mere paradoxical curiosities. For Dionysius plainly says that true knowledge of God is revealed in such states of luminous darkness. Rather, luminous darkness is Dionysius' symbol for *hyper*-mind knowledge of the *hyper*-being God—a transcendent form of knowledge that requires ignorance of the things of being. Thus, whereas simple light stands for knowledge of the things of being and simple darkness signifies ignorance with respect to the things of being, luminous darkness symbolizes both the complete

---

41. *MT* 1.1, 997A–1000A.
42. *MT* 2, 1025A.

The Ineffable God Is Not Ineffable

absence of knowledge from the perspective of being and a *hyper*-mind knowledge of the *hyper*-being God.[43]

Whether described literally or depicted metaphorically, the passages of the last three paragraphs speak clearly of a *hyper-nous* knowing of the *hyper-ousia* God. But what about a *hyper-logos* saying of the *hyper-ousia* God? Admittedly, the textual evidence here is not as robust. Nevertheless, it is hardly nonexistent.[44] *Divine Names* 2.4 in particular identifies both unspeakability and many-namability of the divine unity *hyper*-beingness.

> For example, this is unified and common to the henarchic Trinity with respect to the divine unity, the *hyper*-beingness (ἐπὶ τῆς ἑνώσεως τῆς θείας ἤτοι τῆς ὑπερουσιότητος): the *hyper*-being subsistence, the *hyper*-divine divinity, the *hyper*-good goodness, the identity beyond all of the whole identity beyond all, the *hyper* henarchic unity, the unspeakable (ἄφθεγκτον), the much-speaking (πολύφωνον), the unknowable, the all-intelligible, the positing of all, the removal of all, the *hyper* all positing and removal, the remaining and foundation of the henarchic substances in one another (if I may so speak), wholly *hyper*-unified, and in no part comingled [. . .].[45]

As was the case in chapter 2, one might be tempted here to say that many-namability pertains merely to God *qua* cause of all. But this would be to disregard that this passage says that these predicate-terms are applied to the *hyper*-being divine unity; it would also be to neglect the context of this passage, which indicates that these predicate-terms are applied to the divine unions with respect to the hidden and permanent *hyper*-establishments, not the good-formed processions and manifestations. (For more on this, see section IV of chapter 1.) Rather, I suggest that this passage be interpreted as follows: the *hyper*-being God, the God of the divine names (i.e., the

---

43. Like the basic metaphor *knowing is seeing*, the Dionysian metaphor *divine knowledge is luminous darkness* possesses two stages: a stage of initial darkness or ignorance, and a state of final illumination or knowledge. But unlike the basic metaphor *knowing is seeing*, the Dionysian metaphor *divine knowledge is luminous darkness* does not present these stages as mutually exclusive. To enter into the light of *hyper*-mind knowing is to remain within the darkness of ignorance of the things of being. To enter into the divine darkness is to be illuminated. The power of this Dionysian metaphor is its ability to do double duty, conveying both states at once. See my "Techniques and Rules of Ineffability in the Dionysian Corpus."

44. In addition to the passages quoted below, see especially *MT* 1.3, 1000C; *DN* 1.6, 596A; *DN* 13.3, 981AB.

45. *DN* 2.4, 641A.

hidden and permanent *hyper*-establishments) is both namable as the *hyper*-prefixed divine names themselves and unnamable as the properties that the divine names source. The *hyper*-being God is therefore sayable *hyper-logos* and unsayable *qua logos*. Or, even more elaborately, the *hyper*-being God is (a) sayable *qua logos* as the "positing of all" the properties that the divine names themselves source; (b) unsayable *qua logos* as the "removal of all" the properties that the divine names themselves source; and (c) sayable *hyper logos* as the *hyper*-existent and *hyper*-unified divine names themselves, which are "*hyper* all positing and removal" (insofar as positing and removal are of things of being). As in the case of knowing *hyper nous*, this saying *hyper logos* is, technically speaking, not a saying at all, since all saying is of things of being. Thus it is a silent saying, a saying beyond *logos*.[46] Still, as in the case of *hyper-nous* knowing, it is a communicative something that makes possible the transmission of *hyper-nous* knowledge of divine things.

This interpretation makes good sense of a similar-sounding passage from *Divine Names* 1.1.

> The One *hyper* thought is unthinkable to all thinking, the Good *hyper* speech (λόγον) is ineffable (ἄρρητόν) to all speech (λόγῳ), *henad* uniting every *henad* and *hyper*-being being and un-intelligible intellect and ineffable speech (λόγος ἄρρητος), speechlessness (ἀλογία) and intellectlessness and namelessness (ἀνωνυμία) and being according to nothing of being and cause of all being, but itself not being as beyond all being so that it alone could properly and scientifically manifest itself about itself.[47]

Here, as explicated above in section I, Dionysius qualifies his opening claim that the One *hyper* thought is unthinkable to all thinking and that the Good *hyper* logos is ineffable to all logos by going on to speak of this One-Good as *henad* uniting every *heand*, *hyper*-being being, unintelligible intellect, and ineffable logos. Again, these are not merely mind-bending paradoxes; rather they point to a manner in which the *hyper*-being God *is*, is *known*, and is *said*—not, of course, in some manner of being; rather, in a manner that transcends *ousia*, *nous*, and *logos*. Thus just as the *hyper-ousia* God can be known *hyper-nous*, so the *hyper-ousia* God can be said *hyper-logos*. And this *hyper-ousia* God is, of course, the God of the divine names themselves and persons of the Trinity. This is the preeminence (*hyperochē*) that the

---

46. See especially *MT* 3, 1033BC and *DN* 1.3, 589AB.
47. *DN* 1.1, 588B.

The Ineffable God Is Not Ineffable

logic of *apophasis* reveals. Thus it is appropriate that in one and the same passage Dionysius tells us that among those "things of deprivation" that the theologians negate "in an opposite sense," stand the predicate-terms *ineffable* and *nameless*, which reveal not a deprivation of effability and namability but a many-hymnability and many-namability.

> [. . .] it is customary for theologians to negate (ἀποφάσκειν) the things of deprivation (τὰ τῆς στερήσεως) with respect to God in an opposite sense. Thus Scripture calls the all-shining light invisible, and the many-hymned (πολυύμνητον) and many-named (πολυώνυμον) ineffable (ἄρρητον) and unnamable (ἀνώνυμον), and that which is present in all things and discoverable from all things incomprehensible and inscrutable. In this way, even now, the divine apostle is said to have hymned as foolishness of God that which appears unreasonable and paradoxical in itself, but which uplifts us to the ineffable truth before all reason.[48]

In short and in summary: the *hyper*-being God is not absolutely ineffable and unknowable. It exists *hyper-ousia*, and therefore can be known *hyper-nous* and said *hyper-logos*. This is in part due to the fact that the *hyper*-being God is not absent of all distinctions but rather is both the persons of the Trinity and the *hyper*-prefixed divine names. But it is also due to the fact that this *hyper*-being God reveals itself to the first rank of angels, which then pass this revelation down through the celestial and human hierarchies. In such manner divine things that exist *hyper*-being are known *hyper*-mind and said *hyper*-speech.

IV. The Unknowable and Ineffable God Cannot Be (Absolutely) Unknowable and Ineffable

These textual arguments in place, I turn now to three brief logical arguments against the claim that the Dionysian God is absolutely and unqualifiedly ineffable and unknowable, and in so doing I extend my overall argument from one about what Dionysius actually did say about ineffability and unknowability to what Dionysius logically could say about ineffability and unknowability. The first argument is that the Dionysian God cannot be all the things that it is said to be and do all the things that it is said to do and still be absolutely and unqualifiedly ineffable and unknowable. Here, for the sake of clarity, I will limit the discussion to causation, just as long

48. *DN* 7.1, 865BC.

as we are clear on the fact that a whole lot more than just this is positively said and never taken back about the Dionysian God. My argument in short it this: if the Dionysian God is absolutely and unqualifiedly ineffable and unknowable, then it cannot be the cause of all; and if the Dionysian God is the cause of all, then it cannot be absolutely and unqualifiedly ineffable and unknowable. Given that there is something in the Dionysian cosmos, something that must be caused by God, there is really only one acceptable horn to this dilemma: the Dionysian God is the cause of all and therefore is not absolutely and unqualifiedly ineffable and unknowable—for it is knowable and sayable as the cause of all. And note that causation need not be "horizontal"; it is sufficient that all things be ontologically contingent on the Dionysian God for their formal determinations, for the Dionysian God would then be precisely that on which the beings of the cosmos are dependent for their determinations.[49] And even if causation is a feature of God's "powers" rather than God's "essence," God's essence is still such that it gives rise to powers that are themselves responsible for causation.

The second argument is that an absolutely and unqualifiedly ineffable and unknowable God cannot be predicated in a ranked sequence or metaphorical manner. If some predicate is more true or apt of a subject than some other predicate, then that subject cannot be absolutely and unqualifiedly ineffable and unknowable—it is effable and knowable as more (like) p than q. And if some predicate is metaphorically true or apt of a subject, then that subject cannot be absolutely and unqualifiedly ineffable and unknowable, for a predicate can only be metaphorically true or apt of a subject if it calls to mind a respect in which it is literally true or apt. Both are the case of the Dionysian God. *Mystical Theology* 2–3 not only clearly states that the method of *aphairesis* removes predicate-terms from God in reverse order of similarity or proximity (from last things, to first things) but also plainly says that certain (intelligible) predicate-terms (e.g., life and goodness, speaking and thinking) are more similar or closer to God than other (perceptible) predicate-terms (e.g., air and stone, drunkenness and anger). And *Celestial Hierarchy* 2–3 makes it crystal clear that perceptible symbols are, much like metaphors, "dissimilar similarities"—dissimilar with respect to their perceptible shell, yet similar to their intelligible content. I submit that there is no way for *life* to be more true than *air* of an absolutely and unqualifiedly ineffable and unknowable God, no way for *drunkenness* and *anger* to have an intelligible content that is in some way similar to an absolutely and unqualifiedly ineffable and

---

49. See here Perl, *Theophany*, 17–19.

unknowable God.[50] For all things are equally false (or inapplicable) of an absolutely and unqualifiedly ineffable and unknowable God.

Finally, my third argument is that since the absolute ineffability of something is always relative to some semiotic system in which that thing cannot be said, the ability to know and say that something is absolutely ineffable is only possible from the perspective of some other semiotic system in which that something is not absolutely ineffable.[51] Put in Dionysian terms, if God is absolutely ineffable to beings, then this can only be known and said to be the case from some perspective that is not of being, some perspective that transcends being; without this perspective, the Dionysian God is *absolutely nothing*—not even no-thing. This solution is the only one that is both faithful to the text and logically sound. The Dionysian God can be absolutely and unqualifiedly ineffable and unknowable with respect to the ordinary knowing of the things of being, completely not and *hyper* the things of being, in no way participating in the properties that the divine names source; and the Dionysian God can still be those things which it is said to be with respect to *hyper* being, the persons of the Trinity, the preexistent divine names themselves (as well as their pre-contained effects), the cause of all. All this can be known and said from some other perspective or vantage point; it can be comprehended through *hyper-nous* knowing and said through *hyper-logos* saying.[52] And from this perspective, even if partially knowable and sayable, God is by no means completely knowable and sayable. All this, I think, is what Dionysius has in mind when he refers to divine things as ineffable and unknowable.

---

50. What then do I make of passages that seem to say that God is incomparably beyond all (e.g., those in *DN* 1.2, *DN* 1.4, *DN* 1.5, *DN* 2.7, *DN* 9.6, *DN* 9.7, *DN* 13.3, and *CH* 13.4)? I note that just as perceptible symbols are entirely false with respect to their perceptible shell yet true with respect to their intelligible content, so divine names are entirely false with respect to their intelligible form yet true (in varying degrees) with respect to their unitary content. Thus, the *hyper*-being God is entirely beyond the things of being (since it does not participate in the divine names themselves), yet is (in varying degrees) the divine names themselves (as *hyper*-prefixed).

51. See especially Henle's "Mysticism and Semantics"; see also Proudfoot's *Religious Experience*.

52. Thus the dual meanings of *hyper* can be allowed to sound out in the phrases *hyper-unknowable* and *hyper-ineffable*. On the one hand, God is *beyond* ineffability/unknowability as removed from the ordinary categories in/effable and un/knowable. On the other hand, God is *above* ineffability/unknowability as both preeminently ineffable/unknowable and preeminently effable/knowable in an extraordinary, *hyper*-being manner.

Conclusion

Now that you have reached the end of this book, I would like to tell you a little something about its beginning, more specifically about a couple of its failed beginnings—not for the sake of exposé, but because these failures shed light on what I wanted to accomplish with this book.

The most recent of these failings was titular in nature. For whatever reason, I had a devil of a time settling on a title for this book. Its first title—*Dionysius Against the Grain: Contrarian Readings of the Divine Names, Negation, Hierarchy, and Ineffability*—misleadingly suggested that the book's primary virtue was that of opposing existing interpretations of the Dionysian corpus. My second title—*A Positively Different Dionysius: Apophatic Abandonment and the Rhetoric of Ineffability in the Dionysian Corpus*—overcorrected this error, and at bit too whimsically at that. It was only by the saving grace of my former editor, John N. Jones, that the book received its third and final title: *Negating Negation: Against the Apophatic Abandonment of the Dionysian Corpus*. I would like to think this title "tastes" neither too hot nor too cold.

Nevertheless—and this is the point of my story—the flavors of these discarded titles linger, if only in the fact that they name continuing aims of this book: if this book "negates negation," it does so by arguing "against the grain" for a "positively different Dionysius." Such a Dionysius does not take the divine names to be inadequate metaphors or impotent attributes, but locates them in God as pluralized divine unities and transcendent divine causes. Such a Dionysius therefore does not flatly negate divine names of God, but *aphairetically* removes them as ordinary properties to *apophatically* reveal them as the *hyper*-unified and *hyper*-existent divine sources of these properties. Such a Dionysius utilizes this *aphairetic* method, not to negate and overcome the hierarchical orders and hierurgical rituals, but

Conclusion

as a means of theological preparation for and theurgical participation in the liturgical rites. Such a Dionysius therefore does not find God to be absolutely and unqualifiedly unknowable and ineffable, but knowable *hyper-nous* and sayable *hyper-logos* as these very things. All this, first and foremost, is what this book tried to accomplish: to present textual evidence for a positively different Dionysius, arguing against the grain by opposing the standard interpretation of the Dionysian negation as all-encompassing and all-denying.

This brings me to my book's more distant failing, one that is more substantive than semantic. Initiated not long after the defense of my dissertation, this book was first conceived both in similar form and for similar ends. Its form remained the same: one-third exposition of the history of the study of ineffability, one-third collection of linguistic tools for the analysis of mystical texts, one-third exploration of linguistic techniques employed by Dionysius in speaking about unspeakable things. Thus its ends remained the same: a rejection of the traditional question of ineffability (*Is x ineffable?*) as intractable, an adoption of Michael Sells' program of ineffability-performance investigation as more fruitful, a demonstration of the rule-governed nature of grammatical techniques of ineffability in the Dionysian corpus, and therefore a mitigation of Sells' thesis that apophatically-inclined mystics perform ineffability through the violation of linguistic rules.[1] But not long afterwards, I became increasingly convinced that the traditional question of ineffability was not intractable; it was false—there are no good reasons and no positive evidence for the absolute and unqualified ineffability of any thing that is in some way some thing for us. And so, I tried my hand at a slimmer book of two parts, the first of which offered a series of arguments against recent claims that ultimate realities or mystical experiences are ineffable, the second of which analyzed grammatical techniques and rules of ineffability in the Dionysian corpus for the sake of showing that the presence of such rules constituted evidence not only against the claim that absolute ineffability can be performed through the violation of linguistic rules but also against the claim that ultimate beings or experiences can actually be absolutely ineffable. Despite my best effort at joining these parts, however, they proved too disparate.

Nevertheless—and this is the point of my second story—it should be clear that just as the "flavors" of my discarded titles linger, so do my concerns with ineffability. One of these concerns is with the way in which

1. See Sells, *Mystical Languages of Unsaying*.

the Dionysian corpus is appropriated by our modern-Western discourses of ineffability, be they those that aspire to resolve religious pluralism or rebuff onto-theology. The former look to ineffability to demarcate that which all religions have in common from that about which they differ.[2] According to this line of thinking, whereas religions such as Buddhism and Christianity might disagree both within and between themselves about what is ultimately real, they (ought to) agree that this ultimate "reality" or certain experiences of it are absolutely ineffable, transcending all of our conceptions and articulations about it. Regardless of the merit of this hypothesis, the Dionysian corpus gives it no support. The Dionysian God is not only the cause of all—contra certain Buddhisms—but a cause that sources all things by means of precisely-fixed divine names and returns all things (or at least humans) by means of precisely-fixed hierarchical orders and hierurgical rituals. Nor does the Dionysian corpus give support to our (post)modern-Western projects of anti-onto-theology, at least not those that call upon ineffability as a counter to onto-theology.[3] For even if the Dionysian God is neither a being nor knowable and sayable from the perspective of being, there is still quite a lot that is known and said about its *hyper*-being preeminence, beginning, once again, with the fact that it is the cause of all by means of divine names, about which a "science" is not only possible but actually written. (And the *Divine Names* does not disappear with an anti-onto-theological wave of the hand; rather, the *Mystical Theology* shows us how to interpret it properly, as the science that it is, or at least purports to be.)

My second concern with ineffability is with ineffability itself. This comes out clearest in both the introduction and the fourth chapter, the former of which maintains that the notion of absolute ineffability is not only incoherent but also useless, the latter of which argues that the Dionysius corpus not only does not actually say that God is absolutely ineffable and unknowable but also could not logically say that God is absolutely ineffable and unknowable. I do not wish to rehearse these arguments here. Instead, I want to end this book on a positive note. Indeed, it is good news that ineffability is never absolute but always relative. Relative

---

2. See especially the work of John Hick (especially *An Interpretation of Religion*) and Robert Forman (especially *Mysticism, Mind, Consciousness*). See my "Ineffability Now and Then" for a critique of both Hick's and Forman's appropriations of Dionysius; see also my "Three Misuses of Pseudo-Dionysius" for a lengthier critique of just Hick's appropriation.

3. Per note 4 of my introduction, see especially Jones, "Introduction."

ineffability constitutes both a sounder explanation of the data and a firmer foundation for inquiry—the former, since ultimate realities and experiences can resist and exceed linguistic description only in particular ways for particular reasons as particular "things"; the latter, since ultimate realities and experiences can be investigated and compared only as particular "things" that are similar and different in particular ways and for particular reasons. If ultimate realities and experiences are truly ultimate, then it should come as no surprise that those who think and speak about them should find their means of doing so inadequate. What is interesting and important, though, are the different ways in which such thinkers and writers think and speak this inadequacy. This is to say that if we were to devote attention to the different ways in which humans make thought and language fail ultimate realities, we might learn a good deal about the different ways in which humans take these ultimate realities to be ultimate. This might in turn help lend a more wary eye to some of our religious generalizations, be they popular ones that find all religions fundamentally the same or scholarly ones that operate on the logic of an ahistorical and monolithic theism. And it might also lend a more appreciative eye to the creative ways in which humans speak about unspeakable things, bound on the one hand to a logic of ultimacy that dictates that ultimate things cannot be spoken, and on the other hand to the semiotic fact that anything that is in some way something for us can be somehow spoken. All this too is at stake in my reading of the Dionysian corpus: resistance to the appropriation of the Dionysian corpus by our modern-Western discourse of ineffability, rejection of the notion of absolute ineffability as incoherent and useless, and reinvigoration of the comparative study of (relative) ineffability in a manner that is interesting and important.

Bibliography

De Andia, Ysabel. *Henosis: L'Union à Dieu chez Denys l'Aréopagite*. New York: Brill, 1996.
Aristotle. *The Complete Works of Aristotle: The Revised Oxford Translation*. Edited by Jonathan Barnes. 2 vols. Princeton: Princeton University Press, 1984.
Arthur, Rosemary A. *Pseudo-Dionysius as Polemicist*. Farnham, UK: Ashgate, 2008.
Bradshaw, David. *Aristotle East and West: Metaphysics and the Division of Christendom*. New York: Cambridge University Press, 2004.
Burns, Dylan. "Proclus and the Theurgic Liturgy of Dionysius." *Dionysius* 22 (2004) 111–32.
Dodds, E. R. "Commentary." In *Proclus: The Elements of Theology*, 2nd ed., translation, introduction, and commentary by E. R. Dodds, 187–321. New York: Oxford University Press, 1963.
Forman, Robert K. C. *Mysticism, Mind, Consciousness*. Albany, NY: State University of New York Press, 1999.
Gersh, Stephen. *From Iamblichus to Eriugena: An Investigation of the Prehistory and Evolution of the Pseudo-Dionysian Tradition*. Leiden: Brill, 1978.
Golitizin, Alexander. "Dionysius Areopagita: A Christian Mysticism?" *Pro Ecclesia* 12.2 (2003) 161–212.
———. *Et Introibo Ad Altare Dei: The Mystagogy of Dionysius Areopagita, with Special Reference to Its Predecessors in the Eastern Christian Tradition*. Thessaloniki: Patriarchikon Idryma Paterikon Meleton, 1994.
———. "Suddenly Christ: The Place of Negative Theology in the Mystagogy of Dionysius Areopagites." In *Mystics: Presence and Aporia*, edited by Michael Kessler and Christian Sheppard, 8–37. Chicago: University of Chicago Press, 2003.
Griffith, Rosemary. "Neo-Platonism and Christianity: Pseudo-Dionysius and Damascius." In *Studia Patristica*, vol. 29, edited by Elizabeth A. Livingstone, 238–43. Leuven: Peeters, 1997.
Hathaway, Ronald. F. *Hierarchy and the Definition of Order in the Letters of Pseudo-Dionysius*. The Hague: Nijhoff, 1969.
Henle, Paul. "Mysticism and Semantics." *Philosophy and Phenomenological Research* 9.16 (1949) 416–22.
Hick, John. *The Fifth Dimension: An Exploration of the Spiritual Realm*. Boston: Oneworld, 1999.
———. "Ineffability." *Religious Studies* 36.1 (2000) 35–46.

Bibliography

———. *An Interpretation of Religion: Human Responses to the Transcendent*. New Haven: Yale University Press, 1989.

———. *The New Frontier of Religion and Science: Religious Experience, Neuroscience and the Transcendent*. New York: Palgrave Macmillan, 2006.

———. *Who or What is God? And Other Investigations*. London: SCM, 2009.

Horn, Laurence R. *A Natural History of Negation*. Palo Alto: CSLI, 2001.

Jones, John D. "An Absolutely Simple God? Frameworks for Reading Pseudo-Dionysius Areopagite." *The Thomist* 69.3 (2005) 371–406.

———. "Introduction." In *The Divine Names and Mystical Theology*, translation and introduction by John D. Jones, 15–103. Milwaukee: Marquette University Press, 1980.

Jones, John N. "Sculpting God: The Logic of Dionysian Negative Theology." *The Harvard Theological Review* 89.4 (1996) 355–71.

———. "The Status of the Trinity in Dionysian Thought." *The Journal of Religion* 80.4 (2000) 645–57.

Klitenic, Sarah. "Theurgy in Proclus and Pseudo-Dionysius." *Yearbook of the Irish Philosophical Society* 90 (2001) 85–95.

Knepper, Timothy D. "Ineffability Now and Then: The Legacy of Neoplatonic Ineffability in Twentieth-Century Philosophy of Religion." *Quaestiones Disputatae* 2.1–2 (2011) 263–76.

———. "Techniques and Rules of Ineffability in the Dionysian Corpus." In *Logic in Orthodox Christian Thinking*, edited by Andrew Schumann, 122–73. Piscataway, NJ: Ontos Verlag, 2013.

———. "Three Misuses of Pseudo-Dionysius for Comparative Theology." *Religious Studies* 45.2 (2009) 205–21.

Kügler, Peter. "The Meaning of Mystical 'Darkness.'" *Religious Studies* 41.1 (2005) 95–105.

Lakoff, George, and Mark Johnson. *Metaphors We Live By*. Chicago: The University of Chicago Press, 1980.

———. *Philosophy in the Flesh: The Embodied Mind and its Challenge to Western Thought*. New York: Basic, 1999.

Liddell, Henry George, and Robert Scott. *A Greek-English Lexicon*, revised edition of new (ninth) edition. Oxford: Clarendon, 1968.

Louth, Andrew. *Denys the Areopagite*. Wilton, CT: Morehouse-Barlow, 1989.

———. "Pagan Theurgy and Christian Sacramentalism in Denys the Areopagite." *Journal of Theological Studies* 37.2 (1986) 432–38.

Mortley, Raoul. *The Way of Negation, Christian and Greek*. Vol. 2 of *From Word to Silence*. Bonn: Hanstein, 1986.

Pépin, Jean. "ΥΠΑΡΞΙΣ et ΥΠΟΣΤΑΣΙΣ en Cappadoce." In *Hyparxis e Hypostasis nel Neoplatonismo*, edited by F. Romano and D. P. Taormina, 60–78. Firenze, Italy: Olschki Editore, 1994.

Perczel, István. "Pseudo-Dionysius and the *Platonic Theology*." In *Proclus et la Théologie Platonicienne*, edited by A. Ph. Segonds and C. Steel, 491–532. Leuven: Leuven University Press, 2000.

Perl, Eric. "Dionysius." In *A Companion to Philosophy in the Middle Ages*, edited by Jorge J. E. Garcia and Timothy B. Noone, 540–49. Malden, MA: Blackwell, 2003.

———. "Hierarchy and Participation in Dionysius the Areopagite and Greek Neoplatonism." *American Catholic Philosophical Quarterly* 68.1 (1994) 15–30.

Bibliography

———. "Symbol, Sacrament, and Hierarchy in Saint Dionysios the Areopagite." *Greek Orthodox Theological Review* 39.3–4 (1994) 311–55.

———. *Theophany: The Neoplatonic Philosophy of Dionysius the Areopagite.* Albany, NY: State University of New York Press, 2007.

Plato. *Complete Works.* Edited by John M. Cooper. Indianapolis: Hackett, 1997.

Plotinus. *The Enneads: Loeb Classical Library.* Translated by A. H. Armstrong. 7 vols. Cambridge: Harvard University Press, 1966–88.

Proclus. *The Elements of Theology,* 2nd ed. Translation, introduction, and commentary by E. R. Dodds. New York: Oxford University Press, 1963.

———. *The Platonic Theology.* Translated by Thomas Taylor. 6 vols. 1816. Reprint. Chelmsford, UK: The Prometheus Trust, 1995.

———. *Proclus' Commentary on Plato's* Parmenides. Translated by Glenn R. Morrow and John M. Dillon. Princeton: Princeton University Press, 1987.

Proudfoot, Wayne. *Religious Experience.* New York: University of California Press, 1985.

Pseudo-Dionysius. *Corpus Dionysiacum I: De Divinis Nominibus.* Edited by Beate Regina Suchla. Berlin: de Gruyter, 1990.

———. *Corpus Dionysiacum II: De Coelesti Hierarchia, de Ecclesiastic Hierarchia, de Mystica Theologia, Epistulae.* Edited by Günter Heil and Adolf Martin Ritter. Berlin: de Gruyter, 1991.

———. *Dionysius the Pseudo-Areopagite: The Ecclesiastical Hierarchy.* Translated by Thomas L. Campbell. Lanham, MD: University Press of America, 1981.

———. *The Divine Names and Mystical Theology.* Translation and Introduction by John D. Jones. Milwaukee: Marquette University Press, 1980.

———. *Pseudo-Dionysius: The Complete Works.* Translated by Colm Luibheid. Mahwah, NJ: Paulist, 1987.

———. *The Works of Dionysius the Areopagite.* Translated by John Parker. 1897–99. Reprint. Merrick, NY: Richwood, 1976.

Rist, J. M. "Mysticism and Transcendence in Later Neoplatonism." *Hermes* 92.2 (1964) 213–25.

Rojek, Paweł. "Towards a Logic of Negative Theology." In *Logic in Religious Discourse,* edited by Andrew Schumann, 192–215. Piscataway, NJ: Ontos Verlag, 2010.

Rorem, Paul. *Biblical and Liturgical Symbols within the Pseudo-Dionysian Synthesis.* Toronto: Pontifical Institute of Mediaeval Studies, 1984.

———. "Moses as the Paradigm for the Liturgical Spirituality of Pseudo-Dionysius." *Studia Patristica* 18.2 (1989) 275–79.

———. "The Place of *The Mystical Theology* in the Pseudo-Dionysian Corpus." *Dionysius* 4 (1980) 87–98.

———. *Pseudo-Dionysius: A Commentary on the Texts and an Introduction to their Influence.* New York: Oxford University Press, 1993.

———. "The Uplifting Spirituality of Pseudo-Dionysius." In *Christian Spirituality: Origins to 12th century,* edited by Bernard McGinn, 132–51. New York: Crossroad, 1985.

Rosán, Laurence J. *The Philosophy of Proclus: The Final Phase of Ancient Thought.* New York: Cosmos, 1949.

Schäfer, Christian. *The Philosophy of Dionysius Areopagite.* Boston: Leiden, 2006.

Sells, Michael A. *Mystical Languages of Unsaying.* Chicago: University of Chicago Press, 1994.

Shaw, Gregory. "Neoplatonic Theurgy and Dionysius the Areopagite." *Journal of Early Christian Studies* 7.4 (1999) 573–99.

Bibliography

Sheldon-Williams, I. P. "The *Ecclesiastical Hierarchy* of Dionysius—Part I." *Downside Review* 83.270 (1965) 20–31.

———. "Henads and Angels: Proclus and the Dionysius." *Studia Patristica* 11.2 (1972) 65–71.

Siovanes, Lucas. *Proclus: Neo-Platonic Philosophy and Science*. New Haven: Yale University Press, 1996.

Struck, Peter. "Pagan and Christian Theurgies: Iamblichus, Pseudo-Dionysius, Religion and Magic in Late Antiquity." *The Ancient World* 32.1 (2001) 25–38.

Turner, Denys. "The Art of Unknowing: Negative Theology in Late Medieval Mysticism." *Modern Theology* 14.4 (1998) 473–88.

———. *The Darkness of God: Negativity in Christian Mysticism*. New York: Cambridge University Press, 1995.

———. "How to Read the Pseudo-Denys Today?" *International Journal of Systematic Theology* 7.4 (2005) 428–40.

Van den Berg, R. M. *Proclus' Hymns: Essays, Translations, Commentaries*. Boston: Brill, 2001.

Vanneste, Jan. *Le Mystère de Dieu: Essai Sur la Structure Rationnelle de la Doctrine Mystique du pseudo-Denys l'Aréopagite*. Brussels: Desclée de Brouwer, 1959.

Wear, Sarah Klitenic, and John Dillon. *Dionysius the Areopagite and the Neoplatonic Tradition: Despoiling the Hellenes*. Farnham, UK: Ashgate, 2007.

Williams, Janet. "The Apophatic Theology of Dionysius the Pseudo-Areopagite." *Downside Review* 117.408 (1999) 157–72.

Wolfson, H. A. "Negative Attributes in the Church Fathers and the Gnostic Basilides." In *Studies in the History of Philosophy and Religion*, vol. 1, edited by Isadore Twersky and George H. Williams, 131–42. Cambridge: Harvard University Press, 1973.

Subject Index

An "*n*" after a locator indicates a footnote. A "*t*" after a locator indicates a table.

absolute ineffability-unknowability
   arguments against, 106
   arguments for, lack of, 133
   as concept, 134–35
   God as not, 129–31
   as incoherent and useless, xiv
   nature of, xi
affirmation and negation, terms for, 66*t*
aisthētai symbola. *See* perceptible symbols
all, God as cause of, 38*n*6, 55–59, 130, 134
all-shining light, God as, 45
almighty (divine name), 15
alpha-privative divine names, 42
ambiguity
   of *hyperochē*, 48–53, 55*n*43, 60
   of *hyper*-prefixed divine names, 52–53
ancient of days (divine name), 15
angels, 93, 114–15, 115–19, 129
   See also celestial hierarchy
anti-onto-theology, xiv, xv*n*4, 134
aphairesis (removal)
   apophasis, relationship with, 36, 40–47, 64–68
   description of, 35, 41–42
   grammar of, and unity of Dionysian negation, 61–68
   hierurgical rites, role in, 102
   removal of, in *MT* 5, 43

   syntax of, 43–44
   technē, comparison with, 40–41
   as term, in Dionysian corpus, 40
   union achieved by, 97–99
   See also aphairetic removal; *apophasis* (negation); negation
aphairesis of all [beings], 41; 41*n*13–42*n*13
aphairetic removal
   apophasis, relationship to, 64, 66
   deification-union, role in, 95–96
   as hymning of God, 99–100
   liturgy, role in, 102
   Rorem on, 89*n*54
   as support for hierurgical ritual, 71, 80*n*29
   union achieved by, 97
   See also aphairesis
apophasis (negation)
   aphairesis and, 36, 40–47, 64–68
   description of, 35
   logic of, 64*t*
   meaning of, in Dionysian corpus, 44–45
   as term, 40, 46*n*24
   See also aphairesis (removal); negation
apophatic abandonment, xi, 36–39, 70–71, 94
apophatic ascent, 70
apophatic interpretation, 64
apophatic negation, 46, 89–94

Negating Negation

apophatic predicate-terms, 44–45
Aristotle, 61
assimilation (*aphomoiōsis*), 97n74
attributes, 3, 4, 19–25
auto (intensifier, -itself), 9, 19
auto-prefixed divine names, 20–21, 28

baptism, 75, 84, 88, 92–93, 93–94
beauty (divine name), 17
beauty-itself, 20n49
begetting (*gonos*), 19, 24n60
being, 66, 104n1
   See also *hyper*-being (*hyper-ousia*) God
being (divine name), 1, 16
being-itself, 16, 20, 23–24, 31
being-itself-giving, 23, 32
beings
   divine names and henads as not, 32
   divine names and properties, relationship to, 26
   existence of, 24
   knowledge of, 113
   nature of, xiii
   removal from God, 41–43
Bradshaw, David, 64n64

Campbell, Thomas, 100n86
causes
   causality and pre-containment, 55–61
   causation, 129–30
   cause of all, God as, 38n6, 55–59, 130, 134
   divine causation/support, 38–39
   preeminence, 47–48
   vs. properties, divine names as, 8–10
   properties, relationship to, 47
celestial hierarchy
   angels, 93, 114–15, 115–19, 129
   celestial beings, 106
   hiddenness and manifestation in, 79n29–80n29
   negation of beings of, 94
   order of, 78, 80–81
   parallels with other hierarchies, 74
   ranks of, 73t

Celestial Hierarchy (*CH*)
   2, 90
   2–3, 130
   2.3, 44, 90–91
   2.5, 91–92
   2, Rorem on, 90n55
   3.1, 72
   3.2, 76
   4.1, 55
   6.2, 80–81
   7, 115, 116–17
   7.2, 117–18
   7.3, 118
   7.4, 58
   8.2, 81
   9.2, 78, 79n29
   10.1, 79
   13.4, 52
   contents of, 70
   mentioned, xvi
CH. See *Celestial Hierarchy*
changes of name (metonymies), 7–8, 10–11
cherubim, 116–17
closed set, divine names as, 12
conceptual content of liturgical practices, negation of, 89, 90, 92, 93, 94
contemplation, 117
contrary opposition, 44
creatio ex nihilo, 26

darkness
   divine darkness, 51–52, 125
   hyper-light darkness, 122–23, 125–26
   luminous darkness, 126–27
   metaphor of, 120–21
   nature of, 125
   simple, symbolism of, 126
   See also ray (*aktis*)
The Darkness of God (Turner), 2n1, 43n18
death, *hyper nous* unity after, 112
deification-union (return to God)
   hierarchical mediation of, 72–82
   hierurgical mediation of, 83–89
   means of, xvi–xvii

142

Subject Index

negation as preparation for hierurgies, 95–102
non-negation of hierarchies and hierurgies, 89–94
overview, 69–71, 80n29
deprivation, things of, 129
difference. *See* divine difference
Dionysian corpus
  approaches to, xi–xii
  meshing of two halves of, 71
  modern appropriations of, 134
  nature of, xiii
  principle of negation in, 92
  rhetorical techniques in, 119–20
  terms of affirmation and negation in, 66t
  titles and subtitles in, 73n10
  translations of, xvin5, 35n1, 36n2
  works of, xvi
  See also Celestial Hierarchy; Divine Names; Ecclesiastical Hierarchy; Epistles; Mystical Theology
Dionysian God. *See* God
Dionysian ineffability. *See* ineffability
Dionysian negation, 36–39, 47, 48, 61–68
  See also apophasis; negation
Dionysian unknowability, xiii
dislike (divine name), 15
dissimilar similarities, 130
divine attributes, 19–25
divine causation/support, 38–39
divine darkness, 51–52, 125
divine difference, 29–31
divine knowledge, 127n43
divine law, hierarchical order as, 82
divine light, 79, 79n29–80n30, 82
divinely revealed, ineffable God known as, 106–15
Divine Names (DN)
  1, 106
  1.1, 107–8, 108–9, 113, 128
  1.2, 109–11
  1.3, 56, 58–59, 111, 113
  1.4, 112–13, 115
  1.5, 57, 113–14, 115
  1.5.593B, 53–54
  1.6, 11, 18

  2, 28
  2.1, 28
  2.2, 28
  2.3, 28
  2.4, 29, 127–28
  2.6, 10
  2.8, 24
  4.3, 52–53
  5.2, 32–33
  7.1, 45, 52, 123
  7.2, 54
  7.3, 66–67, 124
  8.2, 56
  9.5, 5
  11.1, 51
  11.6, 20, 21, 31–32
  12.4, 50n31, 51
  13.3, 54
  contents of, 70
  divine names given in, 13–17
  on intelligible divine names, 5–6, 6–7
  interpretation of, 134
divine names (*theōnumia*)
  alpha-privative, 42
  apophatic abandonment of, arguments for, 2–4
  application of things of being to, 62–64
  arbitrary-metaphorical nature of, 11–12
  auto-prefixed divine names, 20–21, 28
  as causes of properties, 1, 17–18, 132
  as causes vs. properties, 8–10
  as divine unities, 19, 28, 31
  dual senses of, xii
  first, 23–24, 31, 33
  God as, 23, 103, 131n50
  God, relationship to, 22–23, 24
  henads, differences from, 3, 27n68
  intelligible names, 1
  list of, 13
  misreadings of, 1–3
  nature of, xii, 1, 4, 61, 103
  Neoplatonic concepts in, 18n48
  non-removal of, 59–60

143

divine names (*theōnumia*) *(cont.)*
   number and order of divine names, 12–19
   perceptible symbols, differences from, 7–8, 11–12
   properties and beings, relationship to, 26
   qua properties, vs. *qua* causes, 60
   removal of, xii–xiii, 25, 59–60
   as sources of intelligible properties, 19
   triadic nature of, 16, 19–20
   truth and falsity of, 130n50
   Turner on, 2n1
   See also divine names, as not names; henads; *hyper*-name; *specific divine names*
divine names, as not names, 1–34
   Neoplatonic henads, differences from, 25–34
   not inessential divine attributes, 19–25
   not perceptible symbols, not metaphors, not names, 5–12
   number and order of, 12–19
   overview, 1–4
divine peace and rest, 51, 63
divine rays, 27n69, 99n78
divine revelation, 106–8
divine union (divine unity), xiii, 19, 28, 29–30
divine work (*theurgy*), 69n1, 88
divinity, as *hyper*-name, 54
divinity-itself, 20n49, 23, 31
divinity-itself-giving, 23, 32
divinization (*theōsis*), 97n74
DN. See *Divine Names*
Dodds, E. R., 27n67
dōros (giving), 19, 24n60

Ecclesiastical Hierarchy (EH)
   1.3, 77, 99
   1.4, 77
   2, 101
   2.I, 76–77, 83–84, 85–86
   2.III.2, 87
   2.III.7, 88
   2.III.8, 99
   3, 101
   3.I, 85, 86, 99
   3.II, 86
   3.III.2, 87
   3.III.4, 56
   3.III.7, 86
   3.III.12, 83, 99
   3.III.13, 88
   5.I.2, 74n14
   5.I.3, 84
   contents of, 70
   on ecclesiastical rituals, 74n11
   mentioned, xvi
   on symbols, 93
ecclesiastical (human) hierarchy
   negation of beings of, 94
   order of, 78, 79, 81
   ranks of, 73–74
   use of term, 73n10–74n10
ecclesiastical rituals, 74
EH. See *Ecclesiastical Hierarchy*
energeia (sacred activity), 72, 73t
epistēmē (science, intellection), 72, 73t, 110
Epistles (EP)
   Epistle 1, 50n31
   Epistle 4, 45
   Epistle 5, 51, 125–26
   Epistle 9.1, 96
   Epistle 9.5, 52
   mentioned, xvi
   on transcendent knowing, 124–25
epistrophē (process of return), 76, 97n74
equality (divine name), 15
eucharist, 75, 84, 85, 86, 101
excluded middle, law of, 44, 61–62

false names, 12
Forms, transcendent, 27
functional order(ing), 14–15, 16t

God
   angels' knowledge of, 115–19
   approaches to understanding of, xi–xii
   as cause of all, 38n6, 55–59, 130, 134

Subject Index

as divine names, 23, 103, 131*n*50
essence of, causation and, 130
as giver of substance to divine names, 20–21, 32
hyper-being (*hyper-ousia*) God, 36, 58, 124–25, 127–29
hyper-being hyparxis of, 64*n*64
hyper-mind knowledge of, 109, 119–29
as *hyper*-named, 25
as *hyper*-names, 23
limited ineffability, xii
mind of, 61–62
mystical negative theology on, 39*n*7
Mystical Theology on, 121–22
naming, 11
persons of the Trinity and, 38*n*5
predictability of, xi–xii
removal of beings of, 41–42
removal of predicate-terms from, 66, 66*n*69
return to, xvi–xvii, 69–71
as source, 22
trinitarian nature of, 5
See also ineffable God, non-ineffability of; Jesus Christ; Trinity; *entries beginning "divine"*
god of gods (divine name), 14
Golitizin, Alexander, 96*n*69
gonos (begetting), 19, 24*n*60
good (divine name), 17
The Good, as *hyper* all beings, 53
goodness-itself, 20*n*49
grammar of *aphairesis*, and unity of Dionysian negation, 61–68
great (divine name), 15
A Greek-English Lexicon (Lidell and Scott), 48

henads
divine names as different from, 3, 27*n*68
Neoplatonic, divine names not qualitatively different from, 25–34
as not beings, 32
as pluralized unities, 26–27
Procline, 27–28
use of term in Dionysian corpus, 33*n*82
henōsis. See union
Hick, John, xv*n*4, 2*n*1, 37*n*4, 70*n*3, 105
hiddenness and manifestation, in celestial hierarchy, 79*n*29–80*n*29
hierarchical order, 78, 80, 82, 103
hierarchical symbols, negation of, not stated, 90
hierarchies and hierurgies
non-negation of, 89–94
return to God via, 69–71
hierarchs, 88, 95, 101
hierarchy
about, 72
constituents and functions of, 75–76
deification-union, mediation of, 72–82
of divine names, 16
problems of parallels in, 74–75
union with God and, 71
See also hierarchies and hierurgies
hierologeō (verbal form of *hierologia* [sacred words]), 85
hierologia (sacred words), 83
hierological illumination, 103–4
hierourgeō (verbal form of hierurgy), 85–86
hierurgy (*hierourgia*, ritual practice, sacred work)
bodily practice of, 86–87, 95
deification-union, effectation of, 83–89
negation as theological preparation for, 71, 95–102
purpose of, 104
return to God via, 69–70
as ritual enactment of theurgy, 88
as term, 69*n*1, 85
See also hierarchies and hierurgies
holy of holies (divine name), 14
holy of holies, God as, 51
Horn, Laurence, 44, 62*n*59
"How to Read the Pseudo-Denys Today?" (Turner), xv*n*4

145

Negating Negation

human hierarchy. *See* ecclesiastical (human) hierarchy
humans, knowledge of ineffable God, 108, 115–19
hymns, 100, 115
hyparxis, 57n48
hyper, 6n10, 19, 20, 48–49, 130n52
hyper and *hyperochē*, 47–55
hyperarchios, 58n52
hyper-being
   as cause of being, 23, 31
   comprehensibility of, 109
   nature of, 21, 22
   as unified thing, 28
hyper-being and hidden divinity (God), 107–10, 113
   See also God
hyper-being (*hyper-ousia*) God, 36, 58, 124–25, 127–29
hyper-being hyparxis, 64n64
hyper-being-itself, 32
hyperbeingly, 62
hyper-beingness, 30
hyper-being preeminence, 66–67
hyper-being science of divine things, 108
hyper-being thearchy, 55
hyperbolē (excess), 49
hyper-divine, 20n49, 21, 22, 28
hyper-good, 20n49, 21, 22
hyperhyparxis, 58n50
hyper-hyparxis thearchy, 57
hyperidrusis (hyper-established, superior), 49n31–50n31
hyperkeimai (hyper-lie, lie above), 49n31, 50n31
hyper-life, 21, 28
hyper-light, 53
hyper-light darkness, 122–23, 125–26
hyper-logos saying, 127–28, 131, 133
hyper-mind, 109
   See also *hyper-nous* knowing
hyper-name (*hyperōnomos*), 22, 23, 53–54
hyper-nature, 20n49
hyper-nous knowing, 106, 113, 122–25, 131, 133
hyperochē (preeminence)
   ambiguity of, 48–53, 55n43, 60
   of causes, 47–48
   meaning of, 38n6–39n6, 49
   morphology of, 48–49
   revealed by logic of *apophasis*, 128–29
hyperochē aphairesis, 67–68
hyperochē mind, 62
hyperōnomos (*hyper*-name), 22, 23, 53–54
hyper-ousia (*hyper*-being) God, 36, 58, 124–25, 127–29
hyperplērēs (overfull), 49
hyper-prefixed divine names
   ambiguity of, 52–53
   as divine unities of the divine unity, 29
   dual meanings of, 36
   God as, 129
   God as substance of divine names, connection to, 21
   henads, similarity to, 28
hyper-prefixed terms, 50–51
hyper-source source, 58
hyper-unknowable, 121
hyper-wise, 21, 28
hypostatis, 57n48

ignorance, in knowledge, 127n43
illumination, in hierarchies, 75
illuminative activities, divine names as, 4
ineffability-unknowability
   Dionysian, 105, 121–22
   Hick on, 2n1
   nature of, xiii
   overcoming of, through divine revelation, 106–8
   as relative, xiv–xv, 134–35
   See also absolute ineffability-unknowability; ineffable God, non-ineffability of
ineffable and unknowable divine knowledge, union with, 98–99
ineffable God, non-ineffability of, 103–31
   better known by angels than by humans, 115–19

Subject Index

as divinely revealed, 106–15
known *hyper* mind, 119–29
not absolutely unknowable and ineffable, 129–31
overview, 103–6
inferiors, 81
intelligible divine name (*noētē theōnumia*), 5–7, 42–43
intelligible names, 1
invisibility, as attribute of God, 44–45

Jesus Christ, 45–46, 63, 88–89, 125
Johnson, Mark, 49*n*30
Jones, John D.
on *apophasis/aphairesis* difference, 36*n*2, 65*n*67
causality, arguments against, 38*n*5
on Dionysius' espousal of mystical negative theology, xv*n*4, 39*n*7
on God as cause or support of all, 38*n*6
on *hyperhyparxis*, 58*n*50
on *hyperochē*, ambiguity of, 55*n*43
justice (divine name), 15

kataphasis (positive predicate-term), 65, 66t
kataphatic theology, 3
kata to kreitton, 122*n*30
knowledge
divine knowledge, 127*n*43
human, limits of, 116
nature of, 113
of unknowable and ineffable things, 105–6
unknowing knowing, 106
See also *hyper-nous knowing*; ineffability-unknowability; unknowability
known *hyper* mind, 119–29
Kügler, Peter, 125*n*39

Lakoff, George, 49*n*30
law of the excluded middle, 44, 61–62
legal hierarchy, 73t, 74–75
life (divine name), 8
life-itself (divine name)
as cause of all, 23, 31

as cause of property of life, xii
as divine cause, 8–9
meaning of, 20
nature of, 25
life-itself-giving, 23, 32
light, 51–52, 79, 82, 126
See also ray (*aktis*)
light (divine name), 17
light-itself, 25
like (divine name), 15
liturgical rituals. See hierurgy
liturgical symbols
cognitive interpretation of, 86, 95
deification-union and, 71
negation of, meaning of, 93–94
negation of, not stated, 92
perceptible symbols for angels, differences from, 93
logion (sacred Scriptures), 108, 110, 113, 115
lord of lords (divine name), 14
Louth, Andrew, 3*n*7, 70*n*2, 100*n*87
love (divine name), 17
luminous darkness, 126–27

manifestation and hiddenness, in celestial hierarchy, 79*n*29–80*n*29
metaphors, 11, 40–41, 66, 120–21
metaphysical negative theology, 39*n*7
metonymies (changes of name), 7–8, 10–11
mind of God, 61–62
more immaterial initiation, 83, 86, 95
Moses, 98, 100*n*87, 120–21, 122
motion (divine name), 15
mountain summits, metaphor of, 120–21
myron consecration, 69*n*1, 75, 84
mystical negative theology, 39*n*7
Mystical Theology (MT)
1, 122
1.1, 53, 126
1.2, 64–65
2, 40, 66, 100–101, 122–23, 126
2–3, 40, 130
3, 41, 100–101
3, Rorem on, 89*n*54–90*n*54
4–5, 40, 42, 57, 105

147

Negating Negation

Mystical Theology (MT) (cont.)
  5, 59
  5.1048B, 57n49
  on conceptual content, removal of, 89–90
  contents of, 70
  Divine Names and, 134
  on God, 121–22
  on kataphatic treatises, 5–6
  mentioned, xvi
  removal of divine names in, 25
  removal of perceptible symbols and divine names, 95
  rhetorical techniques in, 119–20
  as theology, 96
  Turner on names of God in, 37n4
  use of terms *apophasis* and *aphairesis*, 40
  use of terms for process of return, 97

names
  false, 12
  of God (*See* divine names)
  modern interpretations of, 1
  See also divine names, as not names
narrow-scope predicate-term negation, 44, 65n69
negating negation
  divine names as not names, 1–34
  ineffable God, non-ineffability of, 103–31
  negation, non-negation of, 35–68
  ranks, non-bypassing of, 69–94
  rites, non-negation of, 95–102
negation
  apophatic vs. privative, 46
  as means of performing rituals, 71
  ordinary language forms of, 36–37
  principle of, 92
  terms for, 66t
  as theological preparation for hierurgy, 95–102
  See also *aphairesis* (removal); *apophasis*; Dionysian negation
negation, non-negation of, 35–68
  apophasis and *aphairesis*, 40–47

causality and pre-containment, 55–61
grammar of *aphairesis* and unity of Dionysian negation, 61–68
hyper and *hyperochē*, 47–55
overview, 35–40
negative metaphysical theology, 39n7
negative mystical theology, 39n7
negative predicate-terms, 44–48, 54, 61, 65n69–66n69, 119–20
negative theology, xiii, xvii, 70
Neoplatonism
  cause of all in, 32
  Neoplatonic concepts, divine names and, 18n48
  Neoplatonic henads, 25–34
  process of return (*epistrophē*), 76, 97n74
non-ineffability of ineffable God. *See* ineffable God, non-ineffability of
not names, divine names as. *See* divine names, as not names
not unknowable and ineffable, ineffable God as, 129–31
nous. See *hyper-nous* knowing
number and order of divine names, 12–19

one (divine name), 14
One (of Plotinus), 64n64
ontological procession, divine names of, 16t
order
  of divine names, 13–14
  hierarchical order, 78, 80, 82, 103
  and number of divine names, 12–19
order-itself, 9
ōsis (making), 19, 24
ōsis-suffixed divine names, 28
other (divine name), 15
overfull (*hyperplērēs*), 49

pagan dieties, 33
paradeigmata/logoi, 61n58
participations-themselves (participated-themselves), 9, 24n60
Paul, Apostle, 57n49, 125

Paulist Press translation of the Dionysian corpus, xvi*n*5, 35*n*1, 36*n*2
peace (divine name), 14
perceptible symbols (*aisthētai symbola*)
  as dissimilar similarities, 130
  divine names, differences from, 1, 7–8, 11–12
  in *Ecclesiastical Hierarchy*, 93
  of hierurgical rites, 87
  human hierarchy's use of, 74
  interpretation of, 60
  nature of, in apophetic abandonment argument, 94
  not causal, 59
  not divine names, 1, 5–12
  removal of, in *MT*4, 42
  Rorem on, 89*n*54–90*n*54, 92*n*61
  Turner on, 2*n*1
  used of angels and God, 91
perfect (divine name), 14
perfection, 75, 76*n*19, 117–18
Perl, Eric, 27*n*69, 38*n*5, 81*n*32–82*n*32, 104*n*1–105*n*1
Plato, use of term henad, 27*n*67
pluralized unities, 26–27
poēisis (producing), 19, 24*n*60
positive predicate-terms, 65*n*69–66*n*69
power (divine name), 1, 14–15
power, God as cause of, 56
power-itself, 20
powers, divine names as, 24
praise, 27
pre-containment. *See* causes, causality and pre-containment
predicate-term negation, 44–48, 54, 61, 65*n*69–66*n*69, 119–20
predicate-terms, 64, 66, 66*n*69
preeminence. See *hyperochē*
preeminent brightness, 125
preeminent negation, 46–47
privative negation/privation (*sterēsis*), 46, 65, 66*t*
Procline henads, 27–28
Procline theurgy, 102*n*93
Proclus, 27*n*67, 102*n*93
producing (*poēisis*), 19, 24*n*60

proochē (before the having of anything), 55*n*43
properties
  vs. causes, divine names as, 8–10
  causes, relationship to, 47
  divine names, relationship to, 1, 17–18, 26, 132
  locus of, 60
  order of divine names and, 13
"Pseudo-Dionysius and the *Platonic Theology*" (Perczel), 121*n*27
Pseudo-Dionysius the Aeropagite, xvi, 33–34, 132–33
purification, 75, 76*n*19, 78
purification-illumination-perfection, 75, 84
purity, of angels, 117

ranks and rituals. *See* hierarchies and hierurgies
ranks, non-bypassing of, 69–94
  deification-union, hierarchical mediation of, 72–82
  deification-union, hierurgical effectation of, 83–89
  hierarchies and hierurgies, non-negation of, 89–94
  overview, 69–71
  See also rites, non-negation of
ray (*aktis*)
  hyper-being, 112, 113, 126
  hyper-being founding, 110–11
  hyper-brilliant, 124
  hyper-light, 112
  occurrences of, 98*n*78
reality, 12, 134, 135
redemption (divine name), 15
relative ineffability, xiv–xv, 134–35
religious pluralism of Dionysian corpus, xiv
remaining, proceeding, and reverting, 75*n*19
removal. See *aphairesis*
removed properties, 67
rest (divine name), 15
return, Neoplatonic process of (*epistrophē*), 76, 97*n*74
return to God. *See* deification-union

149

Negating Negation

revelation, divine, 106–8
rhetorical techniques in *Mystical Theology*, 119–20
rising from last things to first things, language of, 100–101
rites, non-negation of, 95–102
  See also ranks, non-bypassing of
ritual practices. *See* hierurgy
rituals and ranks. *See* hierarchies and hierurgies
Rorem, Paul, 29n73
  on *apophasis/aphairesis* difference, 36n2
  on *Celestial Hierarchy* 2, 90n55
  mentioned, 70n4
  on more immaterial initiation, 83
  on *Mystical Theology* 3, 89n54–90n54
  on perceptible symbols, 92n61

sacramental rites. *See* baptism; eucharist; myron consecration
sacraments, perfection of, 85
sacred activity (*energeia*), 72, 73t
sacred order (*taxis*), 72, 73t
sacred Scriptures (*logion*), 108, 110, 113, 115
sacred words (*hierologia*), 83
sacred works. *See* hierurgy
salvation (divine name), 15
salvation (*sōtēria*), 77, 97n74
same (divine name), 15
saying, 128
scalar predicates, 62n59
science (intellection, *epistēmē*), 72, 73t, 110
Scriptures, sacred (*logion*), 108, 110, 113, 115
sculpting, metaphor of, 40–41, 66
seals (embossed emblems), 10
Sell, Michael, 133
seraphim, cherubim, and thrones, 80–81
Sheldon-Williams, I. P., 27n67, 73n8
similarity-itself, 9
small (divine name), 15
spatial relations, in meaning of *hyper*, 48–49

sterēsis (privative negation), 46, 65, 66t
Stiglmayr, Josef, 100n86
substance, divine names and God as not, 32n79
summits, metaphor of, 120–21
Symbolic Theology (lost/fictitious work of Dionysian corpus), 6
symbols. *See* hierarchical symbols; liturgical symbols; perceptible symbols
synaxis. *See* eucharist
syntax of removal, 43–44
Syrianus, 27n67

taxis (sacred order), 72, 73t
technē, of sculpting, comparison with *aphairesis*, 40–41
terms of affirmation and negation, 66t
thearchy. *See* God
theologians, 107, 110, 112
Theological Outlines (lost/fictitious work of Dionysian corpus), 5
theological preparation, negation as, 95–102
theological treatises, hierurgical rites and, 99
theology
  Mystical Theology as, 96
  as term, meaning of, 96n69
theōnumia. *See* divine names
Theophany (Perl), 104n1
theōsis (divinization), 97n74
thesis, 41, 43, 65, 66t
theurgy (divine work), 69n1, 88
things of deprivation, 129
Timothy, Saint, 96, 97–98, 126
transcendence, 49
  See also entries beginning "hyper-"
transcendent Forms, 27
transcendent knowing. *See hyper-nous* knowing
transcendent thearchies, 24
transcendent triune thearchies, 19
triads of triads, 13–14, 16
trinitarian properties, 42–43, 60–61
Trinity (including members of)

application of things of being to, 62–63
as God, 30
God as, 129
as guide to Scripture, 126
identified with *hyper*-being God, 38n5
language of difference for, 28
triple immersion in baptism, meaning of, 88, 93–94
true negations, 91–92
Turner, Denys
on darkness, 125n39
on Dionysian God, 105
on divine names, 2n1
divine names, interpretation of, 70n3
on ineffability, xvn4
on names of God in *Mystical Theology*, 37n4–38n4
removed beings, classification of, 43n18

ultimate realities, 135
unapproachable light, darkness as, 125
unification of beings, 14
unificatory return, divine names of, 16t
union (*henōsis*)
divine union, xiii, 19, 27, 28, 29–30
by hierurgical rituals, 99
with ineffable and unknowable divine knowledge, 98–99
with ineffable and unknowable things, 107
use of term, 97n74
unities. *See* henads
unity (divine name), 1
unity-itself, 9
unity of Dionysian negation, grammar of *aphairesis* and, 61–68
unknowability
Dionysian, xiii, 105
hyper-unknowable, 121
unknowable and ineffable things, knowledge of, 105–6
unknowing knowing, 106
unknowable and ineffable God. *See* ineffable God, non-ineffability of
unlike comparisons, 91–92
unspeakable and unknowable things, 107
See also unknowability
up, as term, metaphorical applications of, 49n30, 120n25
uplifting (*anagōgē*), 97n74

visibility, as attribute of God, 44–45

wide-scope propositional negation, 36–37
Williams, Janet, 36n2, 65n67
wisdom-itself, 20
Wolfson, H. A., 36n2

www.ingramcontent.com/pod-product-compliance
Lightning Source LLC
Chambersburg PA
CBHW030859170426
43193CB00009BA/665